REASONING AS MEMORY

There is a growing acknowledgement of the importance of integrating the study of reasoning with other areas of cognitive psychology. The purpose of this volume is to examine the extent to which we can further our understanding of reasoning by integrating findings, theories and paradigms in the field of memory.

Reasoning as Memory consists of nine chapters that make explicit links between basic memory process, and reasoning and decision making. The contributors address a number of key topics including:

- the relationship between semantic memory and reasoning
- the role of expert memory in reasoning
- recognition memory and induction
- working memory and reasoning
- meta-memory in reasoning.

In addition, the chapters provide broad coverage of the field of thinking, and invite the intriguing question of how much there is left to explain in the field of reasoning when one has extracted the variance due to memory.

This book will be of great interest to advanced undergraduates, postgraduates and researchers interested in reasoning or decision making, and to researchers interested in the role played in cognition by a variety of memory processes.

Aidan Feeney is Senior Lecturer at Queen's University Belfast, UK. His research interests include thinking in children and adults, including inductive reasoning, decision making, and counterfactual thinking and regret.

Valerie A. Thompson is Professor of Psychology at the University of Saskatchewan, Canada. Her research interests include intuitive judgments, thinking and decision making, and metacognition.

Current Issues in Thinking and Reasoning
Series Editor: Linden Ball

Current Issues in Thinking and Reasoning is a series of edited books which will reflect the state of the art in areas of current and emerging interest in the psychological study of thinking processes.

Each volume will be tightly focused on a particular topic and will consist of between seven and ten chapters contributed by international experts. The editors of individual volumes will be leading figures in their areas and will provide an introductory overview.

Example topics include thinking and working memory, visual imagery in problem solving, evolutionary approaches to thinking, cognitive processes in planning, creative thinking, decision-making processes, pathologies of thinking, individual differences, neuropsychological approaches and applications of thinking research.

Emotion and Reasoning
Edited by Isabelle Blanchette

New Approaches in Reasoning Research
Edited by Wim De Neys and Magda Osman

The Developmental Psychology of Reasoning and Decision-Making
Edited by Henry Markovits

Aberrant Beliefs and Reasoning
Edited by Niall Galbraith

Reasoning as Memory
Edited by Aidan Feeney and Valerie A. Thompson

REASONING AS MEMORY

Edited by
Aidan Feeney and Valerie A. Thompson

Psychology Press
Taylor & Francis Group
LONDON AND NEW YORK

First published 2015
by Psychology Press
27 Church Road, Hove, East Sussex BN3 2FA

and by Psychology Press
711 Third Avenue, New York, NY 10017

Psychology Press is an imprint of the Taylor & Francis Group, an informa business

British Library Cataloguing in Publication Data
A catalogue record for this book is available from the British Library

Library of Congress Cataloging in Publication Data
Reasoning as memory / edited by Aidan Feeney, Valerie A. Thompson.
Includes bibliographical references and index.
ISBN 978-1-84872-147-0 (hardback) -- ISBN 978-1-84872-148-7
(softcover) 1. Reasoning (Psychology) 2. Memory. I. Feeney, Aidan, 1971-
II. Thompson, Valerie A.
BF442.R423 2015
153.4'3--dc23
2014013285

ISBN: 978-1-84872-147-0 (hbk)
ISBN: 978-1-84872-148-7 (pbk)
ISBN: 978-1-31581-952-5 (ebk)

Typeset in Bembo and Scala Sans
by Saxon Graphics Ltd, Derby

MIX
Paper from
responsible sources
FSC   FSC® C013056
www.fsc.org

Printed and bound in Great Britain by
TJ International Ltd, Padstow, Cornwall

For inspiration past, present and future, we dedicate this book to Ronald Carl Smith and Oliver Feeney.

CONTENTS

ILLUSTRATIONS

Figures

Tables

CONTRIBUTORS

Rakefet Ackerman, Technion-Israel Institute of Technology, Israel.

Glenda Andrews, School of Applied Psychology, Griffith University, Australia.

Daniel R. Buttaccio, Department of Psychology, University of Oklahoma, United States.

Jonathan C. Corbin, Department of Human Development, Cornell University, United States.

Arnaud D'Argembeau, Research Associate of the Fund for Scientific Research, University of Liège, Belgium.

Michael R. Dougherty, University of Maryland, United States.

Aidan Feeney, School of Psychology, Queen's University Belfast, Northern Ireland.

Graeme S. Halford, School of Applied Psychology, Griffith University, Australia.

Isaiah Harbison, Department of Psychology, University of Maryland, United States.

Brett Hayes, University of New South Wales, Australia.

Evan Heit, National Science Foundation, and University of California Merced, United States.

Nicholas D. Lange, Department of Psychological Sciences, University of London, United Kingdom, and Department of Psychology, University of Oklahoma, United States.

Henry Markovits, Université du Québec, Canada.

Valerie F. Reyna, Departments of Human Development and Psychology, Cornell University, United States.

Amber M. Sprenger, Department of Social and Behavioral Sciences, The MITRE Corporation.

Rick P. Thomas, University of Oklahoma, United States.

Valerie A. Thompson, Department of Psychology, University of Saskatchewan, Canada.

Sascha Topolinski, Department of Psychology, Social and Economic Cognition, University of Cologne, Germany.

Nash Unsworth, University of Oregon, United States.

Evan A. Wilhelms, Department of Human Development, Cornell University, United States.

William H. Wilson, School of Computer Science and Engineering, University of New South Wales, Australia.

INTRODUCTION

Reasoning and memory: A case for integration

Valerie A. Thompson and Aidan Feeney

> Memory is the cabinet of imagination, the treasury of reason, the registry of conscience and the council-chamber of thought.
>
> Giambattista Basile

Like many edited books, this one had its origins in a very simple idea: to examine the extent to which we can further our understanding of reasoning by integrating findings, theories, and paradigms from the field of memory. There is a growing acknowledgment of the importance of integrating the study of reasoning with other areas of cognitive psychology, but in many cases, the theorising about such relationships remains vague and only loosely developed. In contrast, this volume consists of nine chapters that make explicit links between basic memory process and reasoning and decision making, addressing topics such as the relationship between semantic memory and reasoning, the role of expert memory in reasoning, recognition memory and induction, working memory and reasoning, and metamemory in reasoning. In addition to providing broad coverage of the contribution of memory to thinking, the chapters also cover the field of thinking, broadly writ, including deductive reasoning, inductive reasoning, expert reasoning, representation in reasoning, hypothetical thinking, intuitive versus analytic thinking, and problem solving. Ideally, anyone interested in thinking, reasoning or decision making ought to find this volume a go-to resource that illustrates how understanding basic memory processes can elucidate and advance theory in their own area of work.

Late in the editing process, it became clear that this lacuna exists in both the popular and the scientific press. When we tried to search for aphorisms or quotations with which to start this preface, we found what appeared to be an endless supply of elegantly expressed views on reason's relationship to emotion; however, there were relatively few on the relationship between reasoning and memory. This was all the more puzzling given that reasoning is often characterised as the process by which we integrate remembered information with newly acquired information, by which we draw out the implications of current knowledge, apply existing knowledge to novel problems, challenge existing assumptions, and make changes to our knowledge base. Reasoning requires short-term memory in which to operate, and it also shares component processes with many types of memory. To take just two examples: Dougherty and colleagues (Dougherty, Thomas & Lange, 2010; Lange et al., this volume) have shown how a global memory model can be adapted to explain probability judgment and decision making. In the field of artificial intelligence, Hélie and Sun (2010) have developed a cognitive architecture (CLARION) based on fundamental principles of memory that can account for a number of key reasoning phenomena.

To be sure, the reasoning literature has long acknowledged the central role of working memory in reasoning. For example, we know that individual differences in cognitive capacity, as measured either by IQ or proxies to IQ (e.g., Stanovich, 2011) or Working Memory Capacity (WMC) (e.g., De Neys 2006a, 2006b) are strong predictors of performance in a wide range of reasoning tasks. This relationship is a critical piece of evidence in support of Dual Process Theories of Reasoning (Evans & Stanovich, 2013), which posit that WMC is necessary to engage higher-order, analytic thinking. Indeed, Evans and Stanovich (2013) have argued that the engagement of WMC is the defining feature of analytic thinking.

Thus, it is not surprising that several of the chapters in this book address the relationship between WM and reasoning. Of interest, however, is that these chapters illustrate how much has been learned about that relationship and how sophisticated theorising in that domain has become. As a point of contrast, an earlier book in this series was Logie and Gilhooly's (1998) book *Working Memory and Thinking*. Comparison between that book and this one is intriguing. As their title suggests, Logie and Gilhooly were primarily concerned with one particular aspect of memory, and the chapters in their book considered questions about strategic use of working memory sub-systems in reasoning, how working memory is involved in age differences in reasoning, and the role of working memory in expertise and problem solving. One very telling fact is that whilst most of the chapters in the earlier book referred to Baddeley's multi-store model, only one of the chapters in this book does. Another telling comparison is between the contributions made by Graeme Halford, who is the only contributor common to both books; Graeme has co-authored a chapter for this volume, and was the author on a chapter in the earlier book. Reading both chapters side by side, one can clearly see how thinking about working memory and its role in reasoning has developed since the late 1990s. Whereas Halford (1998) was concerned with ideas about the development of processing capacity and relational complexity, **Halford, Andrews and Wilson** (this volume) couch their arguments about working memory and relational reasoning in terms of Dual Process Theories (see Evans, 2008) and contemporary ideas about relational binding in working memory (see Oberauer, Süß, Wilhelm & Sander, 2007). The comparison between the two chapters makes it clear that ideas about the relationship between working memory and reasoning have developed in parallel to the development of ideas about working memory. Interestingly, the chapter by **Wilhelms** and colleagues offers an alternative view of the relationship between general cognitive resources and reasoning, which would have been almost unthinkable in 1998.

If working memory provides a source of continuity between our book and Logie and Gilhooly's, our volume nicely illustrates that there are now multiple relations between the literatures on memory and reasoning. One relation is in terms of computational modelling, and two of the chapters in this book (**Lange** et al.; **Feeney** et al.) illustrate how computational models of memory may be applied to the study of hypothetical and inductive reasoning. One very attractive feature of a modelling approach is that it requires one to be very specific about the commonalities and differences. In the case of the **Feeney** et al. chapter, some of the commonalities are surprising. Another relation between memory and reasoning that has recently emerged is the centrality of ideas about metacognition. The chapters by **Topolinski** and **Ackerman and Thompson** illustrate the importance of reasoners' monitoring of their own reasoning to how they regulate their reasoning processes. This is a very new development in the study of reasoning, which illustrates how theoretical advances in the study of memory may lead to analogous advances in the study of reasoning.

In sum, this volume represents continuity and progress in the study of relations between memory and reasoning. We hope that it will be read by reasoning and memory researchers alike, and whilst the questions which have inspired all of the work described here are psychological in nature, we expect cognitive scientists and philosophers to find material to interest them. Logie and Gilhooly started their book by bemoaning the "divide-and-rule" approach that had until that point been taken by cognitive psychologists to the areas of memory and thinking. As the chapters themselves – and the overview below – demonstrate, many more researchers have now considered memory and reasoning side by side: we reason about relations between novel events and things that are important to us; information cued from the environment is often the starting point of hypothesising about an event; we require space in working memory to carry out our reasoning and to integrate the content of current thought with things that we already know, etc. Stated in these terms, one wonders why reasoning researchers would ever have imagined that it could be useful to study reasoning without reference to memory. We look forward to the time when elegant phrases about the relationship between memory and reasoning are easy to find.

Overview of the chapters

A number of different mechanisms have been proposed to mediate the relationship between general cognitive capacity and reasoning: that WMC is needed for a directed search of counter-examples from long-term memory (Markovits, Doyon, & Simoneau, 2002; De Neys, Schaeken & d'Ydewalle, 2005a), that WMC limits the complexity of the representation that can be constructed from the problem information (Johnson-Laird & Byrne, 2002), or that WM capacity is necessary to overturn a pre-potent response and to simulate an alternative answer (Stanovich, 2011). Given the critical position accorded to WM capacity in almost all theories of reasoning, it should not be surprising that four of our nine chapters address the relationship between WM and reasoning.

In the first chapter, **Nash Unsworth** examines the issue from the perspective of a memory researcher, and investigates the mechanisms of working memory that support the relationship between WMC and reasoning. In this chapter, he re-analyses data from a number of published studies involving many hundreds of participants. He obtains a counter-intuitive finding, namely that the relationship between WMC and reasoning is not mediated by the difficulty of the reasoning items, and that WMC is equally implicated in solving easy and difficult items. Instead, a detailed analysis of the components of working memory reveals that individual differences in the scope of attention, attentional control, secondary memory and interference control all contribute to the relationship between WM and reasoning, and that as a collective, they are sufficient to account for the correlation between WMC and reasoning.

The mechanisms identified by Nash resonate with many of those proposed in reasoning theories: secondary memory is involved in the search for counter-examples; resistance to interference is necessary to put aside a pre-potent response as well as to resist using counter-examples that are inappropriate to the task at hand (De Neys, Schaeken & d'Ydewalle, 2005b); differences in the scope of attention will determine the complexity of the representation that one is able to maintain and the success of simulating an alternative representation of a problem. Importantly, however, Unsworth has shown that none of these abilities, in isolation, explains the relationship between WMC and reasoning performance, a finding that should encourage reasoning researchers to adopt a more multifaceted approach to measuring WM. In addition, these findings need to be reconciled with others (Stanovich & West, 2008) showing that capacity (measured as SAT scores) does not correlate with performance on all reasoning tests. Perhaps such correlations would emerge by adopting a broader operational definition of capacity.

In Chapter 2 **Halford, Andrews, and Wilson** develop a theory that addresses the role of relational processes in reasoning and working memory. As with Dual Process theorists, these authors argue that analytic thinking is WM-dependent. Specifically, they argue that all forms of higher cognition depend on processing relations in WM. These relations are used to formulate a model or representation of the premises, which must be represented in WM. In this view, WM is a system that enables the dynamic binding of information to a coordinate system (as per Oberauer et al., 2007), such that reasoning involves the construction of new relational representations in WM. Consequently, limitations to our ability to reason are determined by the complexity of the relations that are bound in WM.

Henry Markovits, Chapter 3, also argues that the key to understanding reasoning is to understand how information is represented in WM. He demonstrates that variability in conditional inferences is a function of the on-line retrieval of counter-examples from semantic memory. This information, which is cued by the premises, is incorporated into a mental model, which can be processed either by a WM-intensive counter-example strategy or by an intuitive probabilistic strategy. Here, the focus is on the interplay between the information presented to the reasoner, an active retrieval process and representations in WM.

The focus of Chapter 4 is also on the role that cued retrieval plays in reasoning outcomes. **Lange, Buttaccio, Sprenger, Harbison, Thomas, and Dougherty** describe a computational model of hypothesis generation (HyGene) in which memory plays the pivotal role. HyGene supposes that hypotheses are cued by information in the environment and that the number of hypotheses that can be actively represented is constrained by WM. This observation is important for a variety of reasoning phenomena, given that many reasoning biases are thought to occur because people represent only a single model of the situation at a time (Evans, 2006). Using a combination of modelling and experimental data, the authors show how HyGene accounts for a number of reasoning phenomena associated with hypothesis generation and testing, including the circumstances under which positive testing is preferred to diagnostic testing.

Whereas the focus of the first four chapters is on the limiting role that WMC plays on reasoning, **Wilhelms, Corbin, and Reyna**, Chapter 5, outline an alternative view. Fuzzy trace theory assumes that deliberate, analytic reasoning requires access to rote, verbatim traces and that intuitions arise from gist-based traces that encode meaning. Wilhelms et al. argue that reliance on gist processes gives rise to both reasoning biases and expert knowledge. Because both gist and verbatim processes are proposed to develop with age and experience, surprising developmental reversals are observed. For example, gist-based representations are posited to be the source of framing effects, which get stronger as people progress from childhood to adolescence. Similarly, expert reasoners (e.g., cardiologists) are posited to rely on gist-based processing, which allows them to make accurate categorical assessments of risk, but none the less be subject to reasoning fallacies, such as the disjunction effect.

The next two chapters also focus on the role of the knowledge structures that support reasoning. **Feeney, Hayes, and Heit** (Chapter 6) explore the proposition that many of the cognitive mechanisms that support recognition memory also underlie category-based induction. For example, the authors argue that it is possible to make inferences about the processes required to make inductive judgments from how well people are subsequently able to recognise the targets of that reasoning. The "inference then recognition" paradigm asks participants to reason about novel or familiar categories. This is followed by a surprise recognition test, which, for example, can help to distinguish between inferences that are made in a category-based way and those that are made on the basis of featural overlap. They go on to argue that a computational model of recognition memory captures many important features of the people's judgments about the strength of inductive arguments. That is, judgments of the strength of simple inductive arguments are captured by a model designed to explain how people recognise those same items.

In Chapter 7, **Arnaud D'Argembeau** addresses the topic of episodic future thinking. Episodic future thinking is the processes of constructing mental representations of possible futures. This chapter explores in detail the memory structures that support such representations. D'Argembeau reviews the evidence that links this ability to the ability to remember past events and shows that deficits in past episodic memory are associated with parallel deficits in the ability to imagine future events. He further argues that the structure of future imaginings parallels that of autobiographical memory. Reasoning researchers should find many useful pointers in these findings, given that the ability to simulate outcomes, consider consequences, judge future probabilities, and to plan are key to many theories of reasoning and have been the object of much study. Mental simulation in particular is a very important, but somewhat poorly understood, ability in reasoning, and ideas in the literature on episodic future thinking will be helpful to reasoning researchers in their theorising.

The final two chapters examine issues of metacognition. **Sascha Topolinski** reviews the evidence showing how intuitions of coherence are mediated by affect. As an example, the Remote Associates Test (Mednick, 1962) requires participants to judge whether there is a common associate for three words, e.g., shine, beam, and struck (moon). The evidence suggests that people are able to tell which triads are coherent and which aren't in less time that it takes them to produce a solution. This intuition of coherence is thought to arise from the fact that coherent triads prime the common remote associate, producing a sense of fluency. Fluency has long been posited to play a central role in metamemory judgments, such as judgments of learning. Topolinski extends this work further by showing that fluency has an affective component, so that fluency-based judgments are basically affective judgments.

The coherence judgments discussed by Topolinski fall into a class of metareasoning judgments that **Ackerman and Thompson** (Chapter 9) call Judgments of Solvability. This chapter summarises the monitoring and regulatory role of metamemory judgments and then develops analogies to metareasoning judgments. Some judgments, such as Judgments of Solvability, are made in advance of attempting a solution to a problem and are proposed to mediate the amount of effort that reasoners will invest in it. The Feeling of Rightness is a judgment that accompanies pre-potent responses, and is proposed to play a gatekeeper function for the degree of subsequent analytic thinking. Judgments of Confidence are posited to play a more dynamic role in regulating reasoning and problem solving than they do in memory, as it is supposed that such judgments are made continuously over a period of thinking and may play a role in regulating the extent of additional thought. This chapter reviews the relatively sparse work on metacognition in reasoning and problem solving, suggests potential lines of investigations and points out specific ways in which research in metamemory can benefit from understanding emerging phenomena in metareasoning.

Conclusions

Our title *Reasoning as Memory* is deliberatively provocative. It implies that viewed from a particular perspective or from sufficient altitude, the wide range of processes that fall under the umbrella of "thinking and reasoning" might ultimately be described in terms of memory. Indeed, several of the phenomena of expert thinking so intensively studied in earlier decades represented exactly that type of possibility. Specifically, early work on problem solving in chess or computer programming emphasised the importance of pattern recognition to expert thinking (Charness, 1991; Chase & Simon, 1973a, 1973b); expert reasoning was shown to be enabled, in large part, by a large long-term memory store whose shelves were stocked through wide experience of the domain. This volume represents the work of a new generation of researchers who hold similar views about a variety of reasoning processes. For example, the view that one cannot hope to understand reasoning without understanding the memory processes that subserve it is nicely exemplified in the following quotation from the chapter by Lange et al. (this volume):

> "Since the generation of hypotheses is not random, but based on retrieval processes, it seems impossible to build an adequate theory of hypothesis-testing behavior without accounting for memory. Thus, understanding hypothesis generation as a memory-retrieval process is necessary to generalize to most real-world hypothesis-testing contexts".

We leave open the question of how much of the phenomena we label reasoning can be explained entirely via concepts from the memory literature. At a minimum, we hope that readers will consider how much richer ideas taken from the study of memory have made the study of reasoning. At a maximum, we invite you to consider the question, "How much about reasoning is there left to explain when one has extracted the variance due to memory?"

References

Charness, N. (1991). Expertise in chess: The balance between knowledge and search. In K. A. Ericsson & J. Smith (eds), *Toward a General Theory of Expertise: Prospects and Limits* (pp. 39–63). New York, NY: Cambridge University Press.

Chase, W. G. & Simon, H. A. (1973a). Perception in chess. *Cognitive Psychology*, 4(1), 55–81. doi: 10.1016/0010-0285(73)90004-2

Chase, W. G. & Simon, H. A. (1973b). The mind's eye in chess. In W. G. Chase (ed.), *Visual Information Processing* (pp. 215–281). New York, NY: Academic Press.

De Neys, W. (2006a). Automatic–heuristic and executive–analytic processing during reasoning: Chronometric and dual-task considerations. *Quarterly Journal of Experimental Psychology*, 59, 1070–1100.

De Neys, W. (2006b). Dual processing in reasoning: Two systems but one reasoner. *Psychological Science*, 17, 428–433. doi: 10.1111/j.1467-9280.2006.01723.x

De Neys, W., Schaeken, W. & d'Ydewalle, G. (2005a). Working memory and counterexample retrieval for causal conditionals. *Thinking & Reasoning*, 11, 123–150.

De Neys, W., Schaeken, W. & d'Ydewalle, G. (2005b). Working memory and counterexample retrieval for causal conditionals. *Thinking & Reasoning*, 11, 349–381.

Dougherty, M. R., Thomas, R. P. & Lange, N. (2010). Toward an integrative theory of hypothesis generation, probability judgment, and hypothesis testing. *The Psychology of Learning and Motivation, Volume 52* (pp. 300–342). Academic Press.

Evans, J. St. B. T. (2006). The heuristic-analytic theory of reasoning: Extension and evaluation. *Psychonomic Bulletin and Review*, 13, 378–395.

Evans, J. St. B. T. (2008). Dual-processing accounts of reasoning, judgment, and social cognition. *Annual Review of Psychology*, 59, 255–278.

Evans, J. St. B. T. & Stanovich, K. E. (2013). Dual-process theories of higher cognition: Advancing the debate. *Perspectives on Psychological Science*, 223–241, 263–271.

Halford, G. S. (1998). Development of processing capacity entails representing more complex relations: Implications for cognitive development. In Logie, R. & Gilhooly, K. (eds) (1998) *Working Memory and Thinking: Current Issues in Thinking and Reasoning* (pp. 139–158). Hove, UK: Psychology Press.

Hélie, S. & Sun, R. (2010). Incubation, insight, and creative problem solving: A unified theory and a connectionist model. *Psychological Review*, 117, 994–1024. doi: 10.1037/a0019532

Johnson-Laird, P. N. & Byrne, R. M. J. (2002). Conditionals: A theory of meaning, pragmatics, and inference. *Psychological Review*, 109, 606–678.

Logie, R. & Gilhooly, K. (eds) (1998). *Working Memory and Thinking: Current Issues in Thinking and Reasoning*. Hove, UK: Psychology Press.

Markovits, H., Doyon, C. & Simoneau, M. (2002). Individual differences in working memory and conditional reasoning with concrete and abstract content. *Thinking & Reasoning*, 8(2), 97–107.

Mednick, S. A. (1962). The associative basis of the creative process. *Psychological Review*, 69, 220–232.

Oberauer, K., Süß, H.-M., Wilhelm, O. & Sander, N. (2007). Individual differences in working memory capacity and reasoning ability. In A. R. A. Conway, C. Jarrold, M. J. Kane, A. Miyake & J. N. Towse (eds), *Variation in Working Memory* (pp. 49–75). New York, NY: Oxford University Press.

Stanovich, K. E. (2011). *Rationality and the Reflective Mind*. New York, NY: Oxford University Press.

Stanovich, K. E. & West, R. F. (2008). On the relative independence of thinking biases and cognitive ability. *Journal of Personality and Social Psychology*, 94, 672–695.

1

WORKING MEMORY CAPACITY AND REASONING

Nash Unsworth

A great deal of research has demonstrated an important link between working memory capacity and reasoning (e.g., Kyllonen & Christal, 1990; Engle et al., 1999; Kane et al., 2004). Despite the large amount of evidence for this relation, the reasons for it remain unclear. In the current chapter, this link is examined primarily from an individual differences perspective, focusing on which working memory components are thought to be important for reasoning. A brief overview of working memory and individual differences in working memory capacity will be given, followed by an examination of several approaches that have been used to better understand the role of working memory in various aspects of reasoning.

Individual differences in working memory capacity

Before discussing the relationship between working memory capacity and reasoning, we will briefly describe working memory capacity, how it is measured, and review the importance of it in predicting performance on both higher-order and lower-order cognitive tasks. Working memory is considered to be a system responsible for active maintenance and on-line manipulation of information over short intervals. In our view, working memory consists of a subset of activated traces above threshold, some of which are highly active strategies for maintaining activation of those traces, and an attention component (e.g., Engle et al., 1999). Thus, our view of working memory emphasizes the interaction of attention and memory in the service of complex cognition. In order to measure the capacity of working memory, researchers have relied on complex working memory span tasks based on the working memory model of Baddeley and Hitch (1974). Beginning with Daneman and Carpenter (1980), these tasks combine a simple memory span task with a secondary processing component. Initially, the idea was that these tasks would better measure a dynamic working memory system that traded off processing and storage resources. Thus, in these tasks participants are required to engage in some form of processing activity while trying to remember a set of to-be-remembered (TBR) items. As an example of such a task, consider the operation span task that requires participants to solve math operations while trying to remember unrelated words in the correct serial order (Turner & Engle, 1989). Several variations exist of this basic paradigm, with most variations consisting of different processing tasks or differences in stimuli.

Despite all these variations, performance on these complex span tasks has been shown to co-vary with performance on a number of both higher-order and lower-order cognitive tasks. Indeed, the original work of Daneman and Carpenter (1980) demonstrated that performance on complex span tasks was highly related to reading comprehension performance as measured by the verbal portion of the SATs. These complex span tasks are also related to other higher-order processes including vocabulary learning (Daneman & Green, 1986), complex learning (Kyllonen & Stephens, 1990), as well as fluid reasoning (Engle, et al., 1999; Kane et al., 2004). This impressive list demonstrates the predictive utility of working memory capacity (WMC) in a number of research domains.

Additional work has shown that WMC is also implicated in performance on many lower-order attentional tasks. This work has demonstrated that individuals who perform well on measures of WMC tend to perform better on basic attention tasks in a variety of conditions. This includes performance on tasks such as Stroop, antisaccade, dichotic listening, and flankers (see Kane et al., 2007; Unsworth & Spillers, 2010, for reviews). Clearly, then, WMC is an important predictor of behavior in a number of different situations.

Based on this prior work we have developed a theory of individual differences in WMC which suggests that these result from multiple components, each of which is important for performance on a variety of tasks (Unsworth & Engle, 2007a; Unsworth & Spillers, 2010). In particular, in our work we have suggested that both attention-control abilities and controlled search from secondary memory are important. In this framework, the attentional component serves to actively maintain a few distinct representations for on-line processing in primary memory. These representations include things such as goal states for the current task, action plans, partial solutions to reasoning problems, and item representations in list-memory tasks. In this view, as long as attention is allocated to these representations, they will be actively maintained in primary memory (Craik & Levy, 1976). This continued allocation of attention serves to protect these representations from interfering internal and external distraction, similar to the attention-control view espoused by Engle and Kane (2004). However, if attention is removed from the representations, due to internal or external distraction or to the processing of incoming information, these representations will no longer be actively maintained in primary memory, and therefore will have to be retrieved from secondary memory if needed. Accordingly, secondary memory relies on a cue-dependent search mechanism to retrieve items (Raaijmakers & Shiffrin, 1981). Additionally, the extent to which items can be retrieved from secondary memory will be dependent on overall encoding abilities, the ability to reinstate the encoding context at retrieval, and the ability to focus the search on target items and exclude interfering items (i.e., proactive interference). Similar to Atkinson and Shiffrin (1968), this framework suggests that working memory is not only a state of activation, but also represents the set of control processes that are needed to maintain that state of activation, to prevent other items from gaining access to this state of activation, and to bring other items into this state of activation via controlled retrieval (Engle et al., 1999). Thus, individual differences in WMC are indexed by both attention-control differences and retrieval differences. Furthermore, we have also suggested that other components are important (Unsworth & Spillers, 2010). These other components include the maximal number of items that can be held in primary memory (or the focus of attention; Cowan, 2001), the ability to rapidly update the contents of working memory and switch items in and out of the primary memory (Oberauer, 2002; Unsworth & Engle, 2008), as well as binding operations that are needed to momentarily bind items (Halford, Cowan, & Andrews, 2007; Oberauer, 2005; see Halford, Andrews, & Wilson in this volume). As will be seen below, a number of components are likely important for reasoning, and likely why WMC and reasoning tend to be so strongly correlated.

Working memory capacity and reasoning

Beginning with the work of Kyllonen and Christal (1990), research has suggested that there is a strong link between individual differences in WMC and reasoning abilities. In particular, this work suggests that at an individual task level, measures of WMC correlate with reasoning measures around .45 (Ackerman, Beier, & Boyle, 2005) and at the latent level, WMC and reasoning are correlated around .72 (Kane, Hambrick, & Conway, 2005). Thus, at a latent level WMC and reasoning seem to share approximately half of their variance. This suggests that there are clearly important links between WMC and reasoning, but also that these two constructs are not isomorphic. Note, for the most part prior research has focused more on inductive reasoning tasks, rather than on deductive reasoning tasks. However, recent work by Wilhelm (2005) suggests that inductive and deductive reasoning are perfectly correlated, and thus load on the same general reasoning factor. Wilhelm (2005) further pointed out that reasoning measures could be delineated based on their content (verbal, numerical, spatial). Given that prior research has primarily focused on inductive reasoning and the fact that inductive and deductive reasoning abilities seem to be strongly correlated, the current chapter will primarily focus on the link between WMC and inductive reasoning abilities. Furthermore, note that in the current chapter we will focus on inductive reasoning measures used primarily in the intelligence literature, rather than other types of inductive reasoning measures. See Feeney, Hayes, and Heit (this volume) for a discussion of the relation between recognition memory and these other inductive reasoning measures.

As an example that WMC is strongly correlated with general reasoning, we reanalyzed data from a prior study (Unsworth et al., 2009) that examined the correlation between WMC and multiple measures of reasoning. Important for the current discussion is the fact that in this study we used three WMC measures, each of which differed in its content, as well as six reasoning tasks that also varied in their content. Shown in Figure 1.1a is the resulting latent variable model. As can be seen, there was a higher-order reasoning factor composed of lower-order content-specific reasoning factors, each of which loaded strongly on the higher-order factor. Importantly, this reasoning factor was strongly correlated with the WMC factor. Thus, consistent with much prior research, WMC and reasoning (broadly defined) were strongly related. As a further example of this relation, we reanalyzed data from 630 participants from our laboratory, each of whom had completed three WMC measures and three reasoning measures. Shown in Figure 1.1b is the resulting latent variable model. As can be seen, WMC and reasoning abilities again were strongly related. These examples demonstrate that WMC and reasoning are strongly related and share a good deal of common variance. Furthermore, these examples demonstrate that this important relation is domain-general in nature, given that both the WMC and reasoning factors were made up by tasks varying in their content. This suggests that whatever the reasons for the relation between WMC and reasoning abilities, they are likely domain-general and cut across multiple different types of tasks.

Not only is it important to demonstrate that WMC and reasoning are related at the latent level, it is also important to demonstrate that similar relations are found at the individual task level, and to explore these task-level relations in more detail. For example, in our sample of 630 participants, the correlation between WMC and the Raven Advanced Progressive Matrices was .40. Likewise, the correlation between WMC and number series was .32, and the correlation between WMC and verbal analogies was .35. These values correspond well with the overall meta-analytic correlation reported by Ackerman et al. (2005), and suggest that the correlation between WMC and reasoning is remarkably similar for different types of reasoning tasks. Thus, it is not simply the case that WMC correlates only with matrix reasoning tasks, or only with analogical reasoning tasks, but rather that WMC seems to be related to various different types of reasoning tasks that vary not only in the type of reasoning required, but also in the content.

Further examination of these task-level correlations is important to rule out various explanations for the correlation between WMC and reasoning. For example, one common explanation for the relation between WMC and measures of reasoning is based on item difficulty, such that on the easiest reasoning problems WMC will not be taxed much, allowing for even low-WMC individuals to get the correct answer. However, as difficulty increases due to an increase in the number of rules or goals that have to be maintained, WMC will be taxed more, allowing only the high-WMC individuals to generate the correct answer (Carpenter, Just, & Shell, 1990). According to these types of views, the correlation between WMC and reasoning should be small to nonexistent on the easiest problems, but the

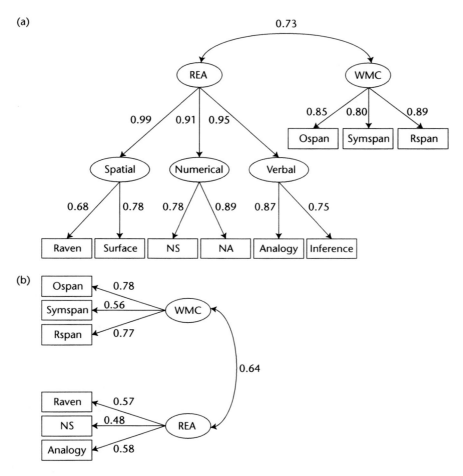

FIGURE 1.1 (a) Confirmatory factor analysis for higher-order reasoning factor (REA) based on lower-order factors composed of spatial, numerical, and verbal reasoning and the relation between the higher-order factor and WMC. Raven = Raven Advanced Progressive Matrices; Surface = surface development; NS = number series; NA = necessary arithmetic operations; Analogy = verbal analogies; Inference = verbal inferences; Ospan = operation span; Symspan = symmetry span; Rspan = reading span. (b) Confirmatory factor analysis for reasoning and WMC. All paths are significant at the $p < .05$ level

correlation should steadily increase as difficulty increases. Given that many reasoning tasks are structured such that the easiest problems are at the beginning and the hardest problems are at the end, these views predict that the correlation between WMC and solution accuracy should increase as a function of problem number. However, prior work has found no such relation. In fact, prior work suggests a nearly flat relation across difficulty levels (Salthouse, 1993; Unsworth &

Engle, 2005; Wiley et al., 2011). One limitation for these prior studies is that they typically only focused on one WMC measure and one reasoning measure (Ravens). Therefore, to examine the notion that item difficulty drives the correlation between WMC and reasoning, we examined the item correlations for the Ravens, number series, and verbal analogies with the composite WMC variable described previously. As shown in Figure 1.2a, the correlations between solution accuracy for each Raven item and WMC, although fluctuating widely, do not appear to increase in any systematic manner as difficulty increases.[1] Indeed, the correlation between WMC and accuracy on the first problem was as high as with the last problem. These results replicate prior research that has specifically focused on the Ravens. Perhaps more interestingly, similar patterns emerged on both the number series (Figure 1.2b) and the verbal analogies (Figure 1.2c) tasks. In all cases there does not seem to be a systematic relation between WMC and solution accuracy as a function of item number.

To explore the notion that as difficulty increases so too should the correlation between WMC and reasoning, we computed quartiles based on solution accuracy, such that the easiest problems in each task were in the first quartile, the next hardest problems in the second quartile, and so forth, as has been done previously (Salthouse, 2000; Unsworth & Engle, 2005). This procedure addresses the issue of item difficulty a bit better than simply looking at problem number, given that the tasks are not always structured based on item difficulty. Looking at the relation between WMC and solution accuracy on the Raven as a function of item difficulty, the results suggested that the correlations do not increase as a function of item difficulty (Raven Quartile 1 = .33, Raven Quartile 2 = .31, Raven Quartile 3 = .32, Raven Quartile 4 = .19), consistent with prior research (Unsworth & Engle, 2005). Similarly the correlations between WMC and solution accuracy on number series did not increase as a function of item difficulty (Number Series Quartile 1 = .31, Number Series Quartile 2 = .20, Number Series Quartile 3 = .23, Number Series Quartile 4 = .16), nor did the correlations for verbal analogies (Analogies Quartile 1 = .23, Analogies Quartile 2 = .19, Analogies Quartile 3 = .27, Analogies Quartile 4 = .23). Thus across all three reasoning tasks the correlation between WMC and solution accuracy was remarkably constant across differing levels of difficulty. This suggests that item difficulty (and whatever likely changes with difficulty levels) is not the driving force for the relation between WMC and reasoning.

The work reviewed thus far suggests that WMC and reasoning are strongly related constructs. This correlation seems to be domain-general in nature, given that the common variance shared across numerical, verbal, and spatial-reasoning tasks correlates strongly with the common variance shared across different WMC tasks. Furthermore, similar relations are found across reasoning tasks differing not only in the types of reasoning involved, but also differing in the content of the items. Finally, this work suggests that variation in item difficulty does not account for the relation between WMC and reasoning, given that the correlation between WMC and reasoning remains remarkably stable across varying levels of difficulty in a number of different reasoning tasks.

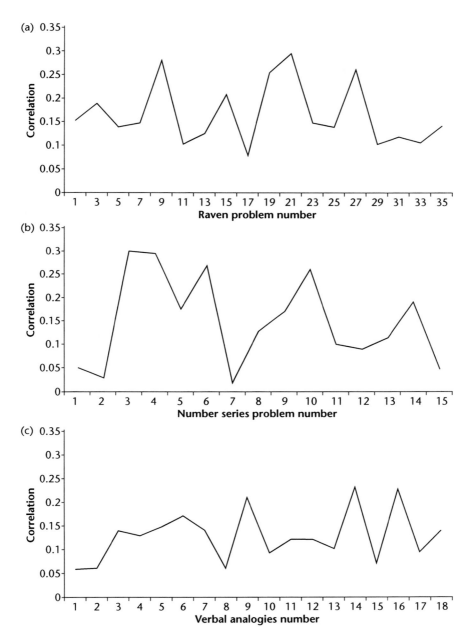

FIGURE 1.2 (a) Point-biserial correlations of solution accuracy with WMC for individual Raven problems. (b) Point-biserial correlations of solution accuracy with WMC for individual number series problems. (c) Point-biserial correlations of solution accuracy with WMC for individual verbal analogies problems.

Assessing the influence of multiple components

Clearly there is a strong link between WMC and reasoning, and this link is unlikely due to simple explanations such as item difficulty. What then is the reason for this strong correlation? Is there a single driving factor that accounts for the relation, or are multiple factors important? In the remainder of the chapter we will explore whether a single component is important or whether multiple components/ mechanisms are important. In doing so we will rely on reanalyses of several data sets that have tended to explore one factor or another. In these reanalyses we will utilize mediation models to examine whether the correlation between WMC and reasoning is reduced or eliminated once another factor thought to be important for the relation is statistically controlled. Specifically, we will rely on bifactor models, in which the common variance between WMC and some other variable (such as attention control) will be extracted and form a factor, and the unique variance associated with WMC only will form another factor. If the shared variance is important for the relation with reasoning, we would expect that the correlation between the residual WMC variance and reasoning should be zero, and the relation between the common variance and reasoning should be quite strong. If, however, multiple components are important for the relation between WMC and reasoning, we should see that the residual WMC variance still predicts reasoning even after controlling for the common variance.

Scope of attention/size of primary memory

According to Cowan and colleagues (Cowan, 2001; Cowan et al., 2005), one reason that WMC and reasoning tend to correlate so well is because WMC tasks partially measure the capacity or scope of the focus of attention. Theoretically, the capacity of the focus of attention is limited to roughly four items, but there are large individual differences in this capacity. Thus, individuals with large capacities can simultaneously maintain more information in working memory than individuals with smaller capacities.

In terms of reasoning, this means that high-capacity individuals can simultaneously attend to multiple goals, sub-goals, hypotheses, and partial solutions for problems that they are working on, allowing them to better solve problems than low-capacity individuals, who cannot maintain/store as much information. Evidence consistent with this hypothesis comes from a variety of studies that have shown that putative measures of this capacity limit are correlated with WMC measures such as complex span tasks, and with various reasoning measures (Cowan et al., 2005, Fukuda, Vogel, Mayr, & Awh, 2010; Shipstead, Redick, Hicks, & Engle, in press). Thus, it seems quite reasonable that the reason WMC correlates with reasoning is due to individual differences in the size or scope of the focus of attention, which limits the ability to effectively solve a variety of reasoning problems.

To examine the notion that the scope of attention is important, we reanalyzed data from Shipstead et al. (in press), in which over 500 individuals completed a version of a change-detection task that has long been thought to provide an estimate of the size of the focus of attention (Cowan, 2001; Luck & Vogel, 1997), along with multiple WMC measures and measures of general reasoning. In this reanalysis we specified a model in which the common variance across the change detection and WMC measures loaded onto a single factor (Scope), and the variance unique only to the WMC measures loaded onto a separate factor (WMC). The correlation between these two factors was set to zero. This model tests the notion that the reason WMC predicts reasoning ability is due to individual differences in the scope of attention. If this is correct, then we should see a substantial relation between the Scope factor and the reasoning factor. Furthermore, if the scope of attention is the sole reason for the relation, we should see that the relation between the residual WMC factor and the reasoning factor is near zero. If, however, the scope of attention only partially accounts for the relation between WMC and reasoning, we should see that the residual WMC factor still predicts reasoning once the scope of attention is statistically controlled for. Shown in Figure 1.3 is the resulting model. As can be seen, the variance theoretically associated with the scope of attention, which cuts across both complex span tasks and change-detection tasks, strongly predicted reasoning, as has been shown previously. Additionally, variance uniquely associated with WMC was also strongly predictive of reasoning. These results suggest that individual differences in the capacity or scope of attention partially account for the relation between WMC and reasoning, but this is not the whole story. There is substantial variance shared between WMC and reasoning over and above that accounted for by variation in scope. Thus, other factors also seem responsible for the relation between WMC and reasoning.

One problem with this analysis is that it is only based on one scope of attention task (change detection), and thus it is not clear whether a broad conclusion on the role of the scope of attention can be made from this data. A theoretically identical concept is that of primary memory, which is also thought to be capacity limited to roughly four items (Craik & Levy, 1976). Traditionally, primary memory has been assessed with immediate free-recall measures as well as serial-recall measures. Thus, to assess whether or not the size of primary memory partially accounts for the relation between WMC and reasoning, we reanalyzed data from Unsworth and Engle (2007b). In this reanalysis we examined performance on three WMC measures along with three measures of primary memory for 133 participants. These included an estimate of primary memory from immediate free recall (Tulving & Colotla, 1970) and estimates of primary memory from two immediate serial-recall tasks (Unsworth & Engle, 2006). Across all three of these measures, the average estimate of primary memory was close to four items, and there was a large amount of variability across individuals. As with the prior model, we specified a bifactor model with the common variance shared across the primary memory estimates and WMC measures loading on one factor (PM), and the unique variance for the WMC measures loading on a separate factor. Shown in Figure 1.4 is the resulting model. Similar to the prior model examining the scope of attention, we see that primary memory significantly predicted reasoning, and the residual variance

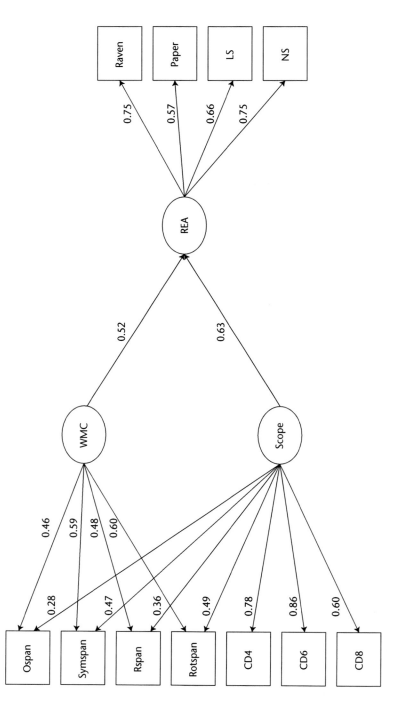

FIGURE 1.3 Structural equation model for the common variance shared across all the tasks thought to represent the scope of attention (Scope), and the residual variance common to only the working memory capacity (WMC) tasks predicting reasoning (REA). Ospan = operation span; Symspan = symmetry span; Rspan = reading span; Rotspan = rotation span; CD4 = change detection set size 4; CD6 = change detection set size 6; CD8 = change detection set size 8; Raven = Raven Advanced Progressive Matrices; Paper = paper folding; LS = letter sets; NS = number series. All paths and loadings were significant at the $p < .05$ level.

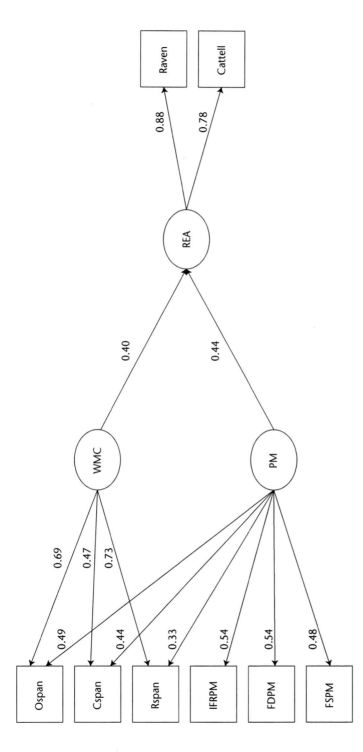

FIGURE 1.4 Structural equation model for the common variance shared across all the tasks thought to represent primary memory (PM) and the residual variance common to only the working memory capacity (WMC) tasks predicting reasoning (REA). Ospan = operation span; Cspan = counting span; Rspan = reading span; IFRPM = primary memory estimate from immediate free recall; FDPM = primary memory estimate from forward span with phonologically dissimilar words; FSPM = primary memory estimate from forward span with phonologically similar words; Raven = Raven Advanced Progressive Matrices; Cattell = Cattell Culture Fair Test. All paths and loadings were significant at the $p < .05$ level.

associated only with WMC also predicted reasoning. Again this suggests that although the size of primary memory/scope of attention partially accounts for the relation between WMC and reasoning, there are other components/mechanisms that account for the relation as well. Thus, although individual differences in the capacity of the focus of attention/primary memory are important, there is more to the story.

Attention control

Another widely held view suggests that the reason WMC and reasoning are so strongly correlated is because of individual differences in attention control (Engle & Kane, 2004). According to attention-control theories of WMC, the primary determinant of individual differences in WMC, and the reason why WMC predicts performance on so many tasks, is attention-control abilities. In particular, Engle, Kane, Conway, and colleagues (Engle & Kane, 2004; Kane et al., 2007) have suggested that domain-general attention-control abilities are needed to actively maintain task-relevant information in the presence of potent internal and external distraction. Attention control is needed to ensure that task goals are maintained in an active state and to prevent attentional capture from other distracting stimuli. According to this attention-control theory of WMC, high-WMC individuals have greater attention-control capabilities than low-WMC individuals, and thus are better at actively maintaining information in the presence of distraction. Evidence consistent with this view comes from a number of studies that have found strong correlations between various attention-control measures and WMC at both the task and latent levels (Engle & Kane, 2004; Unsworth & Spillers, 2010).

In terms of reasoning, this view suggests that high-WMC individuals are better able to solve complex reasoning problems because they are better at maintaining task goals, sub-goals, hypotheses, and partial solutions to problems they are working on in the face of potent distraction. This distraction could be from irrelevant thoughts and feelings leading to mind-wandering, external distraction in the current environment, irrelevant information from prior problems or related semantic content, or distracting information from the current trial. Thus, according to these views, WMC is needed to combat distraction to prevent attentional capture and maintain attentional focus on the current task. Given the difficulty and complexities inherent in reasoning problems, any lapse of attention away from the current task could lead to inabilities to solve the current problem. Although this view is similar to scope of attention views, the main difference is that scope of attention views suggest that it is the size of the focus of attention that matters, whereas attention-control views suggest that it is the ability to control access to the focus of attention that matters. Evidence consistent with this view is the finding that attention-control measures are not only correlated with WMC, but they are also correlated with reasoning (Unsworth & Spillers, 2010). Thus, it seems likely that, at least, part of the reason that WMC and reasoning are so highly correlated is because of the shared influence of attention control.

To assess whether attention control accounts for the relation between WMC and reasoning, we reanalyzed data from Unsworth and Spillers (2010) in which 181 participants performed three different WMC tasks, three reasoning measures, along with four attention-control measures. Like prior models, we specified a bifactor model in which the common variance shared across the WMC and attention-control measures formed an attention-control factor, and the residual WMC variance formed another factor. The correlation between these factors was set to zero and both were allowed to predict the reasoning factor. Shown in Figure 1.5 is the resulting model. As can be seen, attention control strongly predicted general reasoning abilities. Thus, the variance shared across attention-control tasks and measures of WMC was a strong predictor of reasoning abilities consistent with attention-control views. Additionally, the variance shared by WMC measures independent of attention control also predicted reasoning abilities. Similar to the scope of attention results, these results suggest that attention control partially accounts for the relation between WMC and reasoning, but it is not the only reason for the relation.

Secondary memory retrieval

Given that the capacity of the focus of attention (or primary memory) is limited to approximately four items, and given that attention-control abilities are limited in the extent to which they can protect items in the focus of attention, it seems likely that some items will not be able to be maintained, and thus, they will have to be retrieved from secondary memory (or long-term memory). As noted previously, in this view we have suggested that individual differences in WMC are partially due to differences in the ability to retrieve items from secondary memory that could not be actively maintained in the focus of attention. Specifically, we have suggested that high-WMC individuals have better-controlled search abilities than low-WMC individuals. These controlled search abilities include setting up an overall retrieval plan, generating retrieval cues to search memory with, and various monitoring decisions. Thus, WMC is needed not only to actively maintain information in the focus of attention, but also to retrieve items that could not be maintained, or to bring relevant information into the focus from secondary memory (Unsworth & Engle, 2007a). Evidence consistent with this view comes from a number of studies that have demonstrated a strong link between WMC measures and secondary memory measures at both the task and latent levels (Unsworth, 2010a; Unsworth, Brewer, & Spillers, 2009).

In terms of reasoning, this view suggests that part of the reason that WMC and reasoning correlate so well is because both rely, in part, on secondary memory retrieval. That is, high-WMC individuals are better able to solve reasoning problems than low-WMC individuals, because even though some information (goals, hypotheses, partial solutions, etc.) will be displaced from the focus of attention, high-WMC individuals will be better at recovering that information and bringing it back into the focus of attention than low-WMC individuals. Thus, any

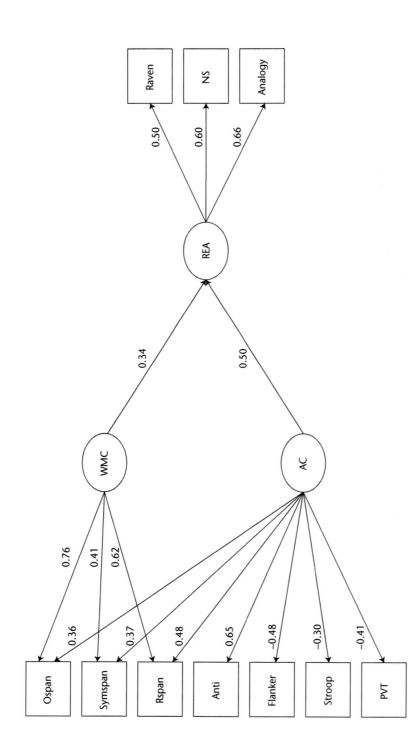

FIGURE 1.5 Structural equation model for the common variance shared across all the tasks thought to represent attention control (AC) and the residual variance common to only the working memory capacity (WMC) tasks predicting reasoning (REA). Ospan = operation span; Symspan = symmetry span; Rspan = reading span; Anti = antisaccade; Flanker = arrow flankers; Stroop = color word Stroop; PVT = psychomotor vigilance task; Raven = Raven Advanced Progressive Matrices; NS = number series; Analogy = verbal analogies. All paths and loadings were significant at the $p < .05$ level.

loss of information can quickly and accurately be recovered by high-WMC individuals, allowing for the correct solution to be made. Low-WMC individuals, however, will be less likely to recover lost information, and thus, will be less likely to correctly solve the problem. A number of recent studies have provided evidence consistent with this view by demonstrating that WMC and secondary memory measures are correlated, and both are correlated with reasoning measures (Unsworth, 2010a; Unsworth, Brewer, & Spillers, 2009; Mogle et al., 2008).

To better examine the notion that individual differences in retrieval from secondary memory partially account for the relation between WMC and reasoning, we reanalyzed data from Unsworth (2010a), in which 165 participants performed three WMC measures, three reasoning measures, and nine secondary memory measures. These secondary memory measures included measures of free recall, cued recall, item recognition, source recognition, and list-discrimination, in order to have a very broad secondary memory factor. A bifactor model was specified in which the common variance shared by the WMC and secondary memory tasks formed a secondary memory factor, and the residual WMC variance formed another factor. The correlation between these two factors was set to zero, and both were allowed to predict the broad reasoning factor. The resulting model is shown in Figure 1.6. Consistent with prior research, the secondary memory factor predicted reasoning abilities, suggesting that part of the reason that WMC correlates with reasoning abilities is due to secondary memory-retrieval abilities. Additionally, as can be seen, WMC still predicted reasoning even after statistically controlling for secondary memory abilities. As with the prior models, this suggests that secondary memory abilities are only part of the reason for the correlation between WMC and reasoning.

In addition to basic secondary memory abilities, another potential component is interference control abilities. It has long been recognized that interference control is an important aspect not only of working memory, but also of cognitive abilities and reasoning (Dempster & Corkill, 1999; Hasher, Lustig, & Zacks, 2007; Unsworth, 2010b). Specifically, recent work has suggested that the ability to deal with interference or conflict from recently presented memories that were once relevant, but are now irrelevant, is one key component of WMC, and one reason why WMC measures tend to correlate so well with measures of reasoning. Note in the current chapter that interference control refers only to interference from competing memory traces and does not index other potential inhibitory constructs such as resistance to prepotent responses (which would be considered more as attention-control rather than secondary memory abilities). A number of studies have demonstrated evidence consistent with this view by suggesting that interference-control measures are related to both WMC and reasoning (Bunting, 2006; Burgess, Braver, Conway, & Gray, 2011; Unsworth, 2010b).

To better examine this notion we reanalyzed data from Unsworth (2010b), in which 161 participants performed three WMC measures, two reasoning measures, and four interference-control measures from four secondary memory tasks. A bifactor model was specified in which the common variance shared by the WMC

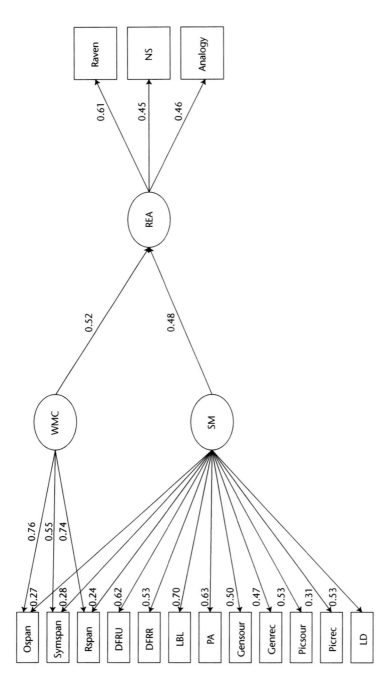

FIGURE 1.6 Structural equation model for the common variance shared across all the tasks thought to represent secondary memory (SM) and the residual variance common to only the working memory capacity (WMC) tasks predicting reasoning (REA). Ospan = operation span; Symspan = symmetry span; Rspan = reading span; DFRU = delayed free recall with unrelated words: LBL = list-before-last recall; PA = paired-associates recall; Gensour = gender source recognition; Genrec = gender recognition; Picsour = picture source recognition; Picrec = picture recognition; LD = list discrimination; Raven = Raven Advanced Progressive Matrices; NS = number series; Analogy = verbal analogies. All paths and loadings were significant at the *p* < .05 level.

and interference-control measures formed an interference-control factor, and the residual WMC variance formed another factor. The correlation between these two factors was set to zero and both were allowed to predict the broad reasoning factor. The resulting model is shown in Figure 1.7. As can be seen, interference control had a strong negative relation with reasoning, suggesting that individuals who experience less interference have higher reasoning scores, consistent with prior research. Importantly, even though the shared variance between WMC and interference control predicted reasoning, the residual WMC variance also predicted reasoning independent of interference control. These results suggest that interference control from competing secondary memory traces partially mediates the relation between WMC and reasoning, but it is not the only factor that is important.

Multifaceted nature of WMC and reasoning

The work reviewed thus far suggests that there is likely not a single factor/ component that accounts for the relation between WMC and reasoning. Specifically, although the scope of attention/size of primary memory, attention control, retrieval from secondary memory, and interference control were all found to account for some of the relation, none was found to fully account for the relation. This suggests that the relation between WMC and reasoning is multifaceted, in that a number of components are likely important. In our work we have suggested that WMC is represented by both primary and secondary memory components (Unsworth & Engle, 2007a; Unsworth & Spillers, 2010). Primary memory reflects both the number of items that can be distinctly maintained, and attention-control processes that actively maintain those items and prevent attentional capture. Secondary memory reflects the need to retrieve items that could not be maintained in primary memory, as well as the need to retrieve other relevant information from secondary memory in the presence of competing memory traces (i.e., interference control). According to this multifaceted model of WMC, there are multiple sources of variance within WMC, and multiple sources of variance that account for the relation between WMC and reasoning (Unsworth & Spillers, 2010; see also Conway et al., 2011). As such, this model nicely explains the reanalyses reviewed thus far, by suggesting that each of these components is important for individual differences in WMC and its relation with reasoning, but no one component is fully responsible for the relation.

To examine the notion that separate components are responsible for the relation between WMC and reasoning, we reanalyzed data from Unsworth and Spillers (2010). As noted previously, in this study participants performed various WMC, attention-control, and reasoning measures. In addition, participants also performed various secondary memory tasks in order to determine if attention control and secondary memory would jointly account for the relation between WMC and reasoning. As before, a bifactor model was specified. In this model we specified one factor as the variance common to WMC and attention-control measures. Another

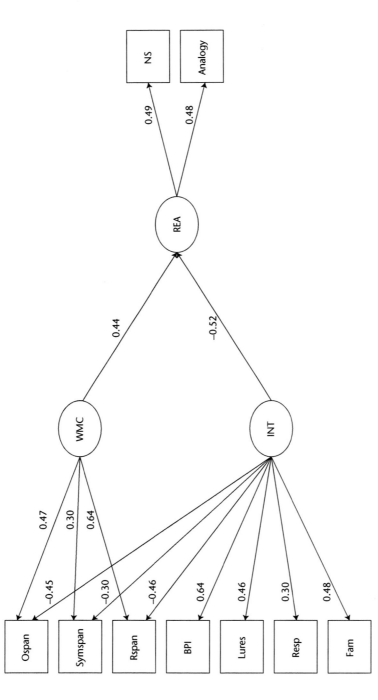

FIGURE 1.7 Structural equation model for the common variance shared across all the tasks thought to represent interference control (INT) and the residual variance common to only the working memory capacity (WMC) tasks predicting reasoning (REA). Ospan = operation span; Symspan = symmetry span; Rspan = reading span; BPI = interference on the Brown–Peterson task; Lures = lure errors on cued-recall task; Resp = response-based interference on recent probes task; Fam = familiarity-based interference on recent probes task; NS = number series; Analogy = verbal analogies. All paths and loadings were significant at the $p < .05$ level.

factor was specified as the variance common to WMC and secondary memory measures. Finally, another factor was composed of the residual WMC variance. The correlations among the three factors were set to zero and all were allowed to predict the general reasoning factor. As shown in Figure 1.8, the WMC measures had significant loadings on all three factors, suggesting at least three sources of variance were present in the WMC measures. Additionally, both the attention-control and secondary memory factors were related with reasoning. Importantly, even after controlling for these two sources of variance, the residual WMC variance still predicted reasoning. These results suggest that WMC is composed of at least three separate sources of variance, and these three sources of variance independently contribute to individual differences in reasoning.

Based on the prior review and our current theoretical model, we suggest that the residual WMC variance reflects the scope of attention/size of primary memory. However, such a claim would be significantly bolstered by work that actually includes capacity measures, rather than only relying on the residual WMC variance. Luckily, recent data collected at the University of Oregon by Keisuke Fukuda, Ed Awh, Ed Vogel, and myself can cast light on this issue. Specifically, in this study 171 participants performed multiple WMC, AC, secondary memory, scope of attention measures (various change-detection tasks), and measures of fluid reasoning. As with previous models, a bifactor model was specified, in which one factor was the variance common to WMC and attention-control measures. Another factor was specified as the variance common to WMC and secondary memory measures. And another factor was specified as the variance common to WMC and the scope of attention measures. Finally, another factor was composed of the residual WMC variance. The correlations among the four factors were set to zero, and all were allowed to predict the general reasoning factor. As shown in Figure 1.9, the WMC measures tended to cross-load on all four factors, suggesting several sources of variance were present in the WMC measures. Furthermore, the attention-control, secondary memory, and Scope factors all predicted unique variance in reasoning. Importantly, the residual correlation between WMC and reasoning was no longer significant.

These results strongly suggest that multiple mechanisms drive the relation between WMC and reasoning. Specifically, these results suggest that the reason WMC is related to reasoning is due to separate sources of variance tied to differences in attention control, differences in secondary memory, and differences in the scope of attention/primary memory. In order to understand why WMC strongly predicts individual differences in reasoning, we must attempt to understand the multifaceted nature of WMC and understand how these various mechanisms independently and jointly lead to variation in broad reasoning abilities.

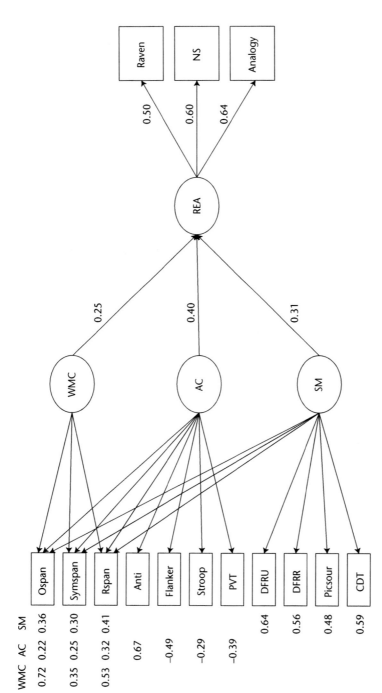

FIGURE 1.8 Structural equation model for the common variance shared across all the tasks thought to represent attention control (AC), common variance shared across tasks thought to represent secondary memory (SM) and the residual variance common to only the working memory capacity (WMC) tasks predicting reasoning (REA). Ospan = operation span; Symspan = symmetry span; Rspan = reading span; Anti = antisaccade; Flanker = arrow flankers; Stroop = color word Stroop; PVT = psychomotor vigilance task; DFRU = delayed free recall with unrelated words; DFRR = delayed free recall with semantically related words; Picsour = picture source recognition; CDT = continuous distractor free recall; Raven = Raven Advanced Progressive Matrices; NS = number series; Analogy = verbal analogies. All paths and loadings were significant at the *p* < .05 level.

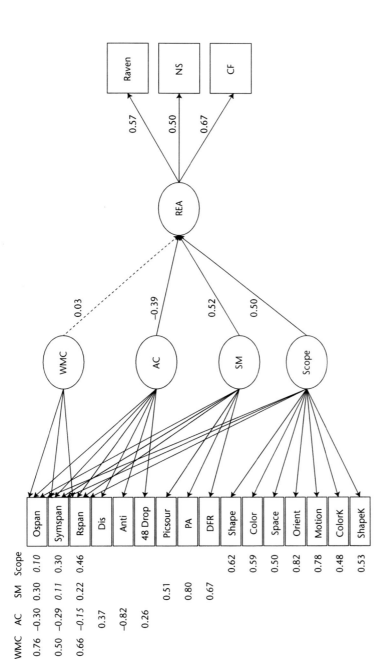

FIGURE 1.9 Structural equation model for the common variance shared across all the tasks thought to represent attention control (AC), common variance shared across tasks thought to represent secondary memory (SM), common variance shared across tasks thought to represent the scope of attention (Scope), and the residual variance common to only the working memory capacity (WMC) tasks predicting reasoning (REA). Ospan = operation span; Symspan = symmetry span; Rspan = reading span; Dis = disengagement task; Anti = antisaccade; 48 Drop = 48 Drop task; Picsour = picture source recognition; PA = paired-associates recall task; DFR = delayed free-recall task; Raven = Raven Advanced Progressive Matrices; NS = number series; CF = Cattell Culture Fair test. Non-significant loadings are italicized, and non-significant paths are shown with a dashed line. All other paths and loadings were significant at the *p* < .05 level.

Conclusions

In the present chapter we have shown that individual differences in WMC are related to individual differences in reasoning. In particular, we have shown that this relation is domain-general in nature. Furthermore, we have shown that this relation is not due to changes in item difficulty, as some theories suggest. Rather, the correlation between WMC and reasoning is constant across varying levels of difficulty for a number of different reasoning tasks. These results suggest that the relation between WMC and reasoning is not likely due to basic factors such as item content or idiosyncratic task effects. Rather, these results suggest that the relation between WMC and reasoning is quite broad and stable across various different types of tasks.

In the present chapter we also explored various unitary accounts of the relation between WMC and reasoning. In particular, we explored whether individual differences in the scope of attention, attention control, secondary memory, or interference control could account for the relation. Reanalyses of several datasets suggested that each of these components was important for the relation, but none of these components fully accounted for the relation between WMC and reasoning. Rather, in each case WMC still predicted reasoning after controlling for the other factor. However, once all three components were accounted for, WMC no longer predicted reasoning. Based on these and similar results, we have argued for a multifaceted view of WMC and its relation to reasoning. According to this multifaceted view, individual differences in WMC are due to variation in primary memory (size and attention control) and secondary memory components, and these components account for unique and shared variance in reasoning. Thus, we suggest that the relation between WMC and reasoning is due to a number of components (see also Conway et al., 2011). Of course, future work is needed to better test this multifaceted view and to better examine how each of these components is needed on various reasoning measures, and whether their contribution to reasoning is due to unique or joint effects. For now, the results from various studies point to the multifaceted nature of WMC and its relation to reasoning. To truly appreciate the WMC–reasoning relation, one must look for multiple sources of variance, rather than just a single source.

References

Ackerman, P. L., Beier, M. E., & Boyle, M. O. (2005). Working memory and intelligence: The same or different constructs? *Psychological Bulletin, 131,* 30–60.

Atkinson, R. C., & Shiffrin, R. M. (1968). Human memory: A proposed system and its control processes. In K. W. Spence (Ed.), *The Psychology of Learning and Motivation, Vol. 2* (pp. 89–195). New York: Academic Press.

Baddeley, A. D., & Hitch, G. (1974). Working memory. In G. H. Bower (Ed.), *The Psychology of Learning and Motivation, Vol. 8* (pp. 47–89). New York: Academic Press.

Bunting, M. F. (2006). Proactive interference and item similarity in working memory. *Journal of Experimental Psychology: Learning, Memory, and Cognition, 32,* 183–196.

Burgess, G. C., Braver, T. S., Conway, A. R. A., & Gray, J. R. (2011). Neural mechanisms of interference control underlie the relationship between fluid intelligence and working memory span. *Journal of Experimental Psychology: General, 140,* 674–692.

Carpenter, P. A., Just, M. A., & Shell, P. (1990). What one intelligence test measures: A theoretical account of the processing in the Raven Progressive Matrices test. *Psychological Review, 97,* 404–431.

Conway, A. R. A., Getz, S. J., Macnamara, B., & Engel de Abreu, P. M. J. (2011). Working memory and fluid intelligence: A multi-mechanism view. In Sternberg, R. J., & Kaufman, S. B. (Eds.), *The Cambridge Handbook of Intelligence.* Cambridge, UK: Cambridge University Press.

Cowan, N. (2001). The magical number 4 in short-term memory: A reconsideration of mental storage capacity. *Behavioral and Brain Sciences, 24,* 97–185.

Cowan, N., Elliott, E. M., Saults, J. S., Morey, C. C., Mattox, S., Hismjatullina, A., & Conway, A. R. A. (2005). On the capacity of attention: Its estimation and its role in working memory and cognitive aptitudes. *Cognitive Psychology, 51,* 42–100.

Craik, F. I. M., & Levy, B. A. (1976). The concept of primary memory. In W. K. Estes (Ed.), *Handbook of Learning and Cognitive Processes* (pp. 133–175). New York: Lawrence Erlbaum Associates.

Daneman, M., & Carpenter, P. A. (1980). Individual differences in working memory and reading. *Journal of Verbal Learning and Verbal Behavior, 19,* 450–466.

Daneman, M., & Green, I. (1986). Individual differences in comprehending and producing words in context. *Journal of Memory and Language, 25,* 1–8.

Dempster, F. N., & Corkill, A. J. (1999). Individual differences in susceptibility to interference and general cognitive ability. *Acta Psychologica, 101,* 395–416.

Engle, R. W., & Kane, M. J. (2004). Executive attention, working memory capacity, and a two-factor theory of cognitive control. In B. Ross (Ed.), *The Psychology of Learning and Motivation, Vol. 44* (pp. 145–199). New York: Elsevier.

Engle, R. W., Tuholski, S. W., Laughlin, J. E., & Conway, A. R. A. (1999). Working memory, short-term memory and general fluid intelligence: A latent-variable approach. *Journal of Experimental Psychology: General, 128,* 309–331.

Fukuda, K., Vogel, E. K., Mayr, U., & Awh, E. (2010). Quantity not quality: The relationship between fluid intelligence and working memory capacity. *Psychonomic Bulletin & Review, 17,* 673–679.

Halford, G. S., Cowan, N., & Andrews, G. (2007). Separating cognitive capacity from knowledge: A new hypothesis. *Trends in Cognitive Sciences, 11,* 236–242.

Hasher, L., Lustig, C., & Zacks, R. T. (2007). Inhibitory mechanisms and the control of attention. In A. R. A. Conway, C. Jarrold, M. J. Kane, A. Miyake, & J. N. Towse (Eds.), *Variation in Working Memory.* New York: Oxford.

Kane, M. J., Conway, A. R. A., Hambrick, D. Z., & Engle, R. W. (2007). Variation in working memory capacity as variation in executive attention and control. In A. R. A. Conway, C. Jarrold, M. J. Kane, A. Miyake, & J. N. Towse (Eds.), *Variation in Working Memory.* New York: Oxford.

Kane, M. J., Hambrick, D. Z., & Conway, A. R. A. (2005). Working memory capacity and fluid intelligence are strongly related constructs: Comment on Ackerman, Beier, and Boyle (2005). *Psychological Bulletin, 131,* 66–71.

Kane, M. J., Hambrick, D. Z., Tuholski, S. W., Wilhelm, O., Payne, T. W., & Engle, R. W. (2004). The generality of working-memory capacity: A latent-variable approach to verbal and visuo-spatial memory span and reasoning. *Journal of Experimental Psychology: General, 133,* 189–217.

Kyllonen, P. C., & Christal, R. E. (1990). Reasoning ability is (little more than) working-memory capacity? *Intelligence, 14,* 389–433.

Kyllonen, P. C., & Stephens, D. L. (1990). Cognitive abilities as determinants of success in acquiring logic skill. *Learning and Individual Differences, 2,* 129–160.

Luck, S. J., & Vogel, E. K. (1997). The capacity of visual working memory for features and conjunctions. *Nature, 390,* 279–281.

Mogle, J. A., Lovett, B. J., Stawski, R. S., & Sliwinski, M. J. (2008). What's so special about working memory? An examination of the relationship among working memory, secondary memory, and fluid intelligence. *Psychological Science, 19,* 1071–1077.

Oberauer, K. (2002). Access to information in working memory: Exploring the focus of attention. *Journal of Experimental Psychology: Learning, Memory, and Cognition, 28,* 411–421.

Oberauer, K. (2005). Binding and inhibition in working memory: Individual and age differences in short-term recognition. *Journal of Experimental Psychology: General, 134,* 368–387.

Raaijmakers, J. G. W., & Shiffrin, R. M. (1981). Search of associative memory. *Psychological Review, 88,* 93–134.

Salthouse, T. A. (1993). Influence of working memory on adult age differences in matrix reasoning. *British Journal of Psychology, 84,* 171–199.

Salthouse, T. A. (2000). Item analyses of age relations on reasoning tests. *Psychology and Aging, 15,* 3–8.

Shipstead, Z., Redick. T. S., Hicks, K. L., Engle, R. W. (in press). The scope and control of attention as separate aspects of working memory. *Memory.*

Tulving, E., & Colotla, V.A. (1970). Free recall of trilingual lists. *Cognitive Psychology, 1,* 86–98.

Turner, M. L., & Engle, R. W. (1989). Is working memory capacity task dependent? *Journal of Memory and Language, 28,* 127–154.

Unsworth, N. (2010a). On the division of working memory and long-term memory and their relation to intelligence: A latent variable analysis. *Acta Psychologica, 134,* 16–28.

Unsworth, N. (2010b). Interference control, working memory capacity, and cognitive abilities: A latent variable analysis. *Intelligence, 38,* 255–267.

Unsworth, N., & Engle, R. W. (2005). Working memory capacity and fluid abilities: Examining the correlation between operation span and raven. *Intelligence, 33,* 67–81.

Unsworth, N., & Engle, R. W. (2006). Simple and complex memory spans and their relation to fluid abilities: Evidence from list-length effects. *Journal of Memory and Language, 54,* 68–80.

Unsworth, N., & Engle, R. W. (2007a). The nature of individual differences in working memory capacity: Active maintenance in primary memory and controlled search from secondary memory. *Psychological Review, 114,* 104–132.

Unsworth N., & Engle, R. W. (2007b). On the division of short-term and working memory: An examination of simple and complex spans and their relation to higher-order abilities. *Psychological Bulletin, 133,* 1038–1066.

Unsworth, N., & Engle, R. W. (2008). Speed and accuracy of accessing information in working memory: An individual differences investigation of focus switching. *Journal of Experimental Psychology: Learning, Memory, and Cognition, 34,* 616–630.

Unsworth, N., & Spillers, G. J. (2010). Working memory capacity: Attention, Memory, or Both? A direct test of the dual-component model. *Journal of Memory and Language, 62,* 392–406.

Unsworth, N., Brewer, G. A., & Spillers, G. J. (2009). There's more to the working memory-fluid intelligence relationship than just secondary memory. *Psychonomic Bulletin & Review, 16,* 931–937.

Unsworth, N., Redick, T. S., Heitz, R. P., Broadway, J., & Engle, R. W. (2009). Complex working memory span tasks and higher-order cognition: A latent variable analysis of the relationship between processing and storage. *Memory, 17,* 635–654.

Wiley, J., Jarosz, A. F., Cushen, P. J., & Colflesh, G. J. H. (2011). New rule use drives the relation between working memory capacity and Raven's advanced progressive matrices. *Journal of Experimental Psychology: Learning, Memory, and Cognition, 37,* 256–263.

Wilhelm, O. (2005). Measuring reasoning ability. In O. Wilhelm, & R. W. Engle (Eds.), *Handbook of Understanding and Measuring Intelligence* (pp. 373–392). London: Sage.

Note

1   There are only 18 problems, given that participants only completed the odd problems for the Raven Advanced Progressive Matrices.

2

RELATIONAL PROCESSING IN REASONING

The role of working memory

Graeme S. Halford, Glenda Andrews and William H. Wilson

There have been some developments in the last three decades that have changed the very foundations of the way we understand reasoning, and have even given us some new conceptions about cognition in general. Halford, Wilson, Andrews and Phillips (2014) have reinterpreted current conceptions of reasoning and working memory to propose a scheme for integrating the conceptual foundation of psychology. In this chapter we will focus on the way changing conceptions of working memory have influenced research on reasoning.

Normative conceptions no longer plausible

Whereas in the 19th century it appeared to be self-evident that thought depended on logic (see, for example, Boole, 1854/1951) in the 20th century it gradually became clear that there was a major mismatch between thought and the laws of logic. Some theorists attempted to deal with this by developing a psycho-logic that provided a closer match to actual human reasoning (Braine, 1978; Piaget, 1950, 1957; Rips, 1994, 2001), but the number of demonstrated mismatches continued to grow. Some of the most celebrated of these included the role of heuristics such as availability and representativeness (e.g. Kahneman & Tversky, 1973, 1982), showing that heuristics play a major role in reasoning. At a more elemental level, discrepancies have been demonstrated between natural language and standard logic. An example would be that in natural language *if A then B* can be interpreted as a conditional $(A \rightarrow B)$ or as a biconditional $(A \leftrightarrow B)$, depending on the context. Thus if I say, "If it is raining, there are clouds," it is clear that the conditional (clouds $\rightarrow$ rain) is intended, because the presence of clouds does not necessarily imply rain, so the reverse implication is ruled out by our world knowledge. On the other hand, if I say, "If the key fits, then the lock opens," it is apparent that the biconditional is intended, because the reverse implication, "If the lock opens, then the key fits," is known to be generally true. The canonical interpretation of *if–then* is as the material conditional, so *if A then B* means that *B* occurs whenever *A* occurs, but the converse, *B implies A*, is not intended. Use of the biconditional interpretation of *if–then* conflicts with the canonical interpretation and is sometimes scored as an error, as in the Wason Selection Task (Cocchi et al., 2013; Evans, 2008; Wason, 1968). The distinction between the conditional and the biconditional is one of many ways that reasoning is influenced by knowledge of the world, including an extensive literature demonstrating the effects of belief-based content in categorical syllogisms (e.g. Evans & Curtis-Holmes, 2005; Stupple & Ball, 2008), relational reasoning (Roberts & Sykes, 2003) and transitive inference (Andrews, 2010). Accounts based on logic alone are insufficient.

Another proposition that seems to have near-universal acceptance is that reasoning is part of our cognitive equipment for adapting to our environment. Piaget (1950) saw intelligence as an extension of biological adaptation, and a similar, but much elaborated view is widely accepted today (Anderson, 1990; Chater & Oaksford, 2004). This has led to an ecological definition of rationality, based on adaptation, as distinct from a normative conception of rationality, judged by conformity to the rules of logic. Thus we switch between modes of reasoning to maximise their utility to our purposes, which are broadly aimed at behaving adaptively in our environment.

Another proposition that has wide acceptance is that reasoning in the real world is probabilistic rather than categorical. Thus conditional premises are interpreted as conditional probabilities. For example the proposition "if *X* is a bird, then *X* flies" is interpreted as "if *X* is a bird, then there is some probability *p* that *X* flies," where *p* will depend on a person's knowledge of the world, being high if *X* is a parrot, zero if *X* is an ostrich (Oaksford & Chater, 2001, 2007).

All these underlying assumptions, including the role of knowledge, and of heuristics based on that knowledge, as well as the adaptive nature of reasoning, and the probabilistic nature of inference, appear to be common ground amongst reasoning theorists as diverse as Evans (2008), Johnson-Laird (2010) and Oaksford and Chater (2007). Contemporary theories differ in the manner in which they implement these characteristics of human reasoning, but there is less debate about the propositions themselves. This can be seen as a welcome step towards consensus and integration. There are, however, a number of controversies that remain active, and we will consider these in the next section.

Types of cognition

One issue about which there has been extensive controversy is the distinction between types of cognition, including reasoning processes. Distinctions have been made between implicit and explicit processes (Clark & Karmiloff-Smith, 1993), associative and rule-based (Sloman, 1996, 2002), subsymbolic versus symbolic (Gentner, 2010; Halford et al., 2012), and analytic versus heuristic (Evans, 2006), amongst others. These distinctions have been reviewed by Evans (2003, 2006,

2008), who crystallised them into Type 1 and Type 2 processes, operating within one system (Evans, 2008). Type 1 processes are fast, automatic and unconscious, while Type 2 are slow, effortful, conscious and require a single, capacity-limited working memory. The working-memory requirement is consistent with a high loading of Type 2 reasoning on intelligence (Stanovich & West, 2000). Empirical evidence of a high correlation between aggregated measures of working memory and fluid intelligence (Gf) is reviewed by Unsworth (in this volume). There has also been dispute about whether distinct categories of cognition exist, or whether they occupy points on a continuum (Bonner & Newell, 2010). However, the distinction between types of cognition does not entail complete discontinuity between processes. For example, one reasoner can operate at two levels of system, with distinct processing demands (De Neys, 2006). For a further review of controversy see Evans and Stanovich (2013). Our position is that it is possible to categorise cognition in a way that provides conceptual coherence (Halford, Wilson, Andrews and Phillips, in press), and higher cognition depends on processing relations, as we will consider below. Any higher-cognitive system necessarily incorporates most properties and processes of lower systems, so there is continuity between systems. For our present purposes it will be sufficient to specify the properties that distinguish the higher system, because it is at this level that working memory has its most significant role.

We have arrived at a position therefore where we find reasonable consensus on some crucial points, these being that:

- Reasoning is knowledge based, including heuristics that depend on knowledge;
- Reasoning is adaptive;
- Reasoning is probabilistic;
- Reasoning can entail a variety of processes; and
- There is a category of reasoning, which we will refer to as *analytic*, that is distinguished crucially by reliance on working memory.

This places us in a position to offer an integrated conception of reasoning. It does not solve all problems, of course, but it avoids relatively unproductive controversy, and highlights some issues that are well worth the effort of investigation. We propose that a conception based on relational knowledge provides a basis for integration and conceptual coherence, so that will be the subject of this chapter.

Relational knowledge forms the foundation of higher cognition, including analytic reasoning (Halford, Wilson & Phillips, 2010). Relational knowledge also provides background theory of the kind that is coming to be recognised as essential to interpretation of empirical findings in psychology (Halford, Wilson, Andrews & Phillips, 2014; Mausfeld, 2012; Stenning & van Lambalgen, 2008). Relational reasoning is positively correlated with fluid intelligence, as measured by the Cattell Culture Fair test. In a study with children, the zero order correlation of fluid intelligence with a relational complexity factor, on which transitive inference and class inclusion had the strongest loadings, was $r = .78$ (Andrews & Halford, 2002).

In an adult study, individuals with higher fluid intelligence were better able to resolve the conflict between belief-based and analytic processes when making transitive inferences (Andrews, 2010, Experiment 3).

Relational representations "can be conceptualised as a binding between a relation symbol and a set of ordered tuples of elements ... For example, the relation symbol *larger* is bound to the set of ordered pairs: { *(elephant, mouse), (pig, cat) ...*}" (Halford, Wilson & Phillips, 2010, p. 497, italics in original). The relation-symbol represents the 'intension' of a relation, and specifies what relation is represented; e.g. the *larger* relation orders things by size. The ordered tuples represent the "extension" of the relation, and specify the instances that are represented (comprised of ordered tuples in which the first element is larger than the second). The ordered tuples can provide information about probabilities, based on the proportion of instances where the relation is true (Halford, Wilson & Phillips, 2010). Thus *larger* (horse, dog) includes instances where the horse is larger than the dog, but there are a minority of instances where a horse is smaller than a dog, and the relative proportions of tuples where the horse is larger provides a probabilistic representation of the relation. The properties of higher cognition that are captured by the theory of relational knowledge include:

Propositions play a significant role in higher cognition including reasoning, and are essentially relational instances. Thus "John loves Mary" is both an instance of the *loves* relation and a proposition.

Explicit cognition: the implicit–explicit distinction is equivalent in many respects to the distinction between associative and relational processing (Phillips, Halford & Wilson, 1995).

Compositionality is a property of relational representations. This means that symbols can be composed into compound representations in which the components retain their identity, and can be retrieved. Thus, given "John loves Mary," we can ask, "Who loves Mary?" (John), "What is the relation between John and Mary?" (loves), and "Who is loved by John?" (Mary). Not all representations are compositional in this way. For example, representations in the hidden units of some neural net models serve to compute input–output functions but are not compositional, in the sense that the components cannot be retrieved. For example, a hidden unit might be activated by inputs "black" and "dog" and can be used to compute outputs appropriate to "black dog", but there might be no function that computes the components "black" or "dog", given the input "black dog".

Higher-order, or hierarchical, representations have lower-order relational representations as components (arguments). Thus "Peter knows that John loves Mary" is a higher-order relation, one component of which is the first-order relation "John loves Mary."

Structural equivalence, another important proposal, is that representations with the same structure form equivalence classes independent of content. Thus transitive inference and class inclusion (e.g. apples and pears are included in fruit) entail different test procedures, but are structurally equivalent, both being defined on three variables (Andrews & Halford, 2002; Halford, Wilson, Andrews & Phillips, 2014; Phillips, Wilson & Halford, 2009).

Strategic modifiability is a property of higher cognition that is captured by relational knowledge. The relation used to provide a plan or strategy for a task can be changed by switching relation symbols. Thus we can switch from an addition operation to a multiplication operation by changing the relation symbol, thus: +(3, 2, 5), +(4, 3, 7) … to ×(3, 2, 6), ×(4, 3, 12) …. The binding between a symbol and the ordered tuples of instances means that a relational representation comprises an integrated structure that can be selected as a whole, so we can switch from addition to multiplication without further learning.

Systematicity is another foundational property of higher cognition that is captured by the theory of relational knowledge (Fodor & Pylyshyn, 1988; Halford et al., 2010; Halford, Wilson, Andrews & Phillips, 2014). In essence, systematicity means that representations have a structure that has some degree of independence of specific instantiations. Thus "John loves Mary" relates not only those entities, but also links the agent role to the patient role, so that a person who understands this proposition can also understand "Mary loves John."

Structural alignment is the property that crucially distinguishes relational cognition from more basic processes such as association (Halford, Wilson, Andrews & Phillips, in press, Chapter 2). The relation "taller" in Figure 2.1a entails assigning elements to slots, one for a taller and one for a shorter element, thus: *taller* = {(*Bob, Tom*), (*Tom, Peter*), (*Bob, Peter*) ….} The structural alignment process applies between representations so that, in Figure 2.1a, the elements Bob, Tom, Peter have to be aligned in a way that matches top, middle, bottom. Structural alignment of representations is the basis of analogy theory (Gentner, 2010; Holyoak, 2012) and the theory of representations (Halford, 1993; Holland et al., 1986). Structural alignment plays a crucial role in similarity, so that "Jane feeds cat" is dissimilar to "cat feeds Jane", despite the identical elements, because the elements are assigned to different roles. On the other hand, "Bob feeds dog" is similar to "Jane feeds cat" because "Bob" and "Jane" are assigned to the agent role and "dog" and "cat" to the patient role. There are numerous computational models of the process, and we cannot consider them in detail here, but see reviews by Gentner (2010), Halford, Wilson, Andrews and Phillips (2014) and Holyoak (2012). Relational knowledge is the core of higher cognition, but entails more than simply responding on the basis of differences such as above–below or left–right, as demonstrated with bees by Avarguès-Weber, Dyer, Combe and Giurfa (2012). These discriminations can be performed by simpler processes (Halford, Wilson et al., 2014).

Working memory and reasoning

Research in the last two decades has shown that aggregated measures of working memory account for a high proportion (approximately 50 per cent) of variance in reasoning (Kane et al., 2004; Oberauer, Süß, Wilhelm & Sander, 2007). Unsworth (this volume) has reviewed the literature on individual differences in working memory and its influence on reasoning. Essentially he conceptualises the role of working memory in reasoning as active maintenance of representations including goal states, action plans, hypotheses, and partial solutions to reasoning problems. Other functions include attention control and controlled search of secondary memory. Working memory is assessed primarily by complex span tasks, including reading span, operation span and counting span. We have no reason to disagree with any aspect of Unsworth's review, but we will focus on a conception of working memory that is complementary in many ways to the model he uses. This is the theory of working memory as dynamic assignment to a coordinate system, proposed by Oberauer (2009; Oberauer et al., 2007).

The proposal by Oberauer et al. (2007) that the central component of working memory depends on dynamic binding of elements to a coordinate system, forming new structures, is highly relevant to reasoning as we conceive it. A working-memory test that assessed recall of words in spatial positions (Oberauer, 2005) provides a clear measure of the dynamic-binding construct. Sets of two to five words were presented, each in a different frame on a screen, followed by a local recognition test, in which participants judged whether probe words appeared in the same frame as previously. The test assessed binding between word and frame (see Figure 2.1c) and was a good measure of working-memory capacity. This binding is dynamic in that it depends on activation of representations, and is not based on enduring links. The words are bound to a coordinate system comprising slots that are linked by a left–right spatial relation.

Oberauer (2009) proposed a conception of working memory that "provides access to representations for goal-directed processing … such as language comprehension, reasoning, planning, and creative problem solving" (p. 47). The proposed system has six properties that Oberauer regards as essential, and which we find highly relevant to analytic cognition, including reasoning. These properties include ability to build and maintain new structural representations, employing a mechanism for dynamic binding. The working-memory system can manipulate representations; it is a general-purpose system rather than a module specialised for particular types of content; it can rapidly update representations; it can draw on contents of long-term memory, and can store new solutions in long-term memory.

Processing capacity is defined by the ability to uphold multiple bindings simultaneously (Oberauer et al., 2008, p. 642). This does not preclude processing and storage, but widens the conception of working memory and makes it more directly applicable to reasoning, which entails building new relational representations.

In the study by Oberauer et al. (2008), dynamic binding was assessed by relational integration. Relations had to be detected in displays containing continuously varying elements, such as a set of three-digit numbers that shared the same final digit. Reasoning was assessed by the Berlin Intelligence Structure with verbal, numerical and visual-spatial content and four functions: reasoning, creativity, memory and speed. The distinctiveness of the dynamic binding construct is indicated by findings that relational integration shared substantial variance with reasoning that was not accounted for by processing and storage, or by processing speed. They also argued that relational integration could not be accounted for by executive functions, only one component of which, updating, predicts fluid intelligence.

Tests that require updating of working memory are likely to be good measures of dynamic binding. An example is the well-known n-back task, in which a series of stimuli, such as words or pictures, are presented, and participants have to say if the current stimulus is the same as the stimulus n items back, where n typically varies from one to three. This requires continuous updating of the working-memory record. However, there is research which specifically addresses the link between updating and higher cognition. Friedman, Miyake et al. (2006) correlated fluid and crystallised intelligence with latent variables corresponding to three executive functions: inhibiting prepotent responses, shifting mental sets and updating working memory. The updating tests required continuous dynamic binding between elements and coordinate systems (e.g. words to categories, letters to ordinal positions in an auditory string, or boxes to spatial positions). Each latent variable was assessed by three tests. Updating was correlated more highly with intelligence than were the other two constructs. They also concluded that the variances that the latter two constructs shared with intelligence were due to updating.

Construction of representations in working memory

Our conception of reasoning includes construction of representations in working memory. Because this notion has been the subject of a number of challenges, we will consider the justification for it first. Oaksford and Chater (2001) suggest that only a small proportion of human reasoning is based on explicit processes such as those that are entailed in Evans (2003) System 2 (approximately equivalent to Evans' 2008 Type 2 processes). Their justification is that the Wason Selection Task, which was developed to assess reasoning, is handled in this way by at most 10 per cent of participants. However, our contention (Cocchi et al., 2013) is that the commonly reported failures reflect a number of misinterpretations of the Wason Selection Task. One of these is the failure to recognise that, as discussed earlier, a biconditional interpretation of *if–then* is not necessarily an error (see also Halford, 1993). Another has been a failure to consider the effect of complexity. The findings with the WST are therefore not truly indicative of human reasoning capabilities. Our position is that heuristic processes enable inferences based on knowledge, they are efficient in the sense that they impose low processing loads, and they are ecologically adaptive (Arkes, 2012). However, analytic processes, approximately equivalent to Evans (2008) Type 2 processes, are based on constructed representations and enable inferences that go beyond previously obtained knowledge. The relation between heuristic and analytic processes is therefore complementary rather than mutually exclusive.

We will develop our argument that reasoning entails representations constructed in working memory by reference to transitive inference and categorical syllogisms.

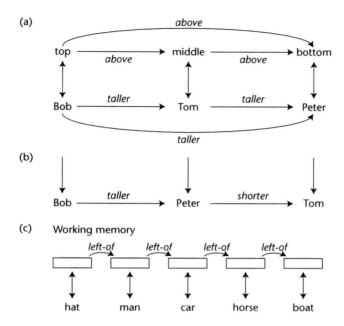

FIGURE 2.1 (a) Mental model for explicit transitive inference (based on Figure 2.2a in Halford et al., 2010, by permission of Elsevier). The premises "Tom is taller than Peter" and "Bob is taller than Tom" are mapped into an ordering schema that provides an integrated representation that captures the relational content of the premises. The relation "Bob is taller than Peter" is not given in the premises and is an analogical inference. (b) *Bob taller-than Peter shorter-than Tom* is precluded because it would not be a structurally consistent mapping (it would mean that *above* would correspond to *taller-than* in one case and *shorter-than* in the other case). (c) Coordinate system in working memory, as used by Oberauer (2005). Words are assigned to slots ordered from left to right on a computer screen.

Transitive inference was regarded by William James (1890) as fundamental to all reasoning, while categorical syllogisms have a long tradition in psychology and philosophy. Both have the essential properties of analytic reasoning, in that they entail representation of premises, they require integration of the premises, and they enable inferences that go beyond stored knowledge. This is illustrated even in the simple transitive inference in Figure 2.1a where the premises "Tom is taller than Peter" and "Bob is taller than Tom" are represented, and are integrated into the ternary relation "Bob taller than Tom taller than Peter". An inference "Bob is taller than Peter" is generated, and this can be done independent of prior knowledge. An example of a categorical syllogism task is *"All X are Y"* and *"All Y are Z"*. The premises can be integrated yielding the inferences *"All X are Z"* and *"Some Z are X"*, as shown in Figure 2.2.

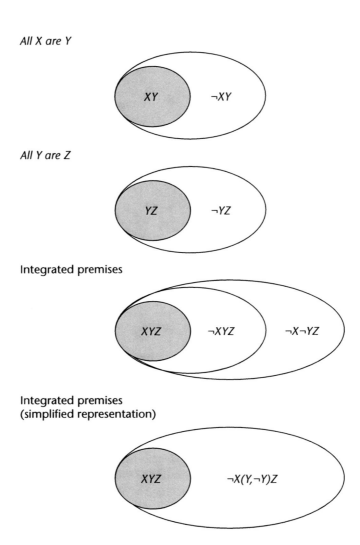

FIGURE 2.2 Representation of premises *"All X are Y"* and *"All Y are Z"*, each represented by diagrams showing the relation between *X* and *Y* and between *Y* and *Z*. The integrated premises are shown as the relation between the three categories that are implied by the premise.

However, people simplify representations according to principles specified in the Method for Analysis of Relational Complexity (Halford, Cowan & Andrews, 2007), so the simplified representation is also shown.

Reproduced from Zielinski, Goodwin and Halford (2010) Figure 1 by permission of Taylor and Francis.

It would be more conventional to represent the categorical syllogism in Figure 2.2 by tokens. The premise *"All X are Y"* could be represented as:

X Y
X Y

"All Y are Z" could be represented as:

Y Z
Y Z

The integrated premises could be represented as:

X Y Z
X Y Z

However, in this context we are mainly concerned that the mental model should correspond to relations in the premises, and this is true for both forms of representation. The only advantage we claim for the style of representation in Figure 2.2 is that it enables categorical syllogisms of all levels of complexity to be represented in a single figure, and does not require more than one mental model for any problem (Zielinski, Goodwin & Halford, 2010).

Our proposal is that the representations shown in Figure 2.1a and Figure 2.2 are constructed in working memory. The construction depends on dynamic assignment to roles (slots), and the validation is by structural correspondence, though it is aided by knowledge and similarity. We will consider this argument first with respect to the transitive inference problem in Figure 2.1a. The roles are locations in an ordering schema such as top, middle, bottom. The assignment of Bob, Tom, Peter to roles is validated by structural correspondence. Notice that the relation *above* in the schema corresponds consistently to the relation *taller* in the premises, and each premise entity is mapped to one and only one slot. Furthermore, the mapping is arbitrary and modifiable so that, for example, it could be reversed, yielding a mental model *Peter shorter-than Tom shorter-than Bob*. This is valid because *shorter-than* corresponds consistently to *above*. However, the ordering *Bob, Peter, Tom* is precluded because, as shown in Figure 2.1b, *above* would have to be mapped to *taller* and to *shorter*, so the mapping is inconsistent. Thus structural correspondence to an ordering schema discriminates between valid and invalid orderings.

Knowledge and similarity can influence this mapping so that, for example, it would be easier to assign Bob to the top slot if we knew Bob was very tall. Element similarity could also play a part. For example, if we were solving a transitive inference problem with premises "the green block is above the red block" and "the red block is above the blue block" it would be easier to assign "green" to a top slot because "above" naturally suggests a top-down arrangement of slots. We fully recognise that knowledge and similarity have important effects, but analytic reasoning can be performed without them. In the transitive inference that we are considering in Figure 2.1a, it is easy to deduce that Bob is taller than Peter without any knowledge of these entities and without the benefit of similarity.

A similar case can be made for the categorical syllogism. As shown in Figure 2.2, the premise *"All X are Y"* can be represented by an ellipse containing X that is embedded with the ellipse containing Y. Similarly for the premise *"All Y are Z"*. The premises are integrated (combined) into a figure containing three classes of entities: XYZ, $\neg XYZ$ and $\neg X \neg YZ$ where $\neg$ means "not". This integrated representation yields the inferences *"All X are Z"* and *"Some Z are X"*, both of which are consistent with the representation. As with the transitive inference example, the relations in the representation correspond to the relations in the premises, and structural correspondence is sufficient for the inference. Categorical syllogisms can also be influenced by heuristics, as Oaksford and Chater (2007) have shown in detail. However, integrated treatments have been proposed (Evans, 2006; Khemlani & Johnson-Laird, 2012a), and Halford, Wilson et al. (2014) have shown in detail that it is not a case of choosing between mental models and heuristic theories, but of defining the respective functions of each. There is evidence from a number of paradigms that establishment of structural correspondence imposes a load on working memory (Blanchette & Dunbar, 2000; Catrambone, 2002; Cho, Holyoak & Cannon, 2007; Waltz, Lau, Grewal & Holyoak, 2000).

The case we have made is essentially a form of mental-models theory, and mental models have been shown to account for a wide range of reasoning (Johnson-Laird, 2010). A review by Khemlani and Johnson-Laird (2012b) concluded that mental-models theory outperforms alternative theories of syllogistic reasoning, while mental models have also been shown to have application in a wide variety of contexts (Halford, 1993). The construction of mental models is influenced by knowledge of instances (Markovits, Forgues & Brunet, 2010; Markovits, this volume) and therefore takes account of world knowledge. Our position does not entail adopting all the characteristics of current mental-models theories, but we adopt one core proposition from that area of theorising. This is that mental models entail construction, in working memory, of representations of structures that reflect the relations entailed in the premises. This is fundamentally in agreement with the theory of Goodwin and Johnson-Laird (2005).

There is a close link between construction of representations by structural correspondence and the working-memory model of Oberauer based on dynamic assignment to a coordinate system. The representation in Figure 2.1a is an application of working memory by dynamic binding. The dynamic-binding conception of working memory has been linked to the reasoning theory of Halford et al. (2007). Mapping to an ordering schema in the transitive inference task in Figure 2.1 makes demands on working memory as envisaged by Oberauer et al. (Oberauer, 2005; Oberauer et al., 2007). In both Figure 2.1a and Figure 2.1c the elements are dynamically bound to spatial-ordering schemas.

Working-memory load imposed by constructing representations

There are studies that specifically address the process of constructing integrated representations in working memory. In transitive inference tasks devoid of semantic cues, as in Figure 2.1a, the premises must be integrated into the ternary relation *monotonically-taller* (*Bob, Tom, Peter*), constrained solely by structural correspondence to relations in the premises. Because the premises are presented only once, the mapping is created dynamically, and continued activation in working memory is required. Integrating premises by mapping between relational representations in Figure 2.1a imposes a processing load (Maybery, Bain & Halford, 1986) and activates the anterior prefrontal cortex (Fangmeier, Knauff, Ruff & Sloutsky, 2006). The processing load occurs because no element can be assigned to a slot on the basis of only one premise, so the premises must be considered jointly. For example, "Tom is taller than Peter" tells us that Tom is in first or second position, but we have to use the second premise to determine which.

The processing load imposed by dynamic binding can be quantified by the complexity of the relations that are bound, according to the relational complexity metric (Halford et al., 1998). The mental model for explicit transitive inference in Figure 2.1a is a ternary relation, *monotonically-taller* (*Bob, Tom, Peter*), which is mapped into the schema *monotonically-higher* (*top, middle, bottom*). There are three dimensions (three slots) to this mapping, and since an n-ary relation is a set of points in n-dimensional space, the number of dimensions corresponds to the *arity* of relations mapped. Dimensionality of relations is associated with processing load, and adult human processing capacity is limited to one quaternary relation in a single cognitive representation (Halford et al., 2005). Complexity of relations that can be processed increases with development between the approximate ages of two and eight years (Andrews & Halford, 2002; Halford et al., 1998, Sections 6.2 and 6.3). Concepts too complex to be processed in parallel are handled by *segmentation* (decomposition into smaller segments that can be processed serially) and *conceptual chunking* (recoding into representations of lower rank), but there is a loss of access to chunked variables. Thus a ternary relation such as speed, defined as distance/time, can be chunked to a single variable; that is speed = distance/time can be reduced to a single variable, as when we say speed = 80 kph. The single variable representation entails a limitation in that access to relations between chunked variables is lost. Thus the question "What happens if we travel the same distance in half the time?" cannot be answered by reference to the single variable, so resort must be had to the ternary relation between speed, distance and time (Halford, Wilson et al., 2014). If decomposition is not possible, there may be a default to implicit processing or heuristics, or to a less complex representation (e.g. processing single premises in transitive inference rather than integrating premises). Explicit processing will be facilitated as capacity increases with age in children (Andrews & Halford, 2002), or by load reduction due to segmentation or conceptual chunking (Halford, Cowan et al., 2007).

The limit to human processing capacity will be observed only where decomposition into simpler tasks by segmentation or conceptual chunking is constrained, as occurs in interpretation of interactions as used by Halford et al. (2005) or, to a lesser extent, in some explicit transitive inference problems. The boundary conditions for processing capacity effects are defined by Halford, Cowan et al. (2007) and Halford, Wilson, Andrews and Phillips (2014, Chapter 5).

Construction of representations in categorical syllogisms has also been shown to entail complexity effects, based on the number of entities that are related in a cognitive representation. Zielinski, Goodwin and Halford (2010) analysed the complexity of categorical syllogisms using the relational complexity metric of Halford et al. (1998) and the Method for Analysis of Relational Complexity (MARC; Halford, Cowan et al., 2007). All 64 syllogisms were classified according to relational complexity, based on the number of related categories implied by the premises, taking account of strategies and heuristics known to be employed in making the inferences. Thus the categorical syllogism based on the premises *"All X are Y"* and *"All Y are Z"* can be represented by the simplified representation in Figure 2.2, which relates two classes of entities, and is binary relational. By contrast, the syllogism *"All X are Y and No Z are Y"*, yielding the conclusion *"Some Z are not X"*, entails four classes of entities and is quaternary relational. Each syllogism was also classified according to the number of mental models required according to the mental-models theory of Johnson-Laird and Byrne (1991). Both relational complexity and mental models accounted for approximately 80 per cent of variance in correct solutions. For example, the binary relational syllogism in Figure 2.2 requires only one mental model and is performed correctly 100 per cent of the time, whereas the quaternary relational syllogism *"All X are Y and No Z are Y"* requires three mental models and is performed correctly 10.5 per cent of the time (Zielinski, Goodwin & Halford, 2010, Table 2). Our position is that valid categorical syllogistic reasoning can be conducted using single models, as in the account of Zielinski, Goodwin & Halford (2010) and illustrated in Figure 2.2, but construction of more than one model plays a role in sophisticated reasoning, such as checking whether an inference is logically necessary. Moreover, the representations required to make the inferences are constructed dynamically in working memory, and the difficulties can be accounted for by the processing loads entailed in that construction.

Working memory and the symbolic transition

Symbolic processes are clearly of fundamental importance to all higher cognition, including reasoning and language. However, the origin of symbolic processes has remained a somewhat intractable problem. Recently a new hypothesis about the origin of symbolic processes has been produced by combining the dynamic-binding conception of working memory with the theory of relational knowledge to reinterpret a classic phenomenon in infant cognition (Halford, Andrews, Wilson & Phillips, 2012; Halford, Wilson, Andrews & Phillips, 2014). There are three main components to this formulation. First, it has been shown that symbols are processor-relative, in the sense that symbols are meaningless unless embedded in some kind of structured process. For example, the numbers "1 ... 3 ... 7" are meaningful in that they are assigned to sets with a given number of members, and the ordering of the numbers corresponds to the ordering of the sets. The numbers are also related by operations such as $3 + 2 = 5$. Second, as structured knowledge entails relations (a structure is a set on which one or more relations are defined), then the onset of symbols will be contingent on ability to represent and process relational knowledge. Third, structured knowledge depends on construction of representations in working memory, which in turn depends on dynamic binding to a coordinate system. It follows that the origin of structured knowledge in infancy will be observed when infants demonstrate dynamic binding to a coordinate system.

There is a classic task, the *A not B* task, that can be reinterpreted as a measure of dynamic binding. Infants are shown an object being hidden a number of times at one location, *A*, and retrieve it each time. Then, in full view of the infants, the object is hidden at location *B*. Infants aged four to eight months have a tendency to search for the object at *A*, despite seeing it hidden at *B*. According to the Hierarchical Competing Systems Model of Marcovitch and Zelazo (2009) there is a *habit system* that causes the infants to perseverate in reaching towards *A*, while a *representational system* creates conscious awareness of the object at *B*. Halford et al. (2012) interpret the representation system as dynamic binding to a coordinate system. That is, infants cease to make the *A not-B* error when they can dynamically bind the representation of the object to their representation of the locations, which has the role of a coordinate system. They make this transition late in their first year, when there is corroborative evidence of dynamic binding of objects to locations (Kaldy & Leslie, 2003). Halford, Wilson, Andrews and Phillips (2014, Chapter 6) suggest that there is a correspondence between dynamic binding of objects to locations and binding of words to roles in language comprehension. For example, comprehension of the proposition "Jane feeds cat" entails binding "Jane" to agent role and "cat" to the patient role, which is structurally similar to binding objects to two different locations. Halford et al. (2012) deduce that dynamic binding between objects and spatial locations would be predictive of the onset of symbols, including acquisition of first words. Based on the relational complexity analysis of theory of mind (Andrews et al., 2003), Halford et al. (2012) also predict that onset of dynamic binding should be linked to attribution of a mental state to another person. This opens up a new landscape for research on acquisition of symbols.

Cognitive complexity and the Wason Selection Task

The Wason Selection Task (Wason, 1968) has been the subject of some decades of intensive research without any clear consensus emerging (for a review, see Evans, 2008). Four cards are presented, each containing one alphanumeric character, such as *A*, 4, *D*, 7. Participants are told there will always be a letter on one side and a digit on the other, and are asked which cards must be turned over to test the validity of a rule such as "if a card has an A on one side, it has a 7 on the other side". The correct response (A and 4 in this example) is typically given by only a small number of participants.

Many different reasoning processes have been blended in the task, and some of the required inferences are quite complex. Cocchi et al. (2013) presented cards one at a time, and used extensive training to ensure that participants performed the prescribed inferences. This included instruction in the conditional interpretation of the rule (i.e. $A \rightarrow 7$ but not $7 \rightarrow A$). Participants had to decide whether a card would (as in cards A and 4) or would not enable testing the validity of the rule (as in cards D and 7). Decisions whether to select one of the cards (yes or no) and fMRI records were obtained for each card separately. Greatly improved performance was obtained, with the poorest being 86 per cent correct for the not-7 card (i.e. card 4 in our example). This card requires the most complex inference, because it is necessary to infer that A and not-7 contradicts A and 7. There are four variables here, comprising A and 7 in the rule and A and not-7 in the card. This is at the limit of relational complexity (Halford et al., 2005). It was also associated with the highest levels of brain activity in the fronto-parietal network, which was the network that was found to be most involved in processing the cards. Thus restructuring the task, ensuring that an appropriate strategy was used, and taking account of cognitive complexity have led to some reconceptualisation of the longstanding enigma associated with performance on this task.

Conclusion

Analytic reasoning depends on construction of representations in working memory that correspond to the relations entailed in the premises of a deductive inference problem. Similar correspondences exist for other types of reasoning. The theory of relational knowledge captures the properties of higher cognition, including representation of propositions, the implicit–explicit distinction, compositionality, higher-order representations, equivalence of distinct tasks at the same level of structural complexity, strategic modifiability and systematicity. Structural alignment of elements into the roles of a relational representation is the factor that crucially distinguishes relational knowledge from more basic processes such as association. The theory of relational knowledge takes account of cognitive complexity as captured in the relational complexity metric and the Method for Analysis of Relational Complexity (MARC). In deductive inference the representation will be influenced by semantic factors, but is also constrained by the requirement that there must be structural correspondence between the representation and the premises. This is essentially consistent with Mental Models accounts of deductive inference, in that both depend on construction of representations in working memory. The role of working memory is based on assignment to a coordinate system, which enables construction of relational representations.

References

Anderson, J. R. (1990). *The adaptive character of thought*. Hillsdale, NJ: Erlbaum.

Andrews, G. (2010). Belief-based and analytic processing in transitive inference depends on premise integration difficulty. *Memory & Cognition, 38*, 928–940.

Andrews, G., & Halford, G. S. (2002). A cognitive complexity metric applied to cognitive development. *Cognitive Psychology, 45*, 153–219.

Andrews, G., Halford, G. S., Bunch, K. M., Bowden, D., & Jones, T. (2003). Theory of mind and relational complexity. *Child Development, 74*, 1476–1499.

Arkes, H. R. (2012). Heuristics can be ecologically rational. *Trends in Cognitive Sciences, 16*, 260–261.

Avarguès-Weber, A., Dyer, A. G., Combe, M., & Giurfa, M. (2012). Simultaneous mastering of two abstract concepts by the miniature brain of bees. *PNAS, 109*, 7481–7486.

Blanchette, I., & Dunbar, K. (2000). How analogies are generated: The roles of structural and superficial similarity. *Memory & Cognition, 28*, 108–124.

Bonner, C., & Newell, B. R. (2010). In conflict with ourselves? An investigation of heuristic and analytic processes in decision making. *Memory & Cognition, 38*, 186–196.

Boole, G. (1854/1951). *An investigation of the laws of thought, on which are founded the mathematical theories of logic and probabilities*. New York: Dover Publications.

Braine, M. D. S. (1978). On the relation between the natural logic of reasoning and standard logic. *Psychological Review, 85*, 1–21.

Catrambone, R. (2002). The effects of surface and structural feature matches on the access of story analogs. *Journal of Experimental Psychology: Learning, Memory, and Cognition, 28*, 318-334.

Chater, N., & Oaksford, M. (2004). Rationality, rational analysis, and human reasoning. In K. Manktelow and M. C. Cheung (eds), *Of reasoning: theoretical and historical perspectives* (pp. 43–74). Hove, East Sussex: Psychology Press.

Cho, S., Holyoak, K. J., & Cannon, T. D. (2007). Analogical reasoning in working memory: Resources shared among relational integration, interference resolution, and maintenance. *Memory & Cognition, 35*, 1445–1455.

Clark, A., & Karmiloff-Smith, A. (1993). The cognizer's innards: A psychological and philosophical perspective on the development of thought. *Mind & Language, 8*, 487–519.

Cocchi, L., Halford, G. S., Zaleski, A., Harding, I. H., Ramm, B., Cutmore, T., David, H. K., & Mattingley, J. B. (2013). Complexity in relational processing predicts changes in functional brain network dynamics. *Cerebral Cortex*. doi: 10.1093/cercor/bht075

De Neys, W. (2006). Dual processing in reasoning: Two systems but one reasoner. *Psychological Science, 17*, 428–433.

Evans, J. S. B. T. (2003). In two minds: Dual-process accounts of reasoning. *Trends in Cognitive Sciences, 7*, 454–459.

Evans, J. S. B. T. (2006). The heuristic-analytic theory of reasoning: Extension and evaluation. *Psychonomic Bulletin & Review, 13*, 378–395.

Evans, J. S. B. T. (2008). Dual-processing accounts of reasoning, judgment, and social cognition. *Annual Review of Psychology, 59*, 255–278.

Evans, J. S. B. T., & Curtis-Holmes, J. (2005). Rapid responding increases belief bias: Evidence for the dual-process theory of reasoning. *Thinking & Reasoning, 11*, 382–389.

Evans, J. S. B. T., & Stanovich, K. E. (2013). Dual-process theories of higher cognition advancing the debate. *Perspectives on Psychological Science, 8*(3), 223–241.

Fangmeier, T., Knauff, M., Ruff, C. C., & Sloutsky, V. (2006). fMRI evidence for a three-stage model of deductive reasoning. *Journal of Cognitive Neuroscience, 18*, 320–334.

Fodor, J. A., & Pylyshyn, Z. W. (1988). Connectionism and cognitive architecture: A critical analysis. *Cognition, 28*, 3–71.

Friedman, N. P., Miyake, A., Corley, R. P., Young, S. E., DeFries, J. C., & Hewitt, J. K. (2006). Not all executive functions are related to intelligence. *Psychological Science, 17*, 172–179.

Gentner, D. (2010). Bootstrapping the mind: Analogical processes and symbol systems. *Cognitive Science, 34*, 752–775.

Goodwin, G. P., & Johnson-Laird, P. N. (2005). Reasoning about relations. *Psychological Review, 112*, 468–493.

Grice, H. P. (1975). *Logic and conversation.* New York: Academic Press.

Halford, G. S. (1993). *Children's understanding: The development of mental models.* Hillsdale, NJ: Erlbaum.

Halford, G. S., Andrews, G., Wilson, W. H., & Phillips, S. (2012). Computational models of relational processes in cognitive development. *Cognitive Development, 27*, 481.

Halford, G. S., Andrews, G., Wilson, W. H., & Phillips, S. (2013). The role of working memory in the subsymbolic–symbolic transition. *Current Directions in Psychological Science, 22*, 210–216.

Halford, G. S., Wilson, W. H., Andrews, G.,& Phillips, S. (2014). *Categorising cognition: Towards conceptual coherence in the foundations of psychology.* Cambridge, MA: MIT Press.

Halford, G. S., Baker, R., McCredden, J. E., & Bain, J. D. (2005). How many variables can humans process? *Psychological Science, 16*, 70–76.

Halford, G. S., Cowan, N., & Andrews, G. (2007). Separating cognitive capacity from knowledge: A new hypothesis. *Trends in Cognitive Sciences, 11*, 236–242.

Halford, G. S., Wilson, W. H., & Phillips, S. (1998). Processing capacity defined by relational complexity: Implications for comparative, developmental, and cognitive psychology. *Behavioral and Brain Sciences, 21*, 803–831.

Halford, G. S., Wilson, W. H., & Phillips, S. (2010). Relational knowledge: The foundation of higher cognition. *Trends in Cognitive Sciences, 14*, 497–505.

Holland, J. H., Holyoak, K. J., Nisbett, R. E., & Thagard, P. R. (1986). *Induction: Processes of inference, learning and discovery.* Cambridge, MA: MIT Press.

Holyoak, K. J. (2012). Analogy and relational reasoning. *Oxford handbook of thinking and reasoning* (pp. 234–259). New York: Oxford University Press.

James, W. (1890). *Principles of psychology.* New York: Holt, Rinehart, & Winston.

Johnson-Laird, P. N. (2010). Mental models and human reasoning. *Proceedings of the National Academy of Sciences, 107*, 18243–18250.

Johnson-Laird, P. N., & Byrne, R. M. J. (1991). *Deduction.* Hillsdale, NJ: Erlbaum.

Kahneman, D., & Tversky, A. (1973). On the psychology of prediction. *Psychological Review, 80*, 237–251.

Kahneman, D., & Tversky, A. (1982). The simulation heuristic. In D. Kahneman, P. Slovic, & A. Tversky (eds), *Judgment under uncertainty: Heuristics and biases* (pp. 3–20). New York: Cambridge University Press.

Káldy, Z., & Leslie, A. M. (2003). Identification of objects in 9-month-old infants: Integrating "what" and "where" information. *Developmental Science, 6*, 360–373.

Kane, M. J., Hambrick, D. Z., Tuholski, S. W., Wilhelm, O., Payne, T. W., & Engle, R. W. (2004). The generality of working memory capacity: A latent-variable approach to verbal and visuospatial memory span and reasoning. *Journal of Experimental Psychology: General, 133*, 189.

Khemlani, S., & Johnson-Laird, P. (2012a). The processes of inference. *Argument and Computation*, 1–17.

Khemlani, S., & Johnson-Laird, P. (2012b). Theories of the syllogism: A meta-analysis. *Psychological Bulletin, 138*, 427.

Marcovitch, S., & Zelazo, P. D. (2009). The need for reflection in theories of executive function: Reply to commentaries. *Developmental Science, 12*, 24–25.

Markovits, H. (this volume). Conditional reasoning and semantic memory retrieval. In A. Feeney and V. Thompson (eds), *Reasoning as memory*. London: Psychology Press.

Markovits, H., Forgues, H. L., & Brunet, M. (2010). Conditional reasoning, frequency of counterexamples, and the effect of response modality. *Memory & Cognition, 38*, 485–492.

Mausfeld, R. (2012). On some unwarranted tacit assumptions in cognitive neuroscience. *Frontiers in Psychology, 3*, 67.

Maybery, M. T., Bain, J. D., & Halford, G. S. (1986). Information processing demands of transitive inference. *Journal of Experimental Psychology: Learning, Memory, and Cognition, 12*, 600–613.

Oaksford, M., & Chater, N. (2001). The probabilistic approach to human reasoning. *Trends in Cognitive Sciences, 5*, 349–357.

Oaksford, M., & Chater, N. (2007). *Bayesian rationality: The probabilistic approach to human reasoning*: New York: Oxford University Press.

Oberauer, K. (2005). Binding and inhibition in working memory: Individual and age differences in short-term recognition. *Journal of Experimental Psychology: General, 134*, 368–387.

Oberauer, K. (2009). Design for a working memory. In B. H. Ross (ed.), *Psychology of learning and motivation: Advances in research and theory, Vol. 51* (pp. 45–100). San Diego, CA: Academic Press.

Oberauer, K., Süß, H.-M., Wilhelm, O., & Sander, N. (2007). Individual differences in working memory capacity and reasoning ability. In A. R. A. Conway, C. Jarrold, M. J. Kane, A. Miyake, & J. N. Towse (eds), *Variation in working memory* (pp. 49–75). New York: Oxford University Press.

Oberauer, K., Süß, H.-M., Wilhelm, O., & Wittmann, W. (2008). Which working memory functions predict intelligence? *Intelligence, 36*, 641–652.

Phillips, S., Halford, G. S., & Wilson, W. H. (1995). The processing of associations versus the processing of relations and symbols: A systematic comparison. In J. D. Moore & J. F. Lehman (eds), *Proceedings of the seventeenth annual conference of the Cognitive Science Society* (pp. 688–691). Pittsburgh, PA: Lawrence Erlbaum.

Phillips, S., Wilson, W. H., & Halford, G. S. (2009). What do transitive inference and class inclusion have in common? Categorical (co) products and cognitive development. *PLOS Computational Biology, 5*(12), e1000599.

Piaget, J. (1950). *The psychology of intelligence* (M. Piercy & D. E. Berlyne, trans.) London: Routledge & Kegan Paul (original work published 1947).

Piaget, J. (1957). *Logic and psychology*. New York: Basic Books.

Rips, L. J. (1994). *The psychology of proof: Deductive reasoning in human thinking*. Cambridge, MA: MIT Press.

Rips, L. J. (2001). Two kinds of reasoning. *Psychological Science, 12*, 129–134.

Roberts, M. J., & Sykes, E. D. (2003). Belief bias and relational reasoning. *The Quarterly Journal of Experimental Psychology: Section A, 56*, 131–154.

Sloman, S. A. (1996). The empirical case for two systems of reasoning. *Psychological Bulletin, 119*, 3–22.

Sloman, S. A. (2002). Two systems of reasoning. In T. Gilovich, D. Griffin, & D. Kahneman (eds), *Heuristics and biases: The psychology of intuitive judgment* (pp. 379–396). New York: Cambridge University Press.

Stanovich, K. E., & West, R. F. (2000). Individual differences in reasoning: Implications for the rationality debate? *Behavioral and Brain Sciences, 23*, 645–665.

Stenning, K., & van Lambalgen, M. (2008). *Human reasoning and cognitive science*. Cambridge, MA: MIT Press.

Stupple, E. J., & Ball, L. J. (2008). Belief–logic conflict resolution in syllogistic reasoning: Inspection-time evidence for a parallel-process model. *Thinking & Reasoning, 14*, 168–181.

Waltz, J. A., Lau, A., Grewal, S. K., & Holyoak, K. J. (2000). The role of working memory in analogical mapping. *Memory & Cognition, 28*, 1205–1212.

Wason, P. C. (1968). Reasoning about a rule. *Quarterly Journal of Experimental Psychology, 20*, 273–281.

Zielinski, T. A., Goodwin, G. P., & Halford, G. S. (2010). Complexity of categorical syllogisms: An integration of two metrics. *European Journal of Cognitive Psychology, 22*, 391–421.

3

CONDITIONAL REASONING AND SEMANTIC MEMORY RETRIEVAL

Henry Markovits

Conditional reasoning involves making inferences based on major premises of the form "If P, then Q". This form of reasoning is important in many contexts, and understanding the nature and processes underlying the way that people make conditional inferences is a critical component of any theory of reasoning. Strikingly, people will respond very differently to conditional inferences that have the same formal structure. One of the more important sources of this variation is related to the pragmatic content of the if–then premises. There is clear evidence from studies using a variety of pragmatic contexts that people do indeed construct a pragmatic meaning for conditionals in just this way. However, while such a mechanism can indeed account for variation between classes of pragmatically different conditionals, it does not allow any explanation for variation within classes. Research has clearly shown the existence of large and consistent variation in conditional inferences within pragmatic classes (e.g. Cummins et al., 1991; Markovits & Vachon, 1990; Thompson, 1994). In the following, I will present evidence that such variation is explicable by an on-line process of information retrieval from semantic memory. Recent studies also indicate that this information can be processed by either a working-memory intensive counterexample strategy, or an intuitive, probabilistic strategy as suggested by Verschueren's dual-process model of conditional reasoning (Verschueren, Schaeken, & d'Ydewalle, 2005a, 2005b).

Deductive reasoning is possibly one of the pinnacles of human reasoning. The ability to make inferences on the basis of purely hypothetical or imaginary statements, and to consider these inferences as having some specific epistemological status, underlies the construction of scientific and mathematical theories. One of the most studied of these forms of inference is conditional reasoning. Conditional reasoning involves making inferences based on major premises of the form "If P, then Q". This form of reasoning is important in many contexts, and understanding the nature and processes underlying the way that people make conditional inferences is a critical component of any theory of reasoning. Both early theoretical conceptions (Inhelder & Piaget, 1958) and some more recent theoretical formulations of conditional reasoning (Braine, 1978; Rips, 1983) consider that this form of reasoning relies on some inferential processes that are essentially syntactic in nature. These suggest that, at least among well-educated older adolescents and adults, conditional inferences should be made in a relatively consistent manner irrespective of the specific content of the premises. Unfortunately, this has not proven to be the case, and deductive reasoning is highly susceptible to variation related to content (Cummins, Lubart, Alksnis, & Rist, 1991; Markovits, 1986; Thompson, 1994), something with both theoretical and educational implications. In the following, we will examine what this variation suggests for the relationship between reasoning and memory.

Many years of research into conditional inferences has shown the existence of a great deal of variability in the way that people make inferences. One of the most striking empirical findings from this research program is the very strong effect of content. Even well-educated university students respond very differently to what are on the surface identical conditional inferences (Cummins et al., 1991; Marcus & Rips, 1979; Markovits, 1986; Thompson, 1994). One of the more important sources of this variation is related to the specific content of the if–then premises. We can in fact distinguish two major forms of content-based variation. The first is related to the pragmatic interpretation that is given to if–then statements. This characterizes classes of conditionals, each of which produces consistent variation in inferential patterns that can be ascribed to the way that people interpret the underlying semantics. The second is intra-class variation, which cannot be easily explained by interpretational factors, and, I will argue, provides the best evidence for an active memory component in reasoning.

Pragmatic influences on the interpretation of conditionals

Making deductive inferences is considered to be a key form of logical reasoning. As such, much of the research looking at the way that people make deductive conditional inferences usually contrasts people's actual inferences with responses that correspond to the textbook definition of the correct, logical response. To be clear, there are four basic conditional inferences that characterize conditional inferences. These are formed by a major premise stating some "if P, then Q" conditional, followed by a minor premise which can be the affirmation or the denial of either the antecedent (P) term or the consequent (Q) term. Each of the resulting four inferences has a correct response, according to standard propositional logic. The affirmation of the antecedent (Modus ponens, MP) inference corresponds to "If P, then Q. P is true", and leads to the logical conclusion that "Q is true". Similarly, the conclusion to the denial of the consequent (Modus tollens, MT) inference is that "P is false". For both the affirmation of the consequent (AC) and the denial of the antecedent (DA) inferences, there is no logical conclusion.

P	Q	If P, then Q
True	True	True
True	False	False
False	True	True
False	False	True

FIGURE 3.1 Truth table.

Now, conditionals are used to express different kinds of relationships between antecedents and consequents. One common way to portray how people understand these relationships is based on truth-table representations. For example, the "standard" understanding of a conditional relationship is often considered to correspond to the truth table (Figure 3.1).

We can translate this truth table into a relatively simple intuitive semantics. A standard conditional expresses a relationship that can be considered to be true if the truth of the antecedent is never associated with the consequent not happening. The opposite relation, that is, how the truth of the consequent might be related to the truth of the antecedent, has no relevance to this. For example, imagine that someone expresses a conditional that says that "If you let a cup drop, then the cup will break". The intuitive meaning of this statement would be that this person would be very surprised to see that a cup had been dropped, but did not break (the P & not-Q combination). On the other hand, a broken cup might be the result of any number of possible events, none of which would disrupt the basic relationship between dropping a cup and breaking it. Thus, if someone said that a cup had broken because a hot liquid had been put into it, this would be irrelevant to the initial conditional. However, it should be noted that there is some dispute over whether this translation of logical criteria does in fact correspond to people's base meaning of conditionals. Probabilistic theorists claim that underlying even deductive reasoning is an analysis of the probability that a conclusion is true given the premises (Evans, Over, & Handley, 2005; Evans, Over, & Handley, 2007; Oaksford & Chater, 2003; Oaksford, Chater, & Larkin, 2000), a very different idea. Thus, in the preceding example, the if–then statement would translate into the intuition that the chances are very high that a cup will break if it has been dropped. Consistent with this notion is the idea that conditionals express the strength of the relation between the antecedent and consequent terms. Probabilistic conditionals do not suppose that relations between antecedent and consequent terms are necessary, and examples of P followed by not-Q are not surprising. Rather, it is the ratio of (P & Q) cases to (P & not-Q) cases that determines the relative strength of a conditional (Evans, Handley, Neilens, & Over, 2007). In other words, when someone says that "If a cup is dropped, it will break", what they really mean is that most of the time, cups being dropped will lead to their breaking, but not always. There is evidence that such a definition is indeed commonly used (Evans et al., 2003), and this is indeed a current source of debate. For the purposes of our specific discussion of the influence of pragmatics, we will continue to use truth-table-based semantics to illustrate pragmatic differences, but the debate over the basic nature of deductive inferences will be discussed later on.

Now, while this intuitive semantics corresponds to many uses of the conditional, people use if–then relations in varied ways, some of which imply quite different semantics. The clearest cases are if–then statements that correspond to clearly defined pragmatic classes; that is, conditional relations whose meaning is defined by commonly shared expectations in well-defined situations. One of the earliest such pragmatic classes to be identified are conditional promises (Fillenbaum, 1975). When someone uses an if–then promise, such as "If you mow the lawn, I'll give you $5", there is a shared expectation that mowing the lawn will invariably be followed by the mower receiving $5. However, in these situations, events that combine a false antecedent with true consequent (not mowing the lawn, but getting $5) are surprising. This is because there is also the shared expectation that not mowing the lawn will invariably be followed by the mower not receiving $5. This shared meaning changes the pattern of inferences that people will reasonably make, since it allows concluding that if the lawn is not mowed, then $5 will not be given, and that if $5 has not been given, then the lawn was not mowed. Thus, in comparison to the standard meaning, promises lead to a "biconditional" interpretation of if–then statements (i.e. what people really mean with a promise is the equivalent of saying that "If, and only if, you mow the lawn, then I'll give you $5"). Exactly the same analysis holds for conditional threats ("If you do this, I'll punch you in the nose").

In fact, when people are asked to make conditional inferences with promises and threats, they produce a pattern of inferences that corresponds to this biconditional meaning; that is, they conclude that "if P is true, then Q is true", "if P is false, then Q is false", "if Q is true, then P is true", and "if Q is false, then P is false". In other words, people make inferences that clearly reflect the intuitive meaning of pragmatic classes. In fact, there is evidence that people can make inferences that mirror the pragmatics of specific forms of if–then relations when simply given pragmatic markers with abstract content: "If you do X, then I'll do Y" (Cheng & Holyoak, 1985). This suggests that semantic memory contains definitions corresponding to pragmatic categories. These definitions are then used to determine just what information is used during reasoning, and how to organize the kinds of inferences that will be commonly made. There are several possible ways of modeling this process. One model that has been used in two important theories of reasoning suggests that people will use their pragmatic interpretations to add information to what is determined by base conditionals. For example, Braine's natural logic theory of reasoning (Braine, 1978) assumes that people have inferential algorithms that translate the semantics of if–then inferences into specific conclusions. In order to account for content-related variation, this theory borrows the Gricean notion of an invited inference (Grice, 1981). This is based on the idea that people will often use linguistic short-cuts to compactly express ideas that are implicitly shared by people because of their shared pragmatic knowledge. Thus, when A tells B, "If you mow the lawn, then I'll give you $5," both A and B understand that if the lawn is not mowed, the money will not be forthcoming. This latter is an invited inference, and it will be added into the explicit meaning of the base conditional. Another related idea is used by Mental Model theory (Johnson-Laird, 2001; Johnson-Laird & Byrne, 1991, 2002). This makes a more general case, suggesting that pragmatics generate abstract semantic representations that can add or subtract truth-table-like elements. Mental Model theory supposes that different forms of conditional are defined by different combinations of states that are possibly true given the pragmatic meaning of the conditional. In other words, the semantics of conditionals essentially comprises a list of potential combinations of antecedent and consequent terms. The meaning of the base conditional is given by the following models, which correspond to the true combinations of P and Q in the truth-table definition:

P   Q
Not-P   Q
Not-P   not-Q

In contrast, the meaning of a conditional promise is:

P   Q
Not-P   not-Q

Johnson-Laird and Byrne (2002) have constructed an extensive description of the way that such forms of pragmatic modulation can affect the nature of people's representation of conditionals, and thus directly affect the kinds of inferences that are made.

Both these ideas suggest that when people reason with conditionals, they will actively interpret the pragmatic content, and that this will in some cases lead to a representation of the premises that differs from that corresponding to people's typical usage of conditionals. Now, this of course requires accessing semantic memory. However, such interpretational processes can be considered to be a preliminary stage of the reasoning process, and might not have any specific impact on the actual processes used during reasoning. There is another form of variation that cannot be so easily explained by preliminary interpretational processes, and which has some clear implications for the way that semantic memory processes are used when people make specific inferences.

Content effects on reasoning within pragmatic classes, evidence for a retrieval model

The previously discussed results show that premise content is pragmatically interpreted in order to construct an understanding of the conditional relationship. These can generate consistent differences in reasoning, depending on what pragmatic class is activated. In addition to these effects, much research has shown the existence of clear and consistent variation in conditional inferences *within* classes of conditionals. For example, causal conditionals (Cummins, 1995; Cummins et al., 1991; Markovits & Vachon, 1990), deontic conditionals (Thompson, 1994, 2000) and conditionals referring to classes and properties (Markovits, 2000) all show the same pattern of content-based variation.

How can this form of variation be understood? Clearly, any simple process of pragmatic interpretation cannot account for variation in reasoning within the same pragmatic class. There is also no reason to suggest that the cognitive load required to reason with premises that only differ in content, but not in pragmatic or logical complexity, is different. Thus, two of the more important factors that have been shown to influence reasoning (pragmatic interpretation and working-memory load (for the latter, see chapters by Unsworth and by Halford, Andrews and Wilson)) are inapplicable here. In the following, I will examine the source of this variation and present evidence consistent with the hypothesis that people construct representations of pragmatically equivalent conditionals by an on-line process of information retrieval from semantic memory (Markovits & Barrouillet, 2002).

The key to understanding how this form of variation functions is the existence of two classes of information that have been shown to correlate very highly with inferential performance. The first such class is that of alternative antecedents. These refer to information about events or classes A, which are different from P, where the conditional relation between A and Q is the same as that between P and Q. For example, for the causal conditional "If a rock is thrown at a window, the window will break", one such alternative antecedent is "Throwing a chair at a window". For the class-based conditional "If an animal is a dog, then it has four legs," one alternative antecedent is "a cat". There are two measures that have been used to categorize premises as to the relative numbers of such alternatives. The first requires people to produce as many alternatives as possible in a limited time frame (Cummins et al., 1991); the second asks people to rate premises along a scale of relative necessity (Thompson, 1994), i.e. to rate the degree to which P is necessary in order to have Q. Although there are no studies that have directly examined the relation between these two, they are conceptually very similar, since the degree of necessity is clearly related to numbers of available alternative antecedents. Critically, these measures have been used to classify premises within the same pragmatic class on a dimension related to the relative accessibility of alternative antecedents. For example, Cummins (1995; Cummins et al., 1991) looked at reasoning with causal conditionals; that is, conditionals of the form "If cause P, then effect Q". She asked participants to independently generate as many alternative antecedents as possible in a limited time for sets of causal conditionals. Premises were then classified as having relatively few or relatively many potential alternatives. Thus, for example, when reasoning with a premise such as "If a rock is thrown at a window, the window will break", people can easily produce many alternatives (chairs, storms, balls, etc.). In contrast, when asked to do so with a premise such as "If a finger is cut, then it will bleed", people find it difficult to produce many alternatives. Critically, when asked to reason with these premises, there is a strong correlation between relative numbers of alternatives and responses to the AC and DA inferences. Premises for which people find it difficult to produce alternatives tend to produce high levels of acceptance of these two inferences, with higher levels of rejection found with premises for which people find it relatively easy to produce alternatives. Similar relations between alternatives generation and reasoning with the AC and DA inferences have also been found with children (Janveau-Brennan & Markovits, 1999; Markovits & Vachon, 1990). This relation is not specific to causal conditionals. Exactly the same pattern is found when examining the way that adults reason with deontic conditionals. These are conditionals that take the basic form "If you want to do P, then you must do Q". Thompson (1994) asked adults to rate the degree of necessity of a set of deontic conditionals. Once again, there was a strong correlation between these ratings and the kinds of inferences made to the AC and DA inferences. The generality of this relation is shown by the existence of exactly the same pattern of relations found among 7- and 8-year-old children when reasoning with class-based premises (Markovits, 2000). Thus responses to AC and DA inferences when reasoning with premises of the form "If something is category P, then it has property Q" varies systematically according to the numbers of categories sharing property Q. Thus, rejection of the AC and DA inferences is much higher with premises such as "If an animal is a dog, then it has legs" than with premises such as "If a plant is a cactus, then it has spines". An important addition to this profile is results that show that reasoning is also related to the individual associative structure of antecedents. Markovits and Quinn (2002) asked people to generate causes to sets of effects. They used this to determine effects for which a single cause is strongly associated with a given effect. For example, when given the effect "a dog scratches a lot", people will very frequently cite "fleas" as a potential cause. People will deny the AC and DA inferences more often when given a premise that has a single highly associated alternative antecedent, compared to a similar premise with a weakly associated alternative. Thus, when reasoning with the premise "If a dog has fleas, then it will scratch a lot," people will accept the AC and DA inferences less often than with the premise "If a dog has a skin condition, then it will scratch a lot." In other words, people are more "logical" when reasoning with the latter premise than with the former. This result is particularly interesting, since the first premise, which contains the highly associated terms, is more familiar. Thus, familiarity by itself has a much weaker effect than the associative structure of alternative antecedents. This result has also been replicated with younger adolescents (Klaczynski, Schuneman, & Daniel, 2004).

The second form of information that has been shown to have a strong within-category effect is potential cases of D, such that P and D together are associated with not-Q. These are known as disablers (Cummins, 1995; Cummins et al., 1991), and have been shown to effect reasoning with the MP and MT inferences. For example, take the causal conditional "If the key is turned in the ignition, the car will start". Normally, if someone is then told that the key was turned in the ignition, they will conclude that the car will start. However, if they are able to easily think of disablers, such as there being no gas in the tank, then they will tend to deny the MP inference, and conclude that it is possible that the car will not start. Similarly, when people consider that a conditional relation does not express a high degree of sufficiency, i.e. that P might be true does not invariably lead to Q being true, they will tend to reject the MP and MT inferences. Available evidence clearly shows that the easier it is for people to generate disablers for a given conditional relation, the greater is their tendency to reject the MP and the MT inferences (De Neys, Schaeken, & d'Ydewalle, 2005). In addition, exactly the same effective associative strength that was found with alternative antecedents has been observed with disablers. Specifically, having a strongly associated disabler to a given conditional relation increases the tendency to reject the MP and the MT inferences (De Neys, Schaeken, & d'Ydewalle, 2002, 2003b).

This pattern of results is clearly consistent with a standard associative retrieval model. This basically suggests that one component of reasoning with concrete, familiar content involves retrieval of information about the premises that will result in activation of alternative antecedents and/or disablers. Although such information is readily available when directly asked for, the high working-memory load required to maintain, and manipulate, premises makes on-line retrieval more difficult. There are different models that can be used to describe such a retrieval-based process. One such model, based on Mental Model theory, has been suggested by Markovits and Barrouillet (2002). This claims that people will use both the major premise and the minor premise as retrieval cues for information concerning potential alternative antecedents and/or disablers that are available in semantic memory. If at least one case of either form of information is successfully retrieved during the reasoning process, then it will be added into the representation of the premises that will be used for making specific inferences. It should be noted that another class of model (which we will examine in more detail further on), which also relies on the same form of associative processes, is that which considers deductive inferences to be basically probabilistic (Evans, Over, & Handley, 2005; Evans & Over, 2004; Oaksford & Chater, 2003; Oaksford & Chater, 2007). Although details might vary (De Neys, Schaeken, & d'Ydewalle, 2003a), the basic retrieval process is similar, resulting in activation of more or less instances of alternatives and/or disablers. However, in this case, the outcome involves modulation of the probability of a given conclusion being empirically true. Thus, if many alternatives are activated, the probability of the AC inference decreases, etc.

All of these models suggest that a basic component of inferential reasoning is an on-line process of information retrieval from semantic memory. However, the evidence that we have cited remains open to different forms of interpretation. For example, it might simply be the case that people who are faster at retrieving information from memory are also better at reasoning. This might simply be due to their combined relation with working memory. Since working-memory capacity is both related to speed of information retrieval (Anderson, Reder, & Lebiere, 1996; Rosen & Engle, 1996) and to the ability to reason logically (Barrouillet & Lecas, 1999; Markovits, Doyon, & Simoneau, 2002; Toms, Morris, & Ward, 1993), this would imply that better reasoning and faster retrieval will be associated. Stronger empirical evidence for a retrieval model would require more nuanced relations between retrieval and reasoning.

There is some clear evidence that this is indeed the case. One specific prediction that is suggested by the previous analyses is that individual differences in retrieval efficiency should be associated with increased retrieval of both alternative antecedents and disablers. Thus, people who are able to retrieve information more efficiently would show more logical responses to the AC and the DA inferences, but they would also show fewer logical responses to the MP and the MT inferences. The strongest evidence for this is given by a study (Janveau-Brennan & Markovits, 1999) examining the development of reasoning with causal conditionals. In this, children varying in age between 8 and 11 years were first asked to generate as many causes as possible for a given effect in a limited time. The content of this generation task was unrelated to the content of the subsequent reasoning problems. At all ages, children who were able to generate relatively more causes showed greater rates of rejection of the AC and DA inferences. In addition, generating more causes was associated with greater rates of rejection of the MP and the MT inferences. This overall pattern of correlations is just what would be predicted by a retrieval model. The fact that children who were more efficient retrievers of alternative causes were more logical with the AC and DA inferences but less logical on the MP and the MT inferences certainly makes any recourse to overall reasoning competence uncertain as an explanatory framework.

Another interesting pattern of results concerning speed of retrieval and reasoning reflects an important distinction found in studies of associative memory. Markovits and Quinn (2002) asked adults to state potential causes for effects for which there was a single strongly associated cause (for example: what makes a dog scratch constantly), and then to reason with unrelated causal conditional premises. Reaction times for the first and second causes generated by each subject were measured. No relation was found between reasoning and time required to produce the first cause. However, time to produce the second cause was related to reasoning with the AC and DA inferences, with people taking more time showing increased acceptance of these inferences. This indicates first that simple speed of retrieval is not a principal factor in reasoning. With the kinds of content used for the retrieval task, generating the initial cause can be done by direct association between the consequent term (the effect) and potential causes. However, the ad hoc category of things that are strong causes of these kinds of effects is limited by choice, and alternative causes must thus be constructed by changing category boundaries

(Barsalou, 1983). When people think of what makes a dog scratch, they think of fleas, but not of other insects, since these do not cause itching. Alternative causes must be constructed by using different categories (e.g. skin disease, etc.). Generating a second cause thus requires being able to activate a different associative network from those that might include the initial, strongly associated cause. This exactly parallels results that have looked at individual differences in working memory and retrieval. These have found that working memory is unrelated to speed of retrieval within category boundaries, but that retrieval involving changing category boundaries is related to working–memory capacity (Anderson et al. 1996; Rosen & Engle, 1996). In other words, the relation between reasoning and retrieval speed is the same as that found between retrieval and working memory, once again strongly suggesting that retrieval does indeed underlie reasoning. Interestingly, the idea that logical reasoning, at least in the case of the uncertain AC and DA inferences, is related to the ability to retrieve information across category boundaries is very similar to one form of creativity called divergent thinking. We will come back to this idea later when we examine some of the implications of a retrieval model for the nature of logical reasoning.

Retrieval and inhibitory processes in reasoning

There is one important factor that has not yet been considered. This concerns the link between retrieval of disablers and MP/MT inferences. When simply asked to make an inference on the basis of conditional relations, the correlation between numbers of disablers and reasoning is very high. However, when people are given logical instructions that require them to "accept the premises", this correlation decreases or even disappears (Vadeboncoeur & Markovits, 1999). In other words, most people will continue to accept the MP inference, even when they are able to generate many potential disablers. Strikingly, people with very high working-memory capacity tend to accept the MP inference even without logical instructions, while those with lower working memory show the usual relation between disabler retrieval and MP acceptance (De Neys et al., 2005). How can one reconcile a retrieval-based model with the effect of logical instructions on MP acceptance? The most direct way of doing this is by assuming that logical instructions prime a process of inhibition. Thus, when reasoning with the two certain inferences under logical instructions, the response can be seen as a combination of retrieval, which would tend to reduce acceptance of these inferences, and inhibitory processes, which would increase acceptance.

How and when does the inhibitory component become activated? The evidence is clear that, in ordinary circumstances, people will activate and process information about disabling conditions in the same way as they do information about alternative antecedents. Thus, when given a conditional statement and asked to evaluate a putative conclusion without any additional instructions, both children and adults will show degrees of rejection of the MP and MT inferences that directly reflect the numbers of available disabling conditions (Cummins et al., 1991; De Neys,

Schaeken, & d'Ydewalle, 2003b; Janveau-Brennan & Markovits, 1999; Thompson, 1994). However, when given explicit instructions to reason logically, they will be much less influenced by disablers and will tend to accept the MP and MT inferences. Nonetheless, they will continue to be strongly influenced by the number of alternative antecedents when responding to the AC and DA inferences (Markovits, Fleury, Quinn, & Venet, 1998; Markovits & Vachon, 1990). Thus, it appears that any inhibitory process primed by logical instructions must be specifically targeted at disablers, and not at information retrieval in general.

A second set of results reinforces this conclusion and suggests that inhibition generated by logical instructions is primed to impede initial retrieval of disablers, before the reasoning process is engaged. Vadeboncoeur and Markovits (1999) specifically examined the effects of strong or weak logical instructions on responding to the four conditional inferences for premises with few or many potential disablers. In one condition, they asked reasoners to explicitly generate disablers before receiving logical instructions. Ordinary logical instructions led to acceptance rates of the MP inference that were high, but nonetheless varied, according to numbers of available disablers. Strong logical instructions led to equally high levels of acceptance of the MP inferences irrespective of numbers of disablers. However, when strong instructions were preceded by generation of potential disabling conditions, their effect was significantly diminished, leading to acceptance rates of the MP inference that varied with numbers of disablers, similar to what was observed with standard instructions. This suggests that the locus of inhibitory control is in the preliminary stage of reasoning, and that the effects of generation and instructions provide directly competing tendencies.

This conclusion is strongly reinforced by a study that examined the effects of information retrieval after logical instructions (Markovits & Potvin, 2001). Simply asking reasoners to generate alternative antecedents after receiving logical instructions and the major premise, created a dramatic decrease in acceptance of the MP inference, while other kinds of retrieval had no effect on reasoning. In addition, the effects of such generation were stronger when premises had many potential disablers. In other words, generating alternative antecedents after logical instructions not only primes retrieval of alternatives, which would be expected, but results in acceptance rates of MP inferences that strongly resemble those found in the absence of logical instructions. This allows two conclusions. First, simply generating alternative antecedents results in activation of the entire semantic field related to the conditional, which includes not only alternative antecedents, but disablers. Second, the inhibitory processes primed by logical instructions limit initial retrieval of disablers, but are less able to inhibit the use of activated information subsequently.

The idea that the ability to accept the MP (and the MT) inferences depends on the ability to successfully inhibit activation of disabling conditions, is given additional support by two separate kinds of studies, which in addition provide some useful nuances. The first involves reasoning with empirically false premises; that is, premises that express a conditional relation that directly contradicts a reasoner's beliefs. Developmental studies have clearly shown that younger children have great difficulties in suppressing their empirical knowledge when given simple inferences based on false conditionals. For example, Dias and Harris (1988; 1990) found that 4- to 5-year-old children, when asked to make inferences such as "If a feather is thrown at a window, the window will break. A feather is thrown at a window. Will the window break?" tend to respond that the window will not break. In other words, they find it very difficult to make inferences that are not directly based on their real-world beliefs. A variety of simple manipulations, including embedding premises into a fantasy context (Markovits & Vachon, 1989), allow these children to reason more logically on such differences. While the most direct interpretation of the effect of manipulations that allow children to accept contrary-to-fact premises and to make MP inferences that do not reflect their real-world knowledge is that these also prime inhibitory processes, there is one important difference. Studies have shown that inserting premises within a fantasy context does indeed increase logical reasoning with the MP inference, but that this same manipulation also increases the acceptance of the AC and the DA inferences with both children (Markovits, Venet, Janveau-Brennan, Malfait, et al., 1996) and adults (Markovits, 1995). In other words, the effect of embedding premises into a fantasy context appears to inhibit retrieval of information both about disablers and about alternative antecedents.

Another form of empirical evidence that supports the role of inhibition in reasoning is correlational studies that show relationships between independent measures of cognitive inhibition in the ability to reason well with empirically false premises. This relationship has been found with both children (Simoneau & Markovits, 2003) and with adults (Markovits & Doyon, 2004).

Overall, what these empirical studies strongly suggest is that when people reason with premises that have specific concrete referents, they will spontaneously activate a network of semantic knowledge that reflects their basic understanding of the structure and the specific content of if–then conditionals. In some cases, this knowledge can be restricted or augmented by people's understanding of different pragmatic classes. However, in most common cases, the kind of knowledge that is readily activated concerns alternative antecedents and potential disabling conditions, something that characterizes reasoning within different pragmatic classes (e.g. Cummins, 1995; Cummins et al., 1991; Markovits, 2000; Markovits & Vachon, 1990; Thompson, 1994, 2000). The fact that we can find these same effects in very young children (Markovits & Thompson, 2008) clearly shows that there is some primitive understanding of the structure of if–then relations that provides semantic pointers to antecedents and disablers. However, the critical conclusion of the many studies that have looked at content effects is that these pointers do not provide access to semantic definitions in the way that pragmatic classes might do. They simply initiate a search in memory for specific forms of information. Whether or not alternative antecedents or disablers are retrieved depends on their quantity and their strength of association with the original premises. In addition, either directed inhibitory processes that target disablers (via logical instructions), or those that target any form of knowledge (embedding into a fantasy context), can reduce retrieval or activation of specific forms of information.

It is useful, in this context, to note that even fairly young children if asked to explicitly retrieve information about alternative antecedents or disabling conditions can readily do so. What makes this form of information retrieval a difficult process when reasoning is two separate characteristics of the inferential process. First, in most reasoning problems there are no specific cues that point directly to any of these forms of information, thus activation remains implicit and not explicit. Second, activation of this knowledge occurs during reasoning, when the cognitive capacities of the reasoner are at least partially taken by the necessity of processing and retaining premises in short-term memory. Both of these factors make retrieval and activation a difficult process that is strongly dependent upon the cognitive capacities of the reasoner, and to some extent their metacognitive abilities (Ackerman & Thompson, this volume; Thompson, Prowse Turner, & Pennycook, 2011).

Dual-process model of information retrieval in reasoning

While these results strongly suggest the relevance of a retrieval and activation model of reasoning, another important question concerns the way that this information is used. There are two classes of theory that can in principle allow us to understand how the kind of information that is activated in semantic memory gets translated into a specific inference. Counterexample theories consider that retrieved information will be used to generate counterexamples to putative conclusions. Probabilistic theories consider that retrieved information is used to generate estimates of the likelihood that a given conclusion is empirically true. Mental Model theory (Johnson-Laird & Byrne, 1991, 2002) is one of the most common instantiations of a counterexample theory. This supposes that people construct models of the premises that summarize the potentially true combinations of the antecedent and the consequent terms. When evaluating a potential conclusion, they will scan these models in order to look for possible counterexamples. Without going into too much detail (see Markovits & Barrouillet, 2002, for further detail), we can summarize the way that information retrieval can affect potential inferences in the following ways. Suppose that someone is given the following AC inference: "If a rock is thrown at a window, the window will break. A window is broken." If the reasoning process allows activation and retrieval of a potential alternative antecedent, then this will be incorporated into the final representation of the premises. This would lead to the following (minimal) set of models:

a rock is thrown   window broken
something else   window broken

The invited conclusion to this inference is that "a rock was thrown". However, scanning this model set shows that there is a counterexample to this inference, leading the reasoner to conclude that there is no logically necessary conclusion. If an alternative antecedent is not retrieved, then the second model will not be constructed.

a rock is thrown   window broken

When examining the remaining model, no counterexample will become available, and the reasoner will conclude that a rock must have been thrown. An exactly analogous explanation of the effects of activation and retrieval of disabling conditions on reasoning with the MP and the MT inferences can be made. The key factor in this analysis is that retrieval of a single counterexample to a potential conclusion is sufficient to deny the validity of this conclusion. In such a model, the quantity and associative strength of alternatives and disablers will affect the probability of retrieving at least one counterexample.

There is, however, another way of conceiving of how this information is used, which is quite different. Probabilistic models of inferential reasoning also imply that exactly the same kinds of information that we have specified are accessed during reasoning. However, these models assume that when people make inferences, they are essentially calculating the real-world probability that a conclusion will be true if the premises are also true. As we can see, relative numbers of alternative antecedents and of disabling conditions are directly related to this probability. For example, the probability that the premises "If a rock is thrown at a window, the window will break. A window is broken" allow the conclusion that "a rock was thrown at a window" varies according to the numbers of alternative ways of breaking a window. The more such potential alternatives there are, the lower is the probability that this conclusion is true, and vice versa. In other words, probabilistic theories of conditional inferences presume accessing exactly the same kinds of information as we have specified previously, but these are used in a very different way. Empirical results indeed support the idea that when making a probabilistic inference, reasoners consider all retrieved information (De Neys, Schaeken, & d'Ydewalle, 2003a), as would be implied by this model. In addition, research with young children has found that they can make explicitly probabilistic inferences in a way that requires considering the totality of available information (Markovits & Thompson, 2008).

On the surface at least, counterexample and probabilistic models appear to describe two different processes: making an explicitly deductive inference where the conclusion is considered to be logically valid; or not or making an explicitly probabilistic inference, which requires a judgment about the relative likelihood that a conclusion is true. However, the fact that content-related variation is just as strong with deductive inferences has been taken to suggest that the underlying process for both forms of inference is essentially probabilistic (e.g. Evans, Over, & Handley, 2005; Oaksford & Chater, 2007). Yet, there is clear evidence that suggests that reasoning strategies differ when making deductive and probabilistic inferences (e.g. Rips, 2001). How can we reconcile these two competing models? One recent theory that has attempted to do exactly that is the dual-process theory of conditional inferences that has been proposed by Verschueren and colleagues (Verschueren, Schaeken, & d'Ydewalle, 2005a, 2005b). This theory suggests that both counterexample and probabilistic models represent different strategies that can be used by people in order to make conditional inferences (note that this theory is not to be confused with the heuristic-analytic distinction used to explain non-logical forms of reasoning such as belief-bias). According to this, both strategies access essentially the same kind of information. A counterexample strategy will use a retrieval process in order to construct a relatively conscious representation of the premises, which must be actively scanned in order to determine whether or not a given conclusion has a counterexample. A probabilistic strategy will rapidly scan the same information in order to construct an intuitive, rapid, likelihood estimation of the probability that a conclusion is true. The former is more working-memory intensive, and is found in more competent reasoners. The latter requires fewer cognitive resources and will be preferentially used by less competent reasoners. Recent studies have provided clear evidence for the existence of these two strategies (Verschueren et al., 2005a, 2005b; Markovits, Lortie Forgues, & Brunet, 2012), and for the relation between individual differences and strategy use. More importantly, Markovits, Brunet, Thompson, & Brisson (2013) have provided evidence that people will preferentially adopt a probabilistic strategy when they are time constrained and unable to perform the metacognitive processing required to successfully use a counterexample strategy. In other words, reasoners have access to both strategies, and the choice of which strategy is used will depend on both cognitive and metacognitive constraints.

In conclusion, there is clear evidence that on-line retrieval of information related to alternative antecedents and to disabling conditions underlies the way that people tend to make inferences with premises that have concrete referents: that is, content for which information is readily available in semantic memory. However, the same information can be used in very different ways. In cases when reasoners lack appropriate metacognitive abilities, or are severely constrained in some way, this information is scanned in order to come up with a real-world estimation of the likelihood that a particular conclusion is true. Otherwise, the same information is processed in a more complex way in order to generate the existence of a potential counterexample, which allows the inference that a particular conclusion is either logically valid or not.

This basic model supposes that one of the key factors in reasoning is the cognitive effort used to access information. When information is readily available (because of a high degree of activation), it can be used in a superficial, rapid way in order to provide quick inferences that basically reflect what a reasoner knows about the world. In contrast, deeper processing leads to a more logical approach, which is less constrained by belief. While we have concentrated on conditional reasoning in this review, this basic dynamic characterizes many other forms of reasoning, which in turn suggests that this model is applicable in a broader context. For example, there are clear similarities between this model and fuzzy-trace theory (Reyna, 2012), which makes an important distinction between surface-level processing and deeper, gist processing. Certainly, understanding the way that memory interacts with reasoning processes is a critical component of any general theory of reasoning and decision making.

References

Anderson, J. R., Reder, L. M., & Lebiere, C. (1996). Working memory: Activation limitations on retrieval. *Cognitive Psychology, 30*, 221–256.

Barrouillet, P., & Lecas, J.-F. (1999). Mental models in conditional reasoning and working memory. *Thinking & Reasoning, 5*(4), 289–302.

Barsalou, L. W. (1983). Ad hoc categories. *Memory & Cognition, 11*(3), 211–227.

Braine, M. D. (1978). On the relation between the natural logic of reasoning and standard logic. *Psychological Review, 85*(1), 1–21.

Cheng, P. W. H., & Holyoak, K. J. (1985). Pragmatic reasoning schemas. *Cognitive Psychology, 17*, 391–416.

Cummins, D. D. (1995). Naive theories and causal deduction. *Memory & Cognition, 23*(5), 646–658.

Cummins, D. D., Lubart, T., Alksnis, O., & Rist, R. (1991). Conditional reasoning and causation. *Memory & Cognition, 19*(3), 274–282.

De Neys, W., Schaeken, W., & d'Ydewalle, G. (2002). Causal conditional reasoning and semantic memory retrieval: A test of the semantic memory framework. *Memory & Cognition, 30*(6), 908–920.

De Neys, W., Schaeken, W., & d'Ydewalle, G. (2003a). Inference suppression and semantic memory retrieval: Every counterexample counts. *Memory & Cognition, 31*(4), 581–595.

De Neys, W., Schaeken, W., & d'Ydewalle, G. (2003b). Causal conditional reasoning and strength of association: The disabling condition case. *European Journal of Cognitive Psychology, 15*(2), 161–176.

De Neys, W., Schaeken, W., d'Ydewalle, G. (2005). Working memory and counterexample retrieval for causal conditionals. *Thinking and Reasoning, 11*(2), 123–150.

Dias, M. G., & Harris, P. L. (1988). The effect of make-believe play on deductive reasoning. *British Journal of Developmental Psychology, 6*(3), 207–221.

Dias, M. G., & Harris, P. L. (1990). The influence of the imagination on reasoning by young children. *British Journal of Developmental Psychology, 8*(4), 305–318.

Evans, J. S. B. T., Over, D. E., & Handley, S. J. (2003). Conditionals and conditional probability. *Journal of Experimental Psychology: Learning, Memory, and Cognition, 29*, 321–335.

Evans, J. S. B. T., & Over, D. E. (2004). *If*. New York, NY: Oxford University Press.

Evans, J. S. B. T., Over, D. E., & Handley, S. J. (2005). Suppositionals, extensionality, and conditionals: A critique of the mental model theory of Johnson-Laird and Byrne (2002). *Psychological Review, 112*, 1040–1052.

Evans, J. S. B. T., Handley, S. J., Neilens, H., & Over, D. E. (2007). Thinking about conditionals: A study of individual differences. *Memory & Cognition, 35*(7), 1785–1800.

Evans, J. S. B. T., Over, D. E., & Handley, S. J. (2007). Rethinking the model theory of conditionals. In A. W. V. Schaeken, W. Schroyens, & G. d'Ydewalle (Eds.), *The mental models theory of reasoning: Refinements and extensions* (pp. 63–83). Mahwah, NJ: Lawrence Erlbaum Associates.

Fillenbaum, S. (1975). If: Some uses. *Psychological Research, 37*, 245–260.

Grice, H. P. (1981). Presupposition and conversational implicature. In P. Cole (Ed.), *Syntax and semantics, Vol. 9: Pragmatics* (pp. 183–198). New York, NY: Academic Press.

Inhelder, B., &. Piaget., J. (1958). *The growth of logical thinking from childhood to adolescence.* New York, NY: Basic Books.

Janveau-Brennan, G., & Markovits, H. (1999). The development of reasoning with causal conditionals. *Developmental Psychology, 35*(4), 904–911.

Johnson-Laird, P. N. (2001). Mental models and deduction. *Trends in Cognitive Sciences, 5*(10), 434–442.

Johnson-Laird, P. N., & Byrne, R. M. J. (1991). *Deduction.* Hove & London: Erlbaum.

Johnson-Laird, P. N., & Byrne, R. M. J. (2002). Conditionals: A theory of meaning, pragmatics and inference. *Psychological Review, 109,* 646–678.

Klaczynski, P. A., Schuneman, M. J., & Daniel, D. B. (2004). Theories of conditional reasoning: A developmental examination of competing hypotheses. *Developmental Psychology, 40*(4), 559–571.

Marcus, S. L., & Rips, L. J. (1979). Conditional reasoning. *Journal of Verbal Learning & Verbal Behavior, 18*(2), 199–223.

Markovits, H. (1986). Familiarity effects in conditional reasoning. *Journal of Educational Psychology, 78*(6), 492–494.

Markovits, H. (1995). Conditioning reasoning with false premises: Fantasy and information retrieval. *British Journal of Developmental Psychology, 13*(1), 1–11.

Markovits, H. (2000). A mental model analysis of young children's conditional reasoning with meaningful premises. *Thinking & Reasoning, 6*(4), 335–347.

Markovits, H., & Barrouillet, P. (2002). The development of conditional reasoning: A mental model account. *Developmental Review, 22*(1), 5–36.

Markovits, H., Brunet, M.-L., Thompson, V., & Brisson, J. (2013). Direct evidence for a dual process model of deductive inference. *Journal of Experimental Psychology: LMC, 39*(4), 1213–1222.

Markovits, H., & Doyon, C. (2004). Information processing and reasoning with premises that are empirically false: Interference, working memory, and processing speed. *Memory & Cognition, 32*(4), 592–601.

Markovits, H., Doyon, C., & Simoneau, M. (2002). Individual differences in working memory and conditional reasoning with concrete and abstract content. *Thinking & Reasoning, 8*(2), 97–107.

Markovits, H., Fleury, M.-L., Quinn, S., & Venet, M. (1998). The development of conditional reasoning and the structure of semantic memory. *Child Development, 69*(3), 742–755.

Markovits, H., Lortie Forgues, H., & Brunet, M.-L. (2012). More evidence for a dual-process model of conditional reasoning. *Memory and Cognition, 40*(50), 736–747.

Markovits, H., & Potvin, F. (2001). Suppression of valid inferences and knowledge structures: The curious effect of producing alternative antecedents on reasoning with causal conditionals. *Memory & Cognition, 29*(5), 736–744.

Markovits, H., & Quinn, S. (2002). Efficiency of retrieval correlates with "logical" reasoning from causal conditional premises. *Memory & Cognition, 30*(5), 696–706.

Markovits, H., & Thompson, V. (2008). Different developmental patterns of simple deductive and probabilistic inferential reasoning. *Memory and Cognition, 36*(6), 1066–1078.

Markovits, H., & Vachon, R. (1989). Reasoning with contrary-to-fact propositions. *Journal of Experimental Child Psychology, 47*(3), 398–412.

Markovits, H., & Vachon, R. (1990). Conditional reasoning, representation, and level of abstraction. *Developmental Psychology, 26*(6), 942–951.

Markovits, H., Venet, M., Janveau-Brennan, G., Malfait, N., et al. (1996). Reasoning in young children: Fantasy and information retrieval. *Child Development, 67*(6), 2857–2872.

Oaksford, M., & Chater, N. (2003). Conditional probability and the cognitive science of conditional reasoning. *Mind & Language, 18*(4), 359–379.

Oaksford, M., & Chater, N. (2007). *Bayesian rationality.* Oxford: Oxford University Press.

Oaksford, M., Chater, N., & Larkin, J. (2000). Probabilities and polarity biases in conditional inference. *Journal of Experimental Psychology: Learning, Memory, and Cognition, 26*(4), 883–899.

Reyna, V. F. (2012). A new intuitionism: Meaning, memory, and development in Fuzzy-Trace Theory. *Judgment and Decision Making, 7*(3), 332–359.

Rips, L. J. (1983). Cognitive processes in propositional reasoning. *Psychological Review, 90*(1), 38–71.

Rips, L. J. (2001). Two kinds of reasoning. *Psychological Science, 12*(2), 129–134.

Rosen, V. M., & Engle., R. W. (1996). The role of working memory capacity in retrieval. *Journal of Experimental Psychology: General, 126*(3), 211–227.

Simoneau, M., & Markovits, H. (2003). Reasoning with premises that are not empirically true: Evidence for the role of inhibition and retrieval. *Developmental Psychology, 39*(6), 964–975.

Thompson, V. A. (1994). Interpretational factors in conditional reasoning. *Memory & Cognition, 22*(6), 742–758.

Thompson, V. A. (2000). The task-specific nature of domain-general reasoning. *Cognition, 76*(3), 209–268.

Thompson, V. A., Prowse Turner, J. A., & Pennycook, G. (2011). Intuition, reason, and metacognition. *Cognitive Psychology, 63*, 107–140.

Toms, M., Morris, N., & Ward, D. (1993). Working memory and conditional reasoning. *The Quarterly Journal of Experimental Psychology A: Human Experimental Psychology. Special Issue: The Cognitive Psychology of Reasoning, 46A*(4), 679–699.

Vadeboncoeur, I., & Markovits, H. (1999). The effect of instructions and information retrieval on accepting the premises in a conditional reasoning task. *Thinking & Reasoning, 5*(2), 97–113.

Verschueren, N., Schaeken, W., & d'Ydewalle, G. (2005a). A dual-process specification of causal conditional reasoning. *Thinking & Reasoning, 11*(3), 239–278.

Verschueren, N., Schaeken, W., & d'Ydewalle, G. (2005b). Everyday conditional reasoning: A working-memory-dependent tradeoff between counterexample and likelihood use. *Memory & Cognition, 33*(1), 107–119.

4

A MEMORY-THEORETIC ACCOUNT OF HYPOTHESIS GENERATION AND JUDGMENT AND DECISION MAKING

Nicholas D. Lange, Daniel R. Buttaccio, Amber M. Sprenger, Isaiah Harbison, Rick P. Thomas and Michael R. Dougherty

Hypothesis generation is a ubiquitous human activity – one that engages a complex set of cognitive processes, ranging from attention and working memory to long-term memory retrieval. The canonical professional example of a hypothesis-generation task is that of clinical diagnosis, wherein the clinician is responsible for rendering diagnoses. Prior to finalizing a diagnosis, physicians are known to, and in fact are instructed to (Sox, Blatt, Higgins, & Marton, 2006), generate plausible alternative hypotheses that can explain the available pattern of symptoms or data (Elstein, 1976). Medical diagnosis provides one example of the many real-world domains involving hypothesis generation: Heuer (1999) identified hypothesis generation as the preeminent step of intelligence analysis within the Central Intelligence Agency; Libby (1985) discussed hypothesis generation in the domain of auditing; and Patrick et al. (1999) described research on fault generation by nuclear-power-plant operators. More informally, hypothesis-generation processes also underlie many everyday social scenarios, such as understanding the personalities of acquaintances, based on behavioral patterns (Zuckerman, Knee, Hodgins, & Miyake, 1995). Given the wide array of domains and tasks in which hypothesis generation is involved, it is arguably a foundational process upon which judgment accuracy depends. In fact, we argue that many common reasoning errors stem from the psychological constraints on the hypothesis-generation process. For example, misdiagnoses in medical decision making can result from, amongst other things, the inability of decision makers to consider multiple diagnostic hypotheses simultaneously.

Despite the ubiquity and importance of hypothesis generation, it has been largely neglected by the mainstream literature on judgment and decision making. The earliest work on hypothesis generation dates back to Elstein (1976), in his work on clinical diagnosis, and work by Gettys and colleagues examining the processes underlying hypothesis and act generation (Gettys & Fisher, 1979). This early work notwithstanding, basic theoretical and empirical research on hypothesis generation has been sparse until recently. The goal of this chapter, therefore, is to review recent advances in our understanding of hypothesis generation. In what follows, we outline a computational model of hypothesis generation, along with supporting empirical data, that positions memory as a central factor underlying hypothesis generation. Specifically, we address the following questions:

- What is the role of memory processes in hypothesis generation?
- How does hypothesis generation impact probability judgment?
- What is the role of hypothesis generation on hypothesis testing?
- What is the influence of the temporal dynamics of working memory (WM) on hypothesis generation?

What is the role of memory processes in hypothesis generation?

Hypothesis generation can be likened to a retrieval process in which the goal is to identify a *set* of possible explanations for an observed pattern of data (Thomas, Dougherty, Sprenger, & Harbison, 2008; Dougherty, Thomas, & Lange, 2010). Thomas et al. (2008) proposed a memory-based computational architecture to capture the memory-retrieval processes underlying hypothesis generation and the effects of hypothesis generation on probability judgment. This model, HyGene (short for **Hy**pothesis **Gene**ration), is based on three principles: (a) Cued recall: Information in the environment prompts retrieval of associated hypotheses from long-term memory; (b) Limited capacity: WM capacity and task characteristics constrain the number of hypotheses that can be actively considered; and (c) Information propagation: Hypotheses maintained in WM serve as input for probability assessment and guide information search (e.g., hypothesis testing). Importantly, the associations between data and hypotheses are stored in memory over repeated experience and are utilized later for structuring decision making.

The hypothesis-generation process can be both divergent, where a single datum implies multiple hypotheses, and convergent, where multiple data imply a single hypothesis. In either case, once hypotheses are generated, they are added to the Set of Leading Contenders (SOC). The SOC is a subset of the total possible set of hypotheses, and the number of hypotheses maintained in the SOC is limited by WM capacity. Individuals may maintain fewer hypotheses in WM because they have a relatively low WM capacity (an individual difference, Dougherty & Hunter, 2003a) or because their WM capacity is being consumed by a secondary task (Sprenger et al., 2011). In keeping with research within the WM literature, we assume that WM includes the ability to actively maintain goal-relevant information (i.e., hypotheses) in the focus of attention while distracted (Unsworth & Engle, 2006; Unsworth & Engle, 2007).

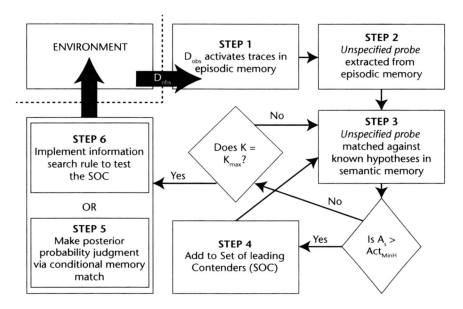

FIGURE 4.1   Flow diagram of computational processing in HyGene.

Episodic memory, semantic memory, and WM operate in concert with a set of retrieval operations to identify a set of plausible hypotheses. The hypotheses maintained in the SOC then serve as input for both probability judgment and information search (Buttaccio, Lange, Hahn, & Thomas, 2014; Dougherty et al., 2010). The basic algorithmic structure of HyGene is illustrated in Figure 4.1, which for convenience can be characterized as a set of discrete steps (for more detail, see Thomas et al., 2008):

Step1: The observed data (D_{obs}) acquired from the environment activates traces in episodic memory representing past experiences sharing features with the D_{obs}.

Step 2: The highly activated traces in episodic memory contribute to the extraction of an *unspecified probe* resembling the hypotheses most commonly and strongly associated with the data. The unspecified probe is much like a prototype representation, but one that has not yet been assigned category membership.

Step 3: The unspecified probe is matched against known hypotheses stored in semantic memory resulting in an activation value for each hypothesis in semantic memory. This is done to identify the set of hypotheses that could explain the D_{obs}.

Step 4: Hypotheses are generated from semantic memory and placed in the SOC if they are sufficiently activated by the unspecified probe. The generation process involves stochastic sampling with replacement, where hypotheses are probabilistically sampled from semantic memory according to their activation values. Hypotheses are recovered from semantic memory and placed into the SOC if their activation values are greater than the activation level of the least active hypothesis in the SOC (Act_{MinH}). Hypotheses in the SOC are referred to as "Leading Contender Hypotheses," because they represent the decision maker's leading explanations for the D_{obs}.

Step 5: The posterior probability of the focal hypothesis, $P(H_i | D_{obs})$, is derived by comparing its memory strength to the summed memory strengths of all hypotheses in the SOC.

Step 6: Hypotheses in the SOC are used to guide the selection of cues for hypothesis testing.

These six processing components allow HyGene to account for a variety of findings in literature, including the effects of long-term and WM on hypothesis generation, probability judgment, and hypothesis testing (for a review see Dougherty et al., 2010).

HyGene predicts that people will generate a small subset of the total number of possible hypotheses. This prediction matches empirical findings (Dougherty, Gettys & Thomas, 1997; Dougherty & Hunter, 2003a; Gettys & Fisher, 1979; Mehle, 1982; Weber, Boeckenholt, Hilton, & Wallace, 1993), and mirrors Evans' (2006) singularity principle, which postulates that many reasoning biases result from people's tendency to consider only a single mental model at a time. One reason HyGene makes this prediction is due to the operation of the threshold for including new hypotheses in WM, where newly sampled hypotheses are only included if they are more highly activated than the least active hypothesis in the current set. Second, HyGene predicts that people will tend to generate hypotheses with higher a priori likelihood *ceteris paribus*, another finding consistent with the literature (Dougherty et al., 1997; Dougherty & Hunter, 2003a; Sprenger & Dougherty, 2012; Weber et al., 1993). This result obtains in HyGene because hypotheses that have occurred more often in the ecology are more prevalent in episodic memory. Thus, the features of the unspecified probe will more strongly reflect the features of the more prevalent hypotheses, resulting in greater semantic activations. In turn, hypotheses with greater a priori likelihood are more likely to be generated.

How does hypothesis generation impact probability judgment?

The most influential and widely applicable theory for understanding probability judgment has been Tversky and Koehler's (1994) support theory. Support theory postulates that the probability judgment for a particular focal hypothesis (H_a) operates via a comparison process where the focal's strength $S(H_a)$ is compared to the strength of its alternatives $S(H_b)$. One consequence of support theory is that judgments should be subadditive, in that the sum of the judgments for an explicit disjunction will exceed the probability of the implicit disjunction. For example, consider someone whose cancer diagnosis has been confirmed, p(cancer=1.0). Subadditivity obtains when the sum of probability judgments for individual cancer types (e.g., prostate, breast, pancreatic, liver, brain, ovarian, etc.) is greater than 1.0. Although support theory provides a general theoretical framework, it has two major shortcomings that preclude it from being a process model: 1) It does not account for how decision makers assess the strength of hypotheses in precise information-processing terms, and 2) it fails to address how hypotheses become part of the comparison process. Subsequent work has addressed both of these issues.

HyGene assumes that the comparison process to derive probability judgment operates only on those hypotheses generated and maintained in WM. Consequently, the probability space is partitioned over only those hypotheses contained in WM – the property of constrained additivity. Constrained additivity implies that probability judgments will be subadditive whenever the decision maker fails to consider all hypotheses within the normative set.

Subadditivity has been found in most studies investigating the additivity of probability judgments (e.g., Dougherty & Hunter, 2003a, 2003b; Tversky & Koehler, 1994; but see Sloman et al., 2004, for an example of superadditivity). However, the level of subadditivity that obtains is dependent upon memory variables. For example, Dougherty and Hunter (2003a, 2003b) showed that the magnitude of subadditivity was *inversely* correlated with WM capacity (see also Sprenger & Dougherty, 2006). This finding is consistent with the notion of a capacity-limited comparison process. Specifically, participants with lower capacity have fewer resources available to maintain alternatives for inclusion in the comparison process, leading them to underestimate the strength of the alternatives compared to those with higher capacity. This account was confirmed by Sprenger et al. (2011), who found that participants showed greater subadditivity when judgments were made under divided attention.

Dougherty & Hunter (2003a) evaluated how the distribution of hypotheses affects probability judgment and subadditivity. Participants showed less subadditivity when the distribution of the to-be-judged hypotheses was characterized by a single strong hypothesis, compared to when the hypotheses were all relatively equal in strength. This finding obtains for two reasons according to our memory-based account: 1) The stronger hypotheses are most likely to be generated (reviewed above), and 2) the capacity to consider alternative hypotheses is limited. These factors make it highly likely that the decision maker will generate the strong alternative hypothesis in the unbalanced condition, which in turn drives down the probability of the focal hypothesis. This finding is similar to the alternative-outcomes effect identified by Windschitl and Wells (1998), but extends the effect to subadditivity.

What is the role of hypothesis generation on hypothesis testing?

Hypothesis testing involves searching for, or selecting information in order to test, the truth of a hypothesis. A common finding in the literature is that of confirmation bias or pseudodiagnostic search (Klayman & Ha, 1987; Mynatt, Doherty, & Tweney, 1977; Sanbonmatsu, Posavac, & Kardes, 1998; Wason, 1968), where people often select information that is relevant for evaluating only a single hypothesis. Although participants commonly select information using a positive test strategy, in a few circumstances diagnostic search has been observed under conditions that facilitate the consideration of alternatives (Mynatt, Doherty, & Dragan, 1993), such as when the alternatives are highlighted in the experimental task or when the participant explicitly considers the alternatives (Kruglanski & Mayseless, 1988; Trope & Mackie, 1987). When the alternatives are not explicitly specified, however, participants tend to search for information pseudodiagnostically (Trope & Mackie, 1987).

We assume that decision makers search for information contingent on their currently held hypotheses – a process we refer to as hypothesis-guided search. If only one hypothesis is maintained in WM, then hypothesis-guided search necessarily follows a positive test strategy. However, if more than one hypothesis is being maintained in WM, then the decision maker can search for information that differentiates amongst the hypotheses under consideration.

We assume that decision makers invoke one of a small number of heuristic processes for guiding information search, all of which function by utilizing hypotheses maintained in WM. We focus on two heuristics and demonstrate the effects of these heuristics on information search: 1) Memory-Strength Heuristic: Choose the cue most highly associated with the focal hypothesis, and 2) Bayesian Diagnosticity: Choose the cue with the highest likelihood ratio.

> *Memory-Strength Heuristic.* When the decision maker generates one hypothesis, information search is assumed to be controlled by the memory strength of cues. That is, cues of the hypothesis with the highest activation, as estimated via memory strength, are searched first (assuming costs of search between information sources are irrelevant).
>
> The cues that have the highest memory strength will tend to be those that are most prevalent, or encoded with higher fidelity, in episodic memory. The memory-strength heuristic can prefer non-diagnostic over diagnostic cues, because the cue that is most strongly associated with the hypothesis being tested does not have to be diagnostic.
>
> *Bayesian Diagnosticity.* When more than one hypothesis is generated, then it is possible for HyGene to directly estimate the Bayesian diagnosticity of the cues and to select the cue with the highest diagnosticity. Importantly, HyGene does not represent conditional probabilities directly, but allows for conditional probabilities to be estimated from episodic memory. HyGene's cue diagnosticity is based on only the hypotheses that populate WM. Thus, the subjective diagnosticity of a test and its objective diagnosticity will be at variance if the set of hypotheses in WM differ from the objectively relevant set. Also, if episodic memory is biased (e.g., through biased sampling or search processes), the subjective diagnosticity of a cue will deviate from its objective diagnosticity (Dougherty et al., 2010).

The heuristic mechanisms presented above represent our first attempt to integrate information-search algorithms within the context of the HyGene architecture. However, do these algorithms make testable predictions that bear out in behavioral studies?

A simulation study was conducted to examine HyGene's hypothesis-testing predictions under varied levels of encoding and experience. Table 4.1 summarizes an ecology of four medical tests, where each test has two possible levels (e.g., normal temperature versus high fever). HyGene's episodic memory "experienced" patients with particular disease hypotheses, with test results generated according to the probability distributions defined in Table 4.1. To simulate differential experience, the number of patients presented to the model was systematically manipulated to be either low (i.e., E=10 patients experienced per disease) or high (i.e., E=50 patients experienced per disease). Also, the encoding fidelity of the memory traces from experience was manipulated at six levels, from high (L=1.0) to low (L=.65).

When the model generated only one hypothesis, information search was based on the memory-strength heuristic. Figure 4.2 illustrates that when one disease (i.e., Disease A *or* Disease B) was generated, HyGene engaged in positive testing. That is, HyGene selected the test (Test 4) that had the highest likelihood of a positive result. Also, more experience (i.e., higher values of E) and better encoding of experiences (i.e., higher value of L) led to more pseudodiagnostic search. Thus, the HyGene information-search model predicts positive testing (Einhorn & Hogarth 1978; Mynatt, Doherty, & Tweney, 1977) when only one hypothesis is generated.

HyGene's diagnosticity search strategy shows a clear preference for more diagnostic cues. Also, as the model gains experience (i.e., higher values of E) or encodes the events with greater fidelity (i.e., higher value of L) HyGene's preference for the most diagnostic cue (Test 1) increases. Although the simulation findings suggest that hypothesis generation is crucial to determining whether diagnostic search will ensue, behavioral evidence is needed.

Thomas, Lange, & Dougherty (unpublished manuscript) tested the effects of self-generated hypotheses on information search. Participants viewed 200 patients suffering from fictitious diseases. Viewing a patient involved observing symptoms and learning which disease the patient suffered from. The patient symptoms were sampled to reflect the statistical ecology presented in Table 4.2.

TABLE 4.1 Associations between the tests and hypotheses A & B, with the diagnosticity of each test presented on the right.

	Hypothesis		*Diagnosticity*
	A	*B*	
Test 1	0.8	0.2	*4.00*
Test 2	0.7	0.3	*2.33*
Test 3	0.6	0.4	*1.50*
Test 4	0.9	0.9	*1.00*

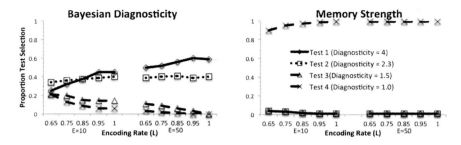

FIGURE 4.2 Simulation result of HyGene-HT demonstrating test selection when the model generated one hypothesis (Memory-Strength Heuristic; left panel) and when the model generated two hypotheses (Bayesian Diagnosticity; right panel) under manipulation of Experience (E) and encoding fidelity (L).

TABLE 4.2 Associations between the hypotheses and data in the hypothesis-testing experiment. Data 1 & 2 were used as memory cues and Data 3, 4, & 5 were tests available for selection.

| | Presenting symptoms | | Available tests | | |
	Data 1	Data 2	Data 3	Data 4	Data 5
Hypothesis 1	0.9	0.1	0.5	0.9	0.9
Hypothesis 2	0.1	0.1	0.5	0.1	0.9
Hypothesis 3	0.1	0.9	0.1	0.5	0.9
Hypothesis 4	0.1	0.9	0.9	0.5	0.9

The first column represents the various hypotheses (diseases). Data columns 1 through 5 refer to medical tests. The numbers below the headings show the probability of an abnormal test result (i.e., a symptom of that disease). The complementary probability represents the probability of a normal test result (i.e., no symptom). Imagine that D1 represents temperature. Hypothesis 1 results in a positive test (i.e., fever) 90% of the time and a normal test (i.e., no fever) 10% of the time. H2, H3, and H4 are each associated with a normal temperature 90% of the time and an abnormal temperature (fever) 10% of the time. In this case, a participant given a test result of "fever" should suspect H1 as the most likely disease, given that fever is nearly always indicative of H1 and very rarely indicative of H2, H3, or H4. Using these distributions, we were able to create and control our own ecology, allowing us to capture some of the dynamics of how hypothesis generation affects testing – particularly preference for positive versus diagnostic search.

After viewing 200 fictitious patients, participants observed a single patient symptom and were asked to select the medical test that they believed would be most informative to evaluate the patient given the presenting symptom. Either D1

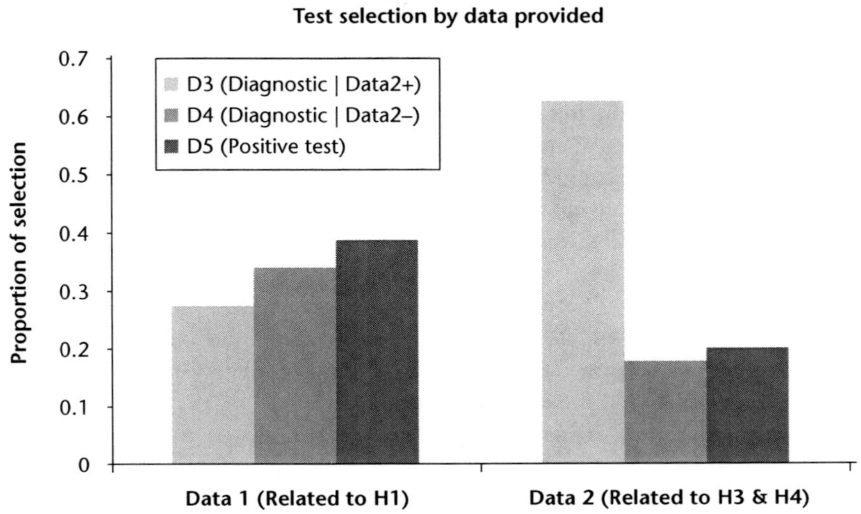

Test selection by data provided

FIGURE 4.3   Data from Thomas, Lange, & Dougherty (unpublished) demonstrating positive test preference when only one hypothesis is strongly associated with the presented data, and strong diagnostic test preference when the presented data was associated with two hypotheses.

or D2 served as the presenting symptoms or cues to prompt the generation of either one disease (where D1 tends to prompt the generation of only H1) or two diseases (where D2 tends to prompt the generation of H3 & H4 or H1 & H2) into WM.

We expected 1) a stronger preference for the positive test (D5) when only one hypothesis was associated with the presenting symptom and generated into WM, and 2) a stronger preference for the diagnostic test (D3) when the presenting symptom was associated with more than one hypothesis. This pattern of results obtained empirically, as illustrated in Figure 4.3.

Hypothesis testing in real-world situations relies on memory retrieval. Previous hypothesis-testing research has ignored memory retrieval, as the experimenter typically provided the to-be-evaluated hypotheses. Since the generation of hypotheses is not random, but based on retrieval processes, it seems impossible to build an adequate theory of hypothesis-testing behavior without accounting for memory. Thus, understanding hypothesis generation as a memory-retrieval process is necessary to generalize to most real-world hypothesis-testing contexts.

What is the influence of the temporal dynamics of working memory (WM) on hypothesis generation?

Time is interwoven with the cognitive operations we perform. As information processing unfolds, there is never a moment at which *time* does not impinge on the deployment of our cognitive faculties. Therefore, learning how time influences hypothesis generation will help build more comprehensive theories of hypothesis generation as it transpires in real-world tasks.

Decision makers are influenced by both external and internal dynamics. Information in the external environment often unfolds over time. Once acquired, this information is then subject to the internal cognitive dynamics of the decision maker as it is maintained and utilized by memory processes. Moreover, as further information is presented in the environment and acquired by the decision maker, this new information can influence the ongoing information-processing and maintenance dynamics. Therefore, in order to understand the temporal dynamics of hypothesis generation, it is necessary to appreciate how internal cognitive dynamics unfold over time, and how these dynamics interact with variation of information presented in the external environment.

Temporal dynamics influence hypothesis generation and maintenance over three stages: 1) Dynamic data acquisition, 2) Hypothesis generation into WM, and 3) Hypothesis maintenance over time as hypotheses are utilized and additional information is acquired. The original HyGene framework (Thomas et al., 2008) readily accounts for the second stage, but in regards to the first and third stages the original model is static: It acquires all of the data available in the environment simultaneously and uses data all to the same degree in the generation of hypotheses. There are no mechanisms in the original model to explore dynamic maintenance and updating processes following the retrieval of hypotheses into WM.

Lange, Thomas, and Davelaar (2012) merged the dynamic WM buffer of Davelaar et al.'s (2005) context-activation model with the original implementation of HyGene in order to allow HyGene to model the dynamics of data acquisition. This integrated model makes predictions about how variation in data acquisition timings and relative serial orders influence hypothesis generation. Davelaar et al. (2005) proposed the context-activation model to account for WM dynamics in routine memory-retrieval paradigms. A critical component of this model is a dynamic memory buffer, in which the memory-activation associated with individual items fluctuates systematically over time. In the context of list-memory paradigms, the buffer models the dynamic rise and fall of individual list items' memory activations over the study phase of a list-recall trial. We suggest that the same dynamic WM processes accounting for the memory activations of list items in the context-activation model may also reflect the processes governing dynamic data acquisition and hypothesis maintenance. We now describe each of the three stages of dynamic hypothesis generation.

Stage 1: data-acquisition dynamics

When engaged in hypothesis-generation tasks, data is acquired serially. As a result, each datum is acquired in some order relative to the rest of the data. These characteristics influence the relative utilization of each piece of data in the generation of hypotheses from LTM. Figure 4.4 portrays the serial acquisition of

Slow presentation rate

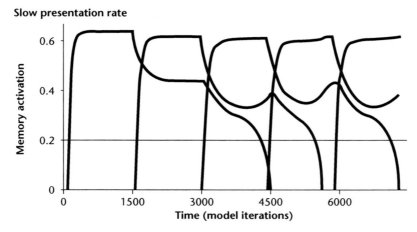

Fast presentation rate

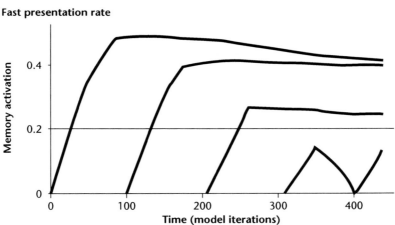

FIGURE 4.4   Two noiseless runs of the dynamic working-memory buffer, in which the model serially acquires five pieces of data at a slow rate (top panel; 1500 iterations/item) or a fast rate (bottom panel; 100 iterations/item). The fast rate causes the earlier items to be more active at the end of the data presentation sequence, unlike the slow rate, in which the later items are more active following the sequence. The solid horizontal line at 0.20 is the threshold for the item being active in WM.

five pieces of data in the dynamic hypothesis-generation model of Lange, Thomas, & Davelaar (2012), with the top panel showing the activations under a slow presentation rate and the bottom panel for a fast presentation rate. In the context of a physician with the goal of rendering a diagnosis, each of the lines in the figure would represent the dynamic memory-activation trajectories of five symptoms sequentially observed by the physician. The data activation level is plotted on the Y-axis, and time (model iterations) is plotted on the X-axis. The activation level of each piece of data is influenced by four factors at each time step of the model: 1) Bottom-up stimulus input, 2) Self-recurrent excitation, 3) Global lateral inhibition from other active items, and 4) Noise. The horizontal line at the 0.2 activation level demarcates the threshold for items to be considered in or out of WM.

As each item is presented to the model, it receives strong bottom-up sensory input. This bottom-up input provides a boost of activation to each item, giving rise to the steep front end of each item's activation trajectory. Additionally, each item recycles some of its activation onto itself. This self-recurrent activation provides the buffer with the ability to maintain items over time, in the absence of bottom-up input. Importantly, the buffer is competitive, in that each item inhibits every other item in proportion with its activation level. The competition instantiated through this global lateral inhibition property drives the dynamic aspect of data acquisition. The competitive nature of the buffer is responsible for producing the subtle ebb and flow of item activations over time. Importantly, inhibition also imposes an emergent capacity limitation on the model (Davelaar, 2007).

The dynamic HyGene model uses the WM buffer's activation levels during acquisition as weights governing the contribution of each piece of data to the generation process. Specifically, the global-memory match between the current set of acquired data and episodic memory is weighted by the data activations in the WM buffer (with data below the 0.2 threshold receiving a weight of 0, as if they were forgotten). Aside from the WM buffer, the dynamic HyGene model operates as in the original version (Thomas et al., 2008).

This integrated model produces two strong predictions representing *temporal biases* in the generation of hypotheses, which arise from the manipulation of sequence and timing in the model. From a normative perspective, time and sequence should have no bearing on the interpretation of the data, but the model is sensitive to these temporal characteristics, as are people.

The first bias predicted by the model is that later data will contribute more to the generation of hypotheses than early data (recency). This is clearly demonstrated in Figure 4.4 (top panel). In this case, the model has acquired five pieces of data. The activation levels of the first three pieces of data dynamically rise into WM, and are eventually pushed out due to the competition of the remaining items. These remaining items, however, survive in WM until the end of the data-presentation sequence. As only the last two items are active in WM at the end of the presentation sequence, only these items can contribute to the hypothesis-retrieval processes. This recency bias of the model predicts that later data will influence hypothesis generation more than earlier data.

Sprenger and Dougherty (2012) examined how differences in data ordering influenced hypothesis generation and probability judgment. In line with the prediction of the dynamic HyGene model, when participants observed cues sequentially, they more often generated hypotheses consistent with the information they most recently acquired. When the most recent evidence was diagnostic of a given hypothesis or cluster of hypotheses, participants tended to generate hypotheses from that cluster and few hypotheses from alternative clusters. In turn, when the most recent information was non-diagnostic, participants tended to generate a more diverse set of hypotheses, even if previously viewed information *was* diagnostic.

In Sprenger and Dougherty's (2012) third experiment, participants were asked to generate psychology courses based on nine sequentially presented descriptive cues. In one condition, early cues were indicative of cognitive/neuroscience courses, and later cues suggested social psychology courses. In another condition, the sequence of data was reversed. As displayed in Figure 4.5, when social psychology cues were presented late in the sequence, participants were more likely to generate social psychology-related courses and less likely to generate cognitive/neuroscience courses; and vice versa when cognitive/neuroscience cues were presented late. These patterns demonstrate that participants' generation was most influenced by recently acquired data. In line with the model prediction this suggests: 1) People do not use all the available evidence equally, and 2) the earlier data was likely displaced from WM by more recent data, thereby allowing the more recent data to exert more influence on generation.

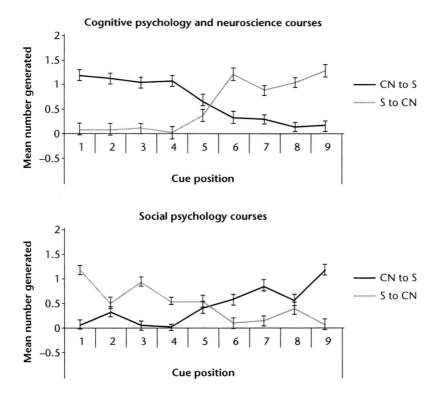

FIGURE 4.5 Data from Sprenger & Dougherty (2012) demonstrating that participants tended to generate items consistent with recently observed information.

An additional experiment by Lange et al. (2012) further bolsters the generality of the data-recency effect in hypothesis generation. In their Experiment 1, participants were sequentially presented with one informative piece of data amongst three uninformative pieces of data. Crucially, the serial position of the useful piece of data was manipulated to appear in each of four possible serial positions. This methodology allows the influence of the data at each serial position to be observed. Figure 4.6 presents the data from this experiment alongside model data from the simulated experiment using dynamic HyGene. As can be seen, the model captures the recency trend evidenced in the data. In comparison to the experiments of Sprenger & Dougherty (2012), the present experiment used a much smaller amount of data (4 as opposed to 9) that is more likely to be within WM capacity limitations. Despite this potential for participants to maintain most (if not all) the presented data, the recency effect still emerged.

The second main prediction of the dynamic HyGene model is that the speed of data acquisition can attenuate and even reverse the data-recency effects. As data acquisition is sped up, there is a shift from the recency profile to a primacy profile of data activation. This prediction suggests that at very fast rates of data acquisition, earlier data will contribute more to the hypothesis-generation process than will later data. These differences in the patterns of data activation are demonstrated in Figure 4.4. The top panel displays the serial data acquisition of five pieces of data at a slow rate. This "early-in, early-out" pattern is the same as demonstrated above. An opposite "early-in, stay-in" pattern is seen in the bottom panel, in which the data presentation rate is fast. The reason for the stark difference in the activation profiles that emerge is due to the truncated period of bottom-up stimulus input received by each item under the fast rate. At slower rates, it is this period of bottom-up input that allows each new item to overcome the inhibition exerted upon it by existing items. Under the fast rate, the truncated period of strong bottom-up input greatly injures the ability of the later items to gain enough activation to gain entry into WM.

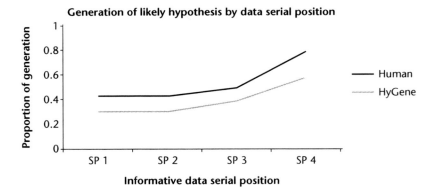

FIGURE 4.6 Empirical and model data from Lange et al. (2012) demonstrating an additional recency bias in generation accounted for by the dynamic HyGene model.

Thus, as presentation rate is increased, earlier data contributes more to the generation process, and under fast rates of data presentation a primacy bias is predicted. This is a unique prediction of the dynamic HyGene model and provides a strong test of the ability of the buffer dynamics to capture dynamic data acquisition in hypothesis-generation tasks.

The above prediction was tested in a diagnosis task in which participants were presented with a sequence of five symptoms and asked to retrieve the most likely of two disease hypotheses (Lange et al., 2012). The sequence of symptoms was set up such that the first two symptoms suggested one hypothesis (Disease A) and the last two symptoms suggested the other hypothesis (Disease B). The middle symptom was uninformative regarding either disease (i.e., it occurred with equal prevalence under each hypothesis). We refer to this data sequence as the "Original Ordering" condition in Figure 4.7. The crucial manipulation was the presentation rate of the individual data in the sequence, which was manipulated to be either a slow rate of 1500 ms (as in the serial position experiment of Lange et al., 2012 above) or a fast rate of 180 ms. The left side of Figure 4.7 shows that under the slow rate we obtain a recency bias in diagnosis, just as expected. Under the fast rate, the recency bias in diagnosis is attenuated, as neither hypothesis is preferred over the other.

This effect of presentation rate is not as strong as the dynamic HyGene model predicts. That is, although there is an attenuation of the recency bias with the increased presentation rate, the predicted primacy effect was not evidenced in the data. We hypothesized that this may be due to the fact that the last item in the presentation sequence may be contributing to the generation process even when the data presentation rate is very fast. This hypothesis was based on data resulting from a free-recall experiment in which the presentation rate of the list items was manipulated to be either fast (200 ms) or slow (1600 ms; Usher, Davelaar,

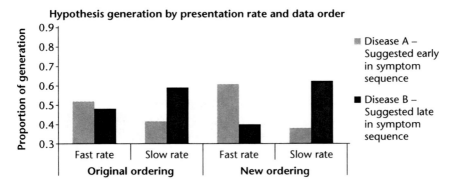

FIGURE 4.7 Data from Lange et al. (2013) in which the presentation rate and data orderings were manipulated. The fast rate attenuated the recency effect evident at slow rates. The predicted primacy effect emerged under the fast rate in the new ordering condition, in which the last item was non-diagnostic.

Haarmann, & Goshen-Gottstein, 2008). In this experiment, the manipulation of presentation rate induced a strong increase in primacy under the fast rate, as predicted. In addition, however, it was also observed that the very last item in the list was recalled a large proportion of the time under both presentation rates. So although primacy was significantly enhanced under the fast rate, recency was not entirely ameliorated. This explains why the data in the "Original Ordering" condition was flat under the fast rate. Although the early items contributed to generation, they likely did so in tandem with the last item, thereby washing out the effect of the early items. In order to test this possibility, Lange et al. (2013) utilized an additional ordering of the data, in which the uninformative data, which previously appeared in the middle of the list, now appeared at the very end of the list. The authors hypothesized that if this item contributed to generation under the fast rate, it would not oppose the hypothesis suggested by the early data and thereby allow the early data to influence generation with greater effect. Indeed, as displayed on the right side of Figure 4.7, this is exactly what the authors found. Under this "New Ordering" condition, the predicted primacy effect clearly emerges under the fast presentation rate as predicted.

Stage 2: hypothesis-generation (sampling) dynamics

HyGene assumes that sampling hypotheses from semantic memory occurs serially and therefore takes time. As mentioned in the introduction, the theory assumes that the number of hypotheses that can be considered at any time is constrained by cognitive limitations and task characteristics. One such task characteristic is the amount of time afforded to a decision maker between the observation of information and the point at which the decision maker must issue her/his response(s) to the task she/he is facing. HyGene predicts that as time pressure increases, people will not be able to populate WM with as many hypotheses as they would under less time pressure or in its absence. This prediction is well supported in light of data from verbal-fluency tasks in which participants are asked to retrieve members of a category. In such tasks, new items are retrieved long into a trial (e.g., after 2 minutes; Walker & Kintsch, 1985).

We demonstrate this point through a simulation in HyGene in which time pressure was manipulated. Time pressure is manipulated in the model through a stopping rule terminating hypothesis generation. The model's stopping rule operates based on the number of retrieval failures the model has suffered (i.e., sampling hypotheses not exceeding the Act_{MinH} threshold or resampling hypotheses which have been generated previously on that trial).[1] Decreasing the number of retrieval failures allowed by the model before generation terminates essentially increases time pressure. Figure 4.8 displays the hypothesis-generation and probability-judgment behavior of the model under conditions of greater and lesser time pressure. In addition, this simulation manipulated the distribution of hypotheses as related to the data. In one condition, the model was provided with a piece of data strongly associated with only one hypothesis, and in the other condition the datum was strongly associated with a few hypotheses.

Figure 4.8 demonstrates effects of both time pressure and hypothesis distribution for the model's hypothesis-generation behavior (left panel) and probability-judgment behavior (right panel). The influence of time pressure on the behavior of the model is evident under both hypothesis distributions. In both cases, greater time pressure results in the model generating fewer hypotheses into the SOC. This relatively impoverished generation then cascades into increases in the probability judgments, as displayed in the right half of Figure 4.8.

The manipulation of hypothesis distribution highlights an additional dynamic aspect of hypothesis sampling in HyGene. As mentioned in the model description above, a dynamic threshold (Act_{MinH}) governs the level of activation that a sampled hypothesis must possess in order to be included in the SOC. On each run of the model, Act_{MinH} is initialized at zero and then takes on the value corresponding to the lowest activation value of the hypotheses in the SOC. Therefore, if the model samples the most highly activated hypothesis first, then it cannot include alternatives in the SOC, as none of the other hypotheses will surpass Act_{MinH}. As there is only one likely hypothesis in the unbalanced condition, generation is likely to be terminated relatively quickly because of retrieval failures due to Act_{MinH}. In the balanced condition, in which hypotheses more readily compete with one another, Act_{MinH} is less likely to take on the highest possible activation value upon sampling the first hypothesis. Therefore, the amount of time the model is provided to sample, and the relative activation values of the hypotheses, both contribute to the number of hypotheses that tend to be generated into the SOC.

Empirical evidence for HyGene's prediction concerning the influence of sampling time comes from Dougherty & Hunter (2003b). In this experiment participants were asked to make probability judgments regarding the likelihood

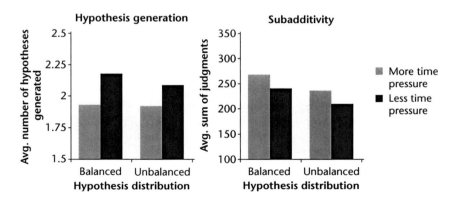

FIGURE 4.8   HyGene simulation demonstrating the effects of time pressure and hypothesis distribution on hypothesis generation (left) and probability judgment (right).

that a randomly chosen person was located in a particular state of the USA, given a particular geographic region of the country. The main manipulation in this experiment was the presence or absence of time pressure. In one block of trials, the participants were allotted as much time as they wanted and could issue their judgment at any time, while in the other block they were required to respond within six seconds. Time pressure resulted in greater subadditivity (i.e., higher judgments), just as produced by HyGene in the above simulation.

Stage 3: hypothesis-maintenance dynamics

The third stage concerns post-generation hypothesis-maintenance dynamics. Once hypotheses are generated and established in WM, it is inevitable that their activations will fluctuate over time and that each hypothesis will be displaced or discarded from WM. Many possible cognitive processes and situational variables may govern the rise and fall of hypothesis activation over time. Although we are beginning to understand the first two stages concerning hypothesis-generation dynamics discussed above, our theoretical understandings and empirical investigations into post-retrieval hypothesis maintenance lags behind. Sprenger and Dougherty (2012), however, noticed that when recent cues suggested different hypotheses than older cues, participants switched, so that the hypotheses they considered were in agreement with the most recent evidence, rather than considering hypotheses consistent with both types of evidence. This finding agrees with Lange et al.'s (2012) Experiment 2. In that experiment, the data presented to the participants was either consistent or inconsistent with a single hypothesis that was likely to have been already generated from previously acquired data. The results showed that the participants tended to no longer include the previously generated hypothesis in their current sets, following the inconsistent data. These results suggest that people discard previously generated hypotheses from WM in light of new information that conflicts with the hypotheses under consideration. Interestingly, these results are discordant with previous findings that people tend to discount new evidence that is inconsistent with currently held beliefs (Lord, Ross, & Lepper, 1979).

One additional insight regarding post-generation behavior comes from a novel eye-tracking methodology, in which attentional "top-down capture" is leveraged to infer WM content activation across time points in a task. It was observed that participants fixated the likely hypothesis first more often when the stimulus array (containing the likely hypothesis, an unlikely hypothesis, and distractor items) was presented shortly after onset of the data suggesting the hypothesis (444 ms), as opposed to slightly later (996 ms; Lange, Buttaccio, Davelaar, & Thomas, 2013). The authors interpreted this finding as suggesting that a hypothesis went through two stages in WM in this task. Shortly after retrieval the hypothesis was highly active, but at the later second stage it was less so, yet still under maintenance in WM for output at the end of the trial sequence. This interpretation is supported by earlier evidence that the initial item fixated in a visual search array is sensitive to WM activation levels (Lange, Thomas, Buttaccio, & Davelaar, 2012).

Given the fact that little empirical data exists regarding the maintenance of hypotheses over time, a plethora of issues currently awaits investigation. Above, we have presented evidence that competitive WM processes govern dynamic data acquisition, and thereby dictate the information that contributes to the retrieval of hypotheses. These processes tell us a great deal concerning how items compete in WM during data acquisition, but there are additional components that warrant research.

One of the most intuitive influences on dynamic data acquisition yet to be addressed behaviorally is the role of WM capacity. Lange, Davelaar, & Thomas (2013) utilized the dynamic HyGene model to demonstrate how varying the dynamic WM buffer's capacity (via the amount of inhibition present in the buffer) influenced hypothesis generation while the presentation rate of a series of five data was presented sequentially. They found that when the model implemented a lower WM capacity, it was more sensitive to the manipulation of data-presentation rate. It remains to be seen, however, if this model prediction can be verified empirically. The role of WM capacity may also be uncovered by investigating the point in a stream of data at which a participant spontaneously generates hypotheses. It is possible that a common strategy in the initial generation of hypotheses is to use as much data as can be maintained in WM. As this capacity is approached or reached, the decision maker may opt to utilize this data before it is displaced. Those with lower WM capacities will generate relatively earlier under such a strategy. This type of strategy would make sense, as generating a hypothesis essentially serves to summarize observed data (Thomas et al., 2008) and would provide a reference to information that would otherwise be lost.

Conclusions

Many situations encountered in everyday life require us to impose structure on the problem space. We suggest that hypothesis–generation processes serve this purpose in a wide variety of circumstances in which one must judge, decide, or act. In the lab, experimental procedures often provide clear options or goals for the participant, and in so doing, they provide task structure that is often lacking in real-world (ecological) environments. HyGene provides a model for how people impose this structure themselves by generating options from memory.

References

Buttaccio, D. R., Lange, N. D., Hahn, S., & Thomas, R. P. (2014). Explicit awareness supports conditional visual search in the retrieval guidance paradigm. *Acta Psychologica*, *145*, 44–53.

Davelaar, E. J. (2007). Sequential retrieval and inhibition of parallel (re)activated representations: A neurocomputational comparison of competitive queuing and resampling models. *Adaptive Behavior*, *15*(1), 51–71. doi: 10.1177/1059712306076250

Davelaar, E. J., Goshen-Gottstein, Y., Ashkenazi, A., Haarmann, H. J., & Usher, M. (2005). The demise of short-term memory revisited: Empirical and computational investigations of recency effects. *Psychological Review*, *112*, 3–42.

Dougherty, M. R. P., & Hunter, J. E. (2003a). Hypothesis generation, probability judgment, and individual differences in working memory capacity. *Acta Psychologica, 113*, 263–282.

Dougherty, M. R. P., & Hunter, J. E. (2003b). Probability judgment and subadditivity: The role of working memory capacity and constraining retrieval. *Memory & Cognition, 31*, 968–982.

Dougherty, M. R. P., Gettys, C. F., & Thomas, R. P. (1997). The role of mental simulation in judgments of likelihood. *Organizational Behavior and Human Decision Processes, 70*, 135–148.

Dougherty, M. R. P., Thomas, R. P., & Lange, N. (2010). Toward an integrative theory of hypothesis generation, probability judgment, and hypothesis testing. In: *The psychology of learning and motivation: Advances in research and theory*, Ross, B. H. (Ed.) 52, pp. 299–342. San Diego, CA: Elsevier Academic Press.

Einhorn, H. J., & Hogarth, R. M. (1978). Confidence in judgment: Persistence of the illusion of validity. *Psychological Review, 85*(5), 395–416. doi: 10.1037/0033-295X.85.5.395

Elstein, A. S. (1976). Clinical judgment: Psychological research and medical practice. *Science, 194* (4266), 696–700.

Evans, J. T. (2006). The heuristic-analytic theory of reasoning: Extension and evaluation. *Psychonomic Bulletin & Review, 13*(3), 378–395. doi: 10.3758/BF03193858

Gettys, C. F., & Fisher, S. D. (1979). Hypothesis plausibility and hypothesis generation. *Organizational Behavior & Human Performance, 24*(1), 93–110. doi: 10.1016/0030-5073(79)90018-7

Harbison, J. I., Dougherty, M. R., Davelaar, E., & Fayyad, B. (2009). The lawfulness of decisions to terminate memory search. *Cognition, 111*, 3, 397–402. doi: 10.1016/j.cognition.2009.03.002

Heuer, R. J. Jr. (1999). *Psychology of Intelligence Analysis.* Unclassified report for the Central Intelligence Agency.

Klayman, J., & Ha, Y. (1987). Confirmation, disconfirmation, and information in hypothesis testing. *Psychological Review, 94*(2), 211–228. doi: 10.1037/0033-295X.94.2.211

Kruglanski, A. W., & Mayseless, O. (1988). Contextual effects in hypothesis testing: The role of competing alternatives and epistemic motivations. *Social Cognition, 6*(1), 1–20.

Lange, N. D., Thomas, R. P., & Davelaar, E. J. (2012). Temporal dynamics of hypothesis generation: The influences of data serial order, data consistency, and elicitation timing. *Frontiers in Cognitive Science, 3*, 1–16.

Lange, N. D., Buttaccio, D. R., Davelaar, E. J., & Thomas, R. P. (2014). Using the memory activation capture (MAC) procedure to investigate the temporal dynamics of hypothesis generation. *Memory & Cognition, 42*, 264–274.

Lange, N. D., Davelaar, E. J., & Thomas, R. P. (2013). Data acquisition dynamics and hypothesis generation. *Cognitive Systems Research.* Invited submission for *Special Issue: Best of International Conference on Cognitive Modeling.* doi: 10.1016/j.cogsys.2012.12.006

Lange, N. D., Thomas, R. P., Buttaccio, D. R., & Davelaar, E. J. (2012). Catching a glimpse of working memory: Top-down capture as a tool for measuring the content of the mind. *Attention, Perception, & Psychophysics, 74*(8),1562–1567. doi: 10.3758/s13414-012-0378-9

Lange, N. D., Thomas, R. P., Buttaccio, D. R., Illingworth, D. A., & Davelaar, E. J. (2013). Working memory dynamics bias the generation of beliefs: The influence of data presentation rate on hypothesis generation. *Psychonomic Bulletin & Review, (20)*1, 171–176. doi: 10.3758/s13423-012-0316-9

Libby, R. (1985). Availability and the generation of hypotheses in analytical review. *Journal of Accounting Research, 23*, 646–665.

Lord, C. G., Ross, L, & Lepper, M. R. (1979). Biased assimilation and attitude polarization: The effects of prior theories on subsequently considered evidence. *Journal of Personality and Social Psychology (37)*11, 2098–2109. doi: 10.1037/0022-3514.37.11.2098

Mehle, T. (1982). Hypothesis generation in an automobile malfunction inference task. *Acta Psychologica, 52*(1), 87–106.

Mynatt, C. R., Doherty, M. E., & Dragan, W. (1993). Information relevance, working memory, and the consideration of alternatives. *The Quarterly Journal of Experimental Psychology, 46*(4), 759–778.

Mynatt, C. R., Doherty, M. E., & Tweney, R. D. (1977). Confirmation bias in a simulated research environment: An experimental study of scientific inference. *The Quarterly Journal of Experimental Psychology, 29*(1), 85–95. doi: 10.1080/00335557743000053

Patrick, J., Grainger, L., Gregov, A., Halliday, P., James, N., & O'Reilly, S. (1999). Training to break the barriers of habit in reasoning about unusual faults. *Journal of Experimental Psychology: Applied, 5*, 314–355.

Raaijmakers, J. G., & Shiffrin, R. M. (1981). Search of associative memory. *Psychological Review, 88*(2), 93–134. doi: 10.1037/0033-295X.88.2.93

Sanbonmatsu, D. M., Posavac, S. S., & Kardes, F. R. (1998). Selective hypothesis testing. *Psychonomic Bulletin & Review, 5*, 197–220.

Sloman, S., Rottenstreich, Y., Wisniewski, E., Hadjichristidis, C., & Fox, C. R. (2004). Typical versus atypical unpacking and superadditive probability judgment. *Journal of Experimental Psychology: Learning, Memory, and Cognition, 30*, 573–582.

Sox, H., Blatt, M. A., Higgins, M. C., & Marton, K. I. (2006). *Medical decision making.* Philadelphia, PA: The American College of Physicians Press.

Sprenger, A., & Dougherty, M. R. (2006). Differences between probability and frequency judgments: The role of individual differences in working memory capacity. *Organizational Behavior and Human Decision Processes, 99*, 202–211.

Sprenger, A., & Dougherty, M. R. (2012). Generating and evaluating options for decision making: The impact of sequentially presented evidence. *Journal of Experimental Psychology: Learning, Memory, and Cognition, 38*, 550–575.

Sprenger, A. M., Dougherty, M. R., Atkins, S. M., Franco-Watkins, A. M., Thomas, R. P., Lange, N., & Abbs, B. (2011). Implications of cognitive load for hypothesis generation and probability judgment. *Frontiers in Cognitive Science, 2*, 1–15.

Thomas, R. P., Lange, N. D., & Dougherty, M. R. (Unpublished manuscript). A memory theoretic account of hypothesis testing behavior.

Thomas, R. P., Dougherty, M. R., Sprenger, A. M., & Harbison, J. I. (2008). Diagnostic hypothesis generation and human judgment. *Psychological Review, 115*, 155–185.

Trope, Y., & Mackie, D. M. (1987). Sensitivity to alternatives in social hypothesis-testing. *Journal of Experimental Social Psychology, 23*(6), 445–459. doi: 10.1016/0022-1031(87)90015-1

Tversky, A., & Koehler, D. J. (1994). Support theory: A nonextensional representation of subjective probability. *Psychological Review, 101*, 547–567.

Unsworth, N., & Engle, R. W. (2006). Simple and complex memory spans and their relation to fluid abilities: Evidence from list-length effects. *Journal of Memory and Language, 54*, 68–80.

Unsworth, N., & Engle, R. W. (2007). The nature of individual differences in working memory capacity: Active maintenance in primary memory and controlled search from secondary memory. *Psychological Review, 114*, 104–132.

Usher, M., Davelaar, E. J., Haarmann, H. J., & Goshen-Gottstein, Y. (2008). Short-term memory after all: Comment on Sederberg, Howard, and Kahana (2008). *Psychological Review, 115*(4), 1108–1116. doi: 10.1037/a0013725

Walker, W. H., & Kintsch, W. (1985). Automatic and strategic aspects of knowledge retrieval. *Cognitive Science, 9*(2), 261–283. doi: 10.1207/s15516709cog0902_3

Wason, P. C. (1968). Reasoning about a rule. *The Quarterly Journal of Experimental Psychology, 20*(3), 273–281. doi: 10.1080/14640746808400161

Weber, E. U., Boeckenholt, U., Hilton, D. J., & Wallace, B. (1993). Determinants of diagnostic hypothesis generation: Effects of information, base rates, and experience. *Journal of Experimental Psychology: Learning, Memory, and Cognition, 19*, 1151–1164.

Windschitl, P. D., & Wells, G. L. (1998). The alternative-outcomes effect. *Journal of Personality and Social Psychology, 75*, 1423–1441.

Zuckerman, M., Knee, C. R., Hodgins, H. S., & Miyake, K. (1995). Hypothesis confirmation: The joint effect of positive test strategy and acquiescence response set. *Journal of Personality and Social Psychology, 68*, 52–60.

Note

1   In current versions of the model we use a stopping rule based on the cumulative number of retrieval failures in a trial, in light of recent evidence suggesting this rule's greater psychological plausibility (Harbison, Dougherty, Davelaar, & Fayyad, 2009). This rule is identical to that used in the Search of Associative Memory model (SAM; Raaijmakers & Shiffrin, 1981).

5

GIST MEMORY IN REASONING AND DECISION MAKING

Age, experience and expertise

Evan A. Wilhelms, Jonathan C. Corbin and Valerie F. Reyna

Expertise, defined here as having domain-specific knowledge (Adam & Reyna, 2005), has been shown to improve decision making in certain tasks (Reyna & Adam, 2003; Reyna & Lloyd, 2006). Although it has been demonstrated that both memory and reasoning improve with expertise in some instances, research has also shown that fallacies in memory, as well as biases in reasoning, have been found to increase with expertise (Gomes & Brainerd, 2012). The overall goal of this chapter is to resolve conflicting evidence about the effects of age and expertise on reasoning, and distinguish paradigms in which one should predict that reasoning would either improve with age and expertise or become more biased.

This chapter introduces basic principles of fuzzy-trace theory (FTT; Reyna & Brainerd, 1995), which is a dual-process theory of both memory and reasoning. FTT predicts that both deliberative, analytic reasoning, which relies on verbatim memory, and intuitive processes, which rely on gist memory, develop with experience. In predicting advances in both verbatim (relying on precise representations) and gist (relying on intuitive, meaningful representations) processes with age, FTT can predict when reasoning biases will decrease and increase with experience, depending on a number of factors relating to the task.

The effects of improved gist processing with age and expertise will then be introduced, including how individuals rely more on gist-based categorical distinctions between no-risk and risk (as opposed to more precise representations of degrees of risk) as they age. We will present research showing that gist reliance can result in taking fewer unhealthy risks in life, and ultimately fewer negative outcomes (Reyna & Farley, 2006). Furthermore, we will extend this work to the realm of expert decision making, showing that experts also rely heavily on gist. Finally, we will introduce some applications of these ideas, for assisting adults in avoiding reasoning biases and improving real-world outcomes, thus simulating expertise for novices. Finally, there will be a brief comparison to standard dual-process theories of reasoning, including discussion of the relationship of bias to intelligence.

Theoretical background

FTT is a theory of cognition that integrates the processing of reasoning and memory. Specifically, FTT proposes that intuition is supported by gist-memory representations that capture bottom-line meaning of experience (e.g., there is a small chance of rain today), and that analytic deliberation is supported by verbatim representations that capture the precise details of experience (e.g., there is a 43% chance of rain today; Reyna, 2012). FTT differs from other dual-process models in that *impulsivity* is distinguished from *intuition*. This theory is based on four foundational principles.

First, information is encoded in multiple representations with varying levels of precision. At one end of the continuum, gist representations preserve the bottom-line meaning of information; at the other end, verbatim representations capture low-level details and surface form, including exact numerical values. These representations form a hierarchy from verbatim to gist, roughly analogous to scales of measurement (exact numerical values, ordinal, and categorical distinctions; Rivers, Reyna, & Mills, 2008).

Second, gist and verbatim representations of experience are encoded, stored, and retrieved independently (Reyna & Brainerd, 2011). This independence allows the possibility that a person may have distinct and even contradictory representations of the same information. The existence of these independent, contradictory representations is supported by research revealing that memory for frequencies is based on verbatim representations and is independent of the accuracy of probability judgments, which are based on gist representations (Reyna & Kiernan, 1994, 1995).

Third, adults and advanced reasoners tend to rely on gist representations in their decision making and judgments, referred to as a fuzzy-processing preference. This preference for the simplest representation necessary to complete a task has been used to explain several other effects, including framing effects and probability judgment (Kühberger & Tanner 2010; Reyna & Brainerd, 2008).

Finally, the preference for reliance on gist representations increases with experience with a given task, also resulting in increases in gist processing with age and expertise (Reyna & Ellis, 1994; Reyna et al., 2011; Reyna, Chick, Corbin, & Hsia, 2014). In contrast to traditional theories that describe development as a progression from intuitive or heuristic processing to analytic deliberative processing (Evans & Stanovich, 2013), this perspective predicts and accounts for several developmental reversals found in memory and reasoning literature, such as reversals in false memories and framing effects (Brainerd, Reyna, & Zember, 2011; Reyna et al., 2011).

These foundational principles have been extended to predict a number of counterintuitive effects, and they also predict several errors in reasoning and judgment. As FTT describes a process of reasoning in which people encode representations in the context of their own background knowledge, and then must retrieve and process these representations, each of these steps (knowledge, representation, retrieval, and processing) can lead to different errors that each demonstrate different patterns of relationships to expertise (more on this below).

Fuzzy-trace theory and developmental reversals

FTT predicts a host of possible reasoning errors that can be attributed to differing types of processing (ranging from simple to complex errors; Reyna, Lloyd, & Brainerd, 2003). This section briefly outlines a number of reasoning errors that have been found to increase with age, from childhood to adulthood. The fact that verbatim and gist memory are independent and develop with age resolves the paradox in memory research that both true and false memory increases with age. In the same way that it accounts for these, it also explains why, in the reasoning literature, both improvements in reasoning as well as increases in biases can be associated with increasing age (De Neys & Vanderputte, 2011; Markovits & Dumas, 1999; Reyna & Farley, 2006). These effects have been termed "developmental reversals," due to the fact that biases are typically considered to decrease from childhood to adulthood (Brainerd & Reyna, 2012; Reyna et al., 2014).

Reasoning errors can be defined by different criteria for reasoning accuracy, including both *coherence* and *correspondence* criteria. Coherence refers to the principle that reasoning and judgments conform to the constraints of logic and probability theory (Gilovich, Griffin, & Kahneman, 2002). Violations of coherence are exemplified by errors such as the conjunction and disjunction fallacies. The conjunction fallacy is the mistaken judgment that a conjunction of events (e.g., P(A and B)) is more likely than one of the events individually; likewise, the disjunction fallacy is the mistaken judgment that the disjunction of events (e.g., P(A or B)) is judged to be less likely than one of the events individually (Lloyd & Reyna, 2001; Wolfe & Reyna, 2010). Both of these errors demonstrate logical impossibilities, and thus violations of coherence. Alternately, correspondence criteria instead refer to the extent to which judgments lead to positive outcomes in reality (Adam & Reyna, 2005). Correspondence criteria generally reflect one's knowledge about real-world outcomes and empirical accuracy of judgments (the likelihood of cancer given a set of symptoms) and the ability to decide on a course of action that leads to the best possible outcome (which treatment will lead to the highest quality of life). A few examples can illustrate some of the reasoning errors that are violations of principles of coherence and that increase with age.

Conjunction fallacy

A large amount of research demonstrates that adults show class-inclusion illusions, specifically the conjunction fallacy. As previously discussed, the conjunction fallacy occurs when an individual mistakenly judges a conjunction of events to be more likely than one of the events individually. The classic example of the conjunction fallacy is the "Linda Problem," in which a description of Linda is given to the participant, which emphasizes her past as a social activist (Tversky & Kahneman, 1983). Participants are then asked to rate how likely it is that Linda is a bank-teller, and how likely it is that Linda is a bank-teller who is also active in the feminist movement. As in the case of the classic Linda Problem – in which people tend to judge the conjoined event of "Linda is a bank-teller and is active in the feminist movement" as more probable than the individual event "Linda is a bank-teller" – people ignore the denominator (i.e., bank-tellers) when estimating the probability of a specific kind of bank-teller (i.e., a feminist bank-teller). Adults will rate the latter as more probable than the former, thus violating the cardinality principle – that if class B (bank-teller) includes class A (feminist), then class B must be as large or larger than class A and B (Tversky & Kahneman, 1983).

FTT proposes that in problems such as this, adults will rely on the overall gist of Linda as a social activist to make their judgments, failing to retrieve the knowledge that the subordinate class cannot outnumber the superordinate class (Reyna, 1991). The world knowledge that is used is the salient gist – the stereotype elicited by the description of Linda – that compels one's intuition. If this were true, we'd find that the error would increase with age, from childhood to adulthood, as the knowledge that will be relied on for this task will also develop with age. This is what is found in practice: adults will actually show more biased judgments than children when given problems that involve representative stereotypes that children have not yet developed (Davidson, 1995; Jacobs & Potenza, 1991). Compelling gists derived from experience lead adults astray when it comes to reasoning with respect to belief bias (acceptance of a believable conclusion irrespective of logical validity) and a number of other similar reasoning tasks (Morsanyi & Handley, 2008; Reyna & Lloyd, 2006). However, adults do answer conjunction problems correctly if the problem is framed in such a way that cues retrieval of the correct reasoning principle (see below; Reyna, 1991).

Risky-choice framing

Framing effects demonstrate how a seemingly superficial aspect of a decision's presentation format can alter how people represent the problem in memory, and therefore alter their decision. This is exemplified in the dread disease framing problem, in which changing the superficial wording of a decision between a sure option and a risky option changes people's choices (Tversky & Kahneman, 1981). Specifically, describing the choice in terms of gains ("200 lives saved for sure" vs. "1/3 chance of 600 saved or 2/3 chance of 0 saved") elicits a preference for a sure option and wording in terms of losses ("400 lost for sure" vs. "2/3 chance of 600 lost or 1/3 chance of 0 lost") elicits a preference for the risky option. Framing problems provide a critical test of FTT's predictions regarding the importance of gist memory in decision making. Specifically, FTT predicts that the framing problem is constructed such that the verbatim information (i.e., the numerical values themselves) leads to indifference, as the expected values (the probability multiplied by the gain or loss) are mathematically equivalent (i.e., $1/3 \times 600 = 200$), and therefore one must rely on the underlying gist of the problem for a decision (Kühberger & Tanner, 2010). People then retrieve underlying values, such as "life is sacred", and apply them to the gist extracted from the problem. In the case of the gains condition, the encoded gist of the choice is between definitely saving some lives and possibly saving no lives (leading to a preference for the sure option), whereas in the loss frame, the gist is a choice between definitely losing some lives and possibly losing no lives (leading to a preference for the risky option).

Research has supported FTT's model of framing effects, demonstrating that emphasizing that categorical nature of the decision (e.g., some saved vs. none saved) increases framing, whereas de-emphasizing it (e.g., 200 saved vs. 1/3 chance 600 saved) can eliminate the framing effect (Kühberger & Tanner, 2010; Reyna & Brainerd, 1991). These changes in the framing pattern are contrary to the predictions of prospect theory, although they are predicted by FTT (Kühberger & Tanner, 2010). Given that these effects would be the result of gist processing, FTT predicts that these effects should also increase with experience. These predictions have been confirmed in experiments showing increases in framing with age (Reyna & Ellis, 1994; Reyna, et al., 2011).

Gist and expertise

Benefits of gist with age

Thus far, we have discussed how increased reliance on gist can result in more biased decision making, according to a coherence criterion of rationality. Although gist processing can lead to predictable violations of coherence, gist has also been associated with real-world benefits. These benefits are typically described by *correspondence* criteria for rationality – that people's decisions lead to healthy or beneficial consequences – and are often displayed through reductions in risk-taking behavior.

One example of the benefits of the greater reliance on gist representations can also be found in real-world situations. Specifically, whether gist or verbatim representations are retrieved and endorsed can be predictive of one's risky lifestyle choices, such as number of sexual partners in adolescent populations. For example, endorsement of the gist principle that represents categorical avoidance of risk, "No risk is better than some risk," is predictive of taking fewer unhealthy risks, as well as decreased intentions to take unhealthy risks, than endorsement of an ordinal gist principle, "Less risk is better than more risk" (Mills, Reyna, & Estrada, 2008). Although both principles express negative views of risk, the ordinal principle makes finer distinctions among risky prospects – thus being closer to verbatim processing on the continuum from gist to verbatim. Regarding one key measure of unhealthy risk in adolescents – initiation of sex – those who endorsed only the ordinal principle (61%) were more than twice as likely to have done so than if they endorsed only the categorical principle (30%). Endorsement of neither or both was associated with an intermediate level of sexual initiation. Therefore, adolescents who endorsed more precise representations of risky decisions were more likely to take those risks than those who endorsed more gist-based, categorical representations.

Further evidence for the protective nature of categorical gist has been demonstrated by relating laboratory tasks (specifically framing tasks) to real-world risky decision making. Given that framing has been shown to result from a reliance on categorical gist (Kühberger & Tanner, 2010), measuring the size of the framing effect (i.e., the difference between the frequencies of picking risky options in equivalent gain- and loss-framed tasks) can be used to measure individual differences in gist reliance. Greater framing effects have been shown to predict less risk taking in adolescents, as measured by initiation of sex and number of sexual partners (Reyna et al., 2011). As previously discussed, this effect was found in the general context of an increase of framing overall from adolescence to adulthood, corroborating prior work that found an increasing reliance on gist representations in framing, from childhood through to adulthood (Reyna & Ellis, 1994).

Benefits of gist with expertise

An illustration of the application of these basic principles of memory – the independent processing of verbatim and gist – to professional expertise can be found by comparing the oral presentation of an experienced clinician to that of a medical student (Lloyd & Reyna, 2009). Whereas the student presents a patient's symptoms as a list of memorized facts (e.g., fever, cirrhosis, pneumonia, and urinary tract infection), the clinician's presentation is organized according to meaningful connections: e.g., the patient's cirrhosis compromises the immune system, which in turn leads to enterococcal bacteremia and concerns about endocarditis. Expressing the symptoms in this way reflects an understanding of the connections of the symptoms, which is the defining characteristic of gist representations. The processing and understanding based on the gist leads to accurate understanding of causes, and appropriate medical decisions (Lloyd & Reyna, 2009). This framework describes and predicts many clinical observations important to expertise and experience, such as lack of significant influence from guidelines, calculators, and continuing education on changing behavior (Reyna, 2008a).

The effect of expertise on various kinds of knowledge and processing errors was evaluated in a study in which health professionals, including physicians, nurses, medical students, graduates students, and a sample of health educators specializing in sexually transmitted infection (STI) risk, were given a questionnaire testing several errors in risk estimation as they pertain to infectious disease (detailed below; Reyna & Adam, 2003, Adam & Reyna, 2005). Some questions, such as whether males or females are more susceptible to contracting a STI when they have had sex with an infected person, are simply questions of knowledge. These errors are predicted to be associated with one's level of experience, specifically that those with the least expertise will exhibit the most errors. This was demonstrated through comparing the groups' accuracy on this question. One hundred percent of the group of health educators were able to correctly answer that females were more biologically susceptible. All the other groups, however, demonstrated lower mean correct answers, demonstrating that accuracy for basic knowledge questions depended on their experience and expertise in STI risk.

The questionnaire also included measures of errors of representation and retrieval like those previously described. Consistent errors were found when participants assessed the effectiveness of condoms in preventing diseases, such as HPV, that are transmitted skin to skin. Every group overestimated the effectiveness of condoms in preventing such infections. This was due to an overextension of the gist of condoms, specifically that they provide a physical barrier, although in reality this barrier is only effective in preventing fluid-borne STIs, not STIs passed on through skin-to-skin contact. All knowledge groups were also susceptible to underestimating their risk estimates for contracting STIs when multiple retrieval cues were absent (e.g., only HPV was given as an example); each group gave a higher answer (closer to the accurate reinfection rate of 50%) when provided with retrieval cues (e.g., HPV, herpes, syphilis). Although only medical students reported an average response that was not significantly different from the correct answer, every group, including those with specific expertise in the subject, benefitted from multiple retrieval cues.

In this questionnaire, participants were given base-rate neglect problems, in which people were asked to make a judgment of the likelihood of a patient having a disease, given a positive test result, and given that the test has an 80% sensitivity (rate of true positives) and 80% specificity (rate of true negatives), and that the disease has a base rate of 10% in the population. Participants only had to select whether the answer was closer to 30% or 70%. People ignored the base rate that the disease is relatively rare in the population, and provided an answer that reflects the perceived accuracy of the test (i.e., that the true chance of having the disease is closer to 70%). Similar to the conjunction/disjunction problems, this error represents a failure to accurately distinguish overlapping classes during processing, such as the class of people with the disease and the class of people with positive test results. Unlike the conjunction/disjunction problems, however, this base-rate neglect problem does not have a misleading semantic gist. According to FTT, this type of error is advanced because it occurs due to processing interference (i.e., confusion due to overlapping classes), and therefore even highly knowledgeable groups should make this error. In fact, group differences were not observed, and nearly all the groups had a minority selecting the correct answer (32% and below). High-school students scored similarly to experienced physicians, at only 33% correct (Reyna, 2004). Although the group of health educators did score higher than the others, their accuracy was at around the level of chance (50%). These results thus demonstrate that many sorts of errors, including those based on retrieval of knowledge, processing of information, as well as overextension of relevant gists can affect even those with high expertise (e.g., physicians).

FTT predicts that experts will rely more on gist, which features rough qualitative distinctions (such as no risk vs. some risk, or more or less risk). This results in the prediction that experts will, given the benefit of their advanced domain-specific knowledge, process information based on fewer dimensions, making simpler, all-or-none distinctions. This prediction has been confirmed in several studies pertaining to medical expertise. Medical experts, for example, will make more accurate diagnostic judgments that rely on fewer pieces of information. This was demonstrated in a study in which physicians from a variety of specialties representing a range of knowledge levels (including cardiology, internal medicine, emergency medicine, family practice, and some medical school students) were asked to evaluate descriptions of nine hypothetical patients that were categorized as either low, medium, or high risk according to the guidelines for unstable angina (Reyna & Lloyd, 2006). The physicians then assessed how likely the patients were to have either imminent risk of myocardial infarction (MI) or coronary artery disease (CAD), the probability of either outcome, as well as the probability of both outcomes. The physicians additionally made triage decisions for each hypothetical patient. Although everyone's treatment decisions were correlated with their assessments of risk (demonstrating internal consistency), the triage and admission decisions of the cardiology experts were related only to the risk assessment for MI, suggesting that they were basing their decisions on only this assessment. All knowledge groups were, however, susceptible to reasoning errors based on class-inclusion confusion, specifically disjunction errors. That is, all the groups estimated the probability of hypothetical patients having both MI *and* CAD to be smaller than either diagnosis individually. However, both those with the highest and lowest cardiovascular expertise (cardiologists and medical students) reported similarly low mean triage levels. It was the middle-knowledge groups (emergency medicine) who reported the highest triage levels. However, the risk group of the patient qualified this relationship. The specialists in cardiology were all more accurate in assessing how likely the patients were to experience adverse cardiac outcomes, even though they used less information (i.e., only considering patients' MI risk alone, rather than risk of MI and CAD). Specifically, they were more likely to place the high-risk patients at a higher triage level, as well as predict a higher probability of admission. The physician judgments were also all significantly different from the protocol guidelines. This study overall demonstrated that although experts were just as susceptible to certain advanced-reasoning errors, they processed fewer dimensions of information in coming to treatment decisions and were more willing to deviate from verbatim protocols.

Experts were also found to rely more on vague, intuitive gist and fewer dimensions of information in preliminary data in other areas. For example, Lazar (2012) conducted a study in which Emergency Medical Technicians (EMTs), who were trained at the level of either Basic Life Support or Advanced Life Support, were given a series of medical case scenarios representing major categories of EMT care. For each case, EMTs were asked to make treatment decisions. Because reliance on gist memory is predicted to increase with expertise, FTT predicts that those with less advanced experience will make decisions that more closely reflect verbatim protocols, and those with more experience will deviate from protocol in conditions which experience has shown to yield better outcomes. Although the care providers demonstrated very accurate knowledge of protocols in control conditions (89% correct on average), they consistently deviated in conditions that were theoretically predicted to elicit desirable deviations based on gist. This deviation was associated with level of experience, in that the more advanced the level of experience the care providers had, the more they deviated from protocol, supporting the hypothesis that experts rely more on gist representations.

Expert knowledge of rheumatology was also associated with gist-based thinking in a preliminary study of expert rheumatologists, in which 30 rheumatologists were given options on how best to characterize the treatment decision for rheumatoid arthritis (Reyna, 2008b). Participants were presented with a series of four descriptions of patients, their medical histories, and their treatment regimens. The rheumatologists were asked to assess the risks and benefits of the medications taken by the patients, as well as select a gist among several options, including examples such as "trade off precise degrees of risk against precise amounts of benefits," "avoid fatal side effects," and "slow down disease progression," that represented the bottom line of the patients' treatment decisions. None of the expert rheumatologists sampled chose the option in which they would trade off risks and benefits, although they demonstrated accurate assessment of the risks and benefits for each patient. Preferring categorical to precise statements provides evidence that few experts endorse the classical decision theory approach that describes rational decision making as a compensatory process in which probabilities and outcomes trade off.

These studies thus demonstrate that experts tend to rely on gist-based evaluations as opposed to verbatim trade-offs or risks and benefits. Further, this evidence demonstrates that development from novice to expert in adulthood can be associated with the increasing reliance on gist. Experts are able to distinguish signal from noise, zeroing in on information that provides them with categorical distinctions between less and more risk, rather than trying to incorporate every bit of information into a precise estimate of risk (Reyna et al., 2014).

Conclusion: how this approach differs from other theories

Other traditional dual-process accounts of have focused more on the relationship between intelligence and rationality (in determining whether or not a person will make an intuitive or deliberate choice (Stanovich, West, & Toplak, 2012). This emphasis is in the context of a dual-system account in which Type 1 processes are automatic, fast, and intuitive, and Type 2 processes are "slow, sequential, and correlated with measures of general intelligence" (Evans & Stanovich, 2013, p. 235). Many of these dual-system structures are *default-interventionist*, meaning that the cognitive capacities found in Type 2 thinking only operate if a need for an override of Type 1 thinking is detected (as opposed to processes running in parallel, as in FTT; Evans & Stanovich, 2013; Kahneman, 2011; Kahneman & Frederick, 2002). Type 2 processes include not only the cognitive capacities that tend to result in accurate judgments, but also the reflective capacities that monitor processing and determine if an override of automatic thinking is necessary, as captured in individual differences in constructs such as *need for cognition* (Stanovich, West, & Toplak, 2011, Figure 1).

Although there are a variety of other traditional dual-process theories with varying details and theoretical differences, many common elements of these theories distinguish these two types of processes (for a summary, see Figure 1 in Kahneman, 2003). A recent review concluded that a common characteristic of dual-process theories is that Type 1 processes do not require controlled attention, and thus make minimal demands on working memory (Evans & Stanovich, 2013). This dual-process account allows for an association between experience and Type 1 processing by arguing that rules, principles, or tasks that have been practiced to the point of automaticity will become intuitive and automatic under Type 1 processes (Kahneman & Klein, 2009). This explanation, however, appears to be indistinct from purely associative processing (e.g., resulting from "implicit learning and conditioning," Evans & Stanovich, 2013, p. 236), and does not predict a relationship between Type 1 processing and insight (Brainerd, Yang, Reyna, Howe, & Mills, 2008).

In this perspective, Type 2 processing is dependent on general and fluid intelligence, which is highly correlated with working memory capacity. According to the aforementioned review, "Type 2 thinking became uniquely developed in human beings, effectively forming a new mind … which coexists with an older mind based on instincts and associative learning and gives humans the distinctive forms of cognition that define the species" (Evans & Stanovich, 2013, p. 236). These cognitive capacities are often required to achieve normative responses because, for many tasks, people must inhibit automatic responses and simulate alternative responses (Stanovich & West, 2008). Many tasks, however, do not require such cognitive capacity for a Type 2 response, and thus for these tasks, bias does not always correlate with measures of cognitive capacity such as working memory and intelligence. In these cases, people must have access to the analytic rules and procedures required for a Type 2 response, and must also detect a need to override an automatic heuristic response, and thus errors can arise from either lacking access to relevant rules, or a failure to override.

The predictions described above can be easily illustrated using the example of framing experiments. In a series of experiments testing the relationship between intelligence and bias, participants were given either gain- or loss-framed versions of the aforementioned dread disease problem (i.e., a between-subjects experiment) in which people selected between a sure or risky option whose expected values were equal (Stanovich & West, 2008). In an ANOVA that used both the framing of the problem and a bivariate split of SAT scores to predict risk preference in the problem, the frame of the problem was the primary determinant of whether people picked the sure or risky option. SAT score did not interact with frame to determine risk preference. In other words, participants demonstrated the same framing effect regardless of their SAT score.

According to this dual-process account of reasoning, this between-subject framing effect is a failure to recognize a need to override a Type 1 response, since participants only see one of the frames, and thus do not recognize that there is a reasoning principle that could be violated. Even if participants may have knowledge of rules and procedures of how to calculate a better option, there is no conflict to cue use of those rules and procedures if they only see one version of the problem. Thus intelligence and working memory do not become relevant to determining consistency of choices between framing conditions. This changes, however, when the experiment is done within-subjects (e.g., Bruine de Bruin, Parker, & Fischhoff, 2007). In this case, measures of cognitive capacity, such as working memory, determine whether participants are aware that the two frames of the problem are equivalent numeric responses. This requires both remembering the past versions of the problem and sustaining a calculation to determine that the versions are equivalent. The resulting prediction of this account is that intelligence and working memory are related to the size of the framing effect when the different frames are presented within-subjects, as in the previously mentioned experiment.

This dual-process model thus makes predictions regarding when cognitive ability is associated with normative responses and when it is not. Specifically, cognitive ability will not be correlated with normative responses "when participants are not appropriately motivated or when success can be achieved by Type 1 processing" (Evans & Stanovich, 2013, p. 234). This does not include any prediction that ability may be positively correlated with bias and negatively correlated with normative responses. An exception may be that "when a problem is too difficult for everyone, however, the correlation [between intelligence and susceptibility to judgment biases] is likely to reverse because the more intelligent respondents are more likely to agree on a plausible error than to respond randomly" (Kahneman & Frederick, 2002, p. 68). However, that explanation does not account for developmental reversals such as that exhibited with the framing task. As it is the same task being used both when a relationship is found between intelligence and the normative response (e.g., Stanovich and West, 2008), and when a reversal is found between development and the normative response (e.g., Reyna et al., 2011), the reversal of the relationship cannot be because of increase in difficulty. These mechanisms thus do not explain why adults fail to override Type 1 biases with Type 2 analysis, and why they can do so more than adolescents and children.

Dual-process theorists have addressed some of the above concerns (e.g., developmental reversals), however, and have adapted their theories in turn. For example, Type 1 processing has been clarified as best interpreted as a plural set of multiple systems, perhaps best characterized with the abbreviation TASS – the autonomic set of systems (Evans & Stanovich, 2013, p. 226). This allows for the possibility that autonomic impulsivity and intuition may in fact be separate processes – though Stanovich does not clearly delineate that distinction. Additionally, clarification has been made that Type 2 modes of thinking may include both reflective capacities (characterized by individual differences such as need for cognition) as well as cognitive capacities (e.g., intelligence, working memory), and that these capacities also operate independently. The authors also addressed the need for dual-process theories to make the distinction between defining and correlating features of a process. The asserted defining characteristics, however – that Type 1 is automatic and Type 2 is demanding of cognitive abilities such as intelligence and working memory – would not predict developmental reversals a priori as shown above.

FTT accounts for findings that demonstrate independent encoding and retrieval of gist and verbatim representations, as well as their simultaneous improvement with age (though individuals increasingly rely on gist with development, they are also able to retrieve more precise verbatim representations when needed). These effects also illustrate the importance of understanding and insight (the defining components of gist in FTT; Reyna & Brainerd, 2011) for the development of expertise. These results emphasize the differences between knowledge, representation, retrieval, and processing, and how these concepts account for counterintuitive findings in the literature. Advanced knowledge tends to lead to better decision making when the reasoning task requires specific background knowledge. However, knowledge does not necessarily mean better decision making, as processing and retrieval errors can occur even with complete knowledge (Reyna & Lloyd, 2006). Expert decision making relies on imprecise, meaningful representations resulting in qualitative distinctions that can lead to both improvements (Reyna & Lloyd, 2006) and predictable errors (Reyna et al., 2014) in reasoning and decision making. Class-inclusion errors represent one of the primary examples of how having expert knowledge does not prevent the error. This is because class-inclusion errors – such as base-rate neglect – occur from a combination of an overextension of relevant gists as well as processing interference. Without tools to distinguish overlapping classes, experts can be as susceptible to class-inclusion errors as those without experience.

Thus, although many people may presume that the reasoning that is associated with expertise is based on precise, complex representations, the evidence appears to demonstrate the opposite. The argument from standard dual-process mechanisms is that "when we are evaluating important risks – such as the risk of certain activities and environments for our children – we do not want to substitute vividness for careful thought about the situation" (Evans & Stanovich, 2013, p. 236). FTT makes explicit predictions that oppose those assumptions, specifically that the advanced processing exhibited by experts in their domain of knowledge will occur automatically and unconsciously, rather than through careful thought about the situation (Reyna, in press). Although experts certainly can deliberate, in the normal course of events they rely on gist, meaning they rely on representations of meaningful, semantic connections.

The evidence reviewed above has demonstrated that experts and novices encode verbatim and gist representations when making decisions. Furthermore, experts have been shown to preferentially rely on less complex gist representations, that can lead to improved outcomes. However, expertise can also be unhelpful in situations in which gist leads to bias, and processing demands are high (e.g., class-inclusion problems). In these circumstances, theoretically motivated tools (as described above) can help to improve decision making. Overall, the findings emphasize the importance of understanding expert gist in order to better understand when it leads to bias, as well as when it can be used to improve decision making.

Authors' note

Valerie F. Reyna, Departments of Human Development and Psychology, Center for Behavioral Economics and Decision Research and Cornell Magnetic Resonance Imaging Facility, Cornell University; Evan A. Wilhelms, Department of Human Development, Cornell University; Jonathan C. Corbin, Department of Human Development, Cornell University. Correspondence concerning this article should be addressed to Valerie F. Reyna, Departments of Human Development and Psychology, Center for Behavioral Economics and Decision Research, Cornell University, B44 Martha Van Rensselaer Hall, Ithaca, NY 14853, USA. Email: vr53@cornell.edu.

Preparation of this chapter was supported in part by the National Institutes of Health under Awards R21CA149796 and R01NR014368–01 to V. F. Reyna. The content is solely the responsibility of the authors and does not necessarily represent the official view of the National Institutes of Health.

References

Adam, M. B., & Reyna, V. F. (2005). Coherence and correspondence criteria for rationality: Experts' estimation of risks of sexually transmitted infections. *Journal of Behavioral Decision Making, 18*, 169–186. doi: 10.1002/bdm.493

Barrouillet, P. (2011). Dual process theories of reasoning: The test of development, *Developmental Review, 31*, 151–179.

Brainerd, C. J., & Reyna, V. F. (1992). Explaining "memory free" reasoning. *Psychological Science, 3*, 332–339. doi: 10.1111/j.1467-9280.1992.tb00042.x

Brainerd, C. J., & Reyna, V. F. (2012). Reliability of children's testimony in the era of developmental reversals. *Developmental Review, 32*, 224–267. doi: 10.1016/j.dr.2012.06.008

Brainerd, C. J., Reyna, V. F., & Ceci, S. J. (2008). Developmental reversals in false memory: A review of data and theory. *Psychological Bulletin, 134*, 343–382. doi: 10.1037/0033-2909.134.3.343

Brainerd, C. J., Reyna, V. F., & Mojardin, A. H. (1999). Conjoint Recognition. *Psychological Review, 106*(1), 160–179.

Brainerd, C. J., Reyna, V. F., & Zember, E. (2011). Theoretical and forensic implications of developmental studies of the DRM illusion. *Memory & Cognition, 39*(3), 365–380. doi: 10.3758/s13421-010-0043-2

Brainerd, C. J., Stein, L., & Reyna, V. F. (1998). On the development of conscious and unconscious memory. *Developmental Psychology, 34*, 342–357. doi: 10.1037/0012-1649.34.2.342

Brainerd, C. J., Wright, R., Reyna, V. F., & Mojardin, A. H. (2001). Conjoint recognition and phantom recollection. *Journal of Experimental Psychology: Learning, Memory, and Cognition, 27*(2), 307–327.

Brainerd, C. J., Wright, R., Reyna, V. F., & Payne, D. G. (2002). Dual retrieval processes in free and associative recall. *Journal of Memory and Language, 46*, 120–152. doi: 10.1006/jmla.2001.2796

Brainerd, C. J., Yang, Y., Reyna, V. F., Howe, M. L., & Mills, B. A. (2008). Semantic processing in "associative" false memory. *Psychonomic Bulletin & Review, 15*, 1035–1053. doi: 10.3758/PBR.15.6.1035

Brewer, N. T., Richman, A. R., DeFrank, J. T., Reyna, V. F. & Carey, L. A. (2012). Improving communication of breast cancer recurrence risk. *Breast Cancer Research and Treatment, 133*(2), 553–561. doi: 10.1007/s10549-011-1791-9

Bruine de Bruin, W., Parker, A. M., & Fischhoff, B. (2007). Individual differences in adult decision-making competence. *Journal of Personality and Social Psychology, 92*, 938–956.

Davidson, D. (1995). The representativeness heuristic and conjunction fallacy effect in children's decision-making. *Merrill-Palmer Quarterly, 41*, 328–346.

De Neys W. (2006). Dual processing in reasoning – two systems but one reasoner. *Psychological Science, 17*, 428–433.

De Neys, W. (2012). Bias and conflict: A case for logical intuitions. *Perspectives on Psychological Science, 7*(1), 28–38.

De Neys, W., & Vanderputte, K. (2011). When less is not always more: Stereotype knowledge and reasoning development. *Developmental Psychology, 47*, 432–441. doi: 10.1037/a0021313

Evans, J. S. B. T. (2003). In two minds: Dual process accounts of reasoning. *Trends in Cognitive Sciences, 7*, 454–459.

Evans, J. S. B. T. (2007). On the resolution of conflict in dual process theories of reasoning. *Thinking & Reasoning, 13*, 321–339.

Evans, J. S. B. T. (2008). Dual-processing accounts of reasoning, judgment, and social cognition. *Annual Review of Psychology, 59*, 255–278.

Evans, J. S. B. T., & Curtis-Holmes J. (2005). Rapid responding increases belief bias: Evidence for the dual-process theory of reasoning. *Think. Reasoning, 11*(4), 382–389.

Evans, J. S. B. T., & Stanovich, K. E. (2013). Dual-process theories of higher cognition: Advancing the debate. *Perspectives on Psychological Science, 8*(3), 223–241. doi: 10.1177/1745691612460685

Evans, J. S. B. T., Barston, J. L., & Pollard, P. (1983). On the conflict between logic and belief in syllogistic reasoning. *Memory & Cognition, 11*, 295–306.

Giedd, J. N., Stockman, M., Weddle, C., Liverpool, M., Wallace, G. L., Lee, N. R., Lalonde, F., & Lenroot, R. K. (2012). Anatomic magnetic resonance imaging of the developing child and adolescent brain. In V. F. Reyna, S. B. Chapman, M. R. Dougherty, & J. Confrey (Eds.), *The adolescent brain: Learning, reasoning, and decision making* (pp. 15–35). Washington, DC: American Psychological Association. doi: 10.1037/13493-001

Gigerenzer, G., & Gaissmaier, W. (2011). Heuristic decision making. *Annual Review of Psychology, 62*, 451–482.

Gigerenzer, G., & Regier, T. (1996). How do we tell an association from a rule? Comment on Sloman (1996). *Psychological Bulletin, 119*, 23–26.

Gilovich, T., Griffin, D. W., & Kahneman, D. (2002). The psychology of intuitive judgment: Heuristic and biases. Cambridge: Cambridge University Press.

Gomes, C. F. A., & Brainerd, C. J. (2012). Dual processes in the development of reasoning: The memory side of the story. In C. Gauffroy & P. Barrouillet (Eds.), *The development of thinking and reasoning*. New York: Psychology Press.

Green, L., Myerson, J., Lichtman, D., Rosen, S., & Fry, A. (1996). Temporal discounting in choice between delayed rewards: The role of age and income. *Psychology and Aging, 11*(1), 79–84.

Jacobs, J. E., & Potenza, M. (1991). The use of judgment heuristics to make social and object decisions: A developmental perspective. *Child Development, 62,* 166–178.

Kahneman, D. (2003). A perspective on judgment and choice: mapping bounded rationality. *The American psychologist, 58*(9), 697–720. doi: 10.1037/0003-066X.58.9.697.

Kahneman, D. (2011). *Thinking, fast and slow.* New York: Farrar, Straus, and Giroux.

Kahneman, D., & Frederick, S. (2002). Representativeness revisited: Attribute substitution in intuitive judgment. In T. Gilovich, D. Griffin, & D. Kahneman (Eds.), *Heuristics and biases: The psychology of intuitive judgment* (pp. 49–81). New York: Cambridge University Press.

Kahneman, D., & Klein, G. (2009). Conditions for intuitive expertise: A failure to disagree. *The American Psychologist, 64*(6), 515–26. doi: 10.1037/a0016755.

Kirby, K. N. (2009). One-year temporal stability of delay-discount rates. *Psychonomic Bulletin & Review, 16,* 457–462. doi: 10.3758/PBR.16.3.457.

Kühberger, A., & Tanner, C. (2010). Risky choice framing: Task versions and a comparison of prospect theory and fuzzy-trace theory. *Journal of Behavioral Decision Making, 23*(3), 314–329.

Lazar, A. N. (2012). *Desirable deviations in medical decision making in the pre-hospital setting: A fuzzy-trace theory approach* (Unpublished master thesis). Cornell University, Ithaca, NY.

Liberali, J. M., Reyna, V. F., Pardo, S. T., Furlan, S., & Stein, L. M. (2012). Individual differences in numeracy and cognitive reflection, with implications for biases and fallacies in probability judgment. *Journal of Behavioral Decision Making, 25*(4), 361–381.

Lloyd, F. J., & Reyna, V. F. (2001). A web exercise in evidence-based medicine using cognitive theory. *Journal of General Internal Medicine, 16*(2), 94–99. doi: 10.1111/j.1525-1497.2001.00214.x.

Lloyd F. J., & Reyna, V. F. (2009). Clinical gist and medical education: Connecting the dots. *Journal of the American Medical Association, 302*(12), 1332–1333. doi: 10.1001/jama.2009.1383.

Markovits, H., & Dumas, C. (1999). Developmental patterns in the understanding of social and physical transitivity. *Journal of Experimental Child Psychology, 73,* 95–114. doi: 10.1006/jecp.1999.2496.

Metcalfe J., & Mischel W. (1999). A hot/cool system analysis of delay of gratification: Dynamics of willpower. *Psychological Review, 106,* 3–19.

Mills, B., Reyna, V.F., & Estrada, S (2008). Explaining Contradictory Relations Between Risk Perception and Risk Taking. *Psychological Science, 19,* 429–33. doi: 10.1111/j.1467-9280.2008.02104.x .

Morsanyi, K., & Handley, S. J. (2008). How smart do you need to be to get it wrong? The role of cognitive capacity in the development of heuristic-based judgment. *Journal of Experimental Child Psychology, 99,* 18–36.

Nelson, W., Reyna, V. F., Fagerlin, A., Lipkus, I., & Peters, E. (2008). Clinical implications of numeracy: Theory and practice. *Annals of Behavioral Medicine, 35*(3), 261–274. doi: 10.1007/s12160-008-9037-8.

Osman, M. (2004). An evaluation of dual-process theories of reasoning. *Psychonomic Bulletin & Review, 11,* 988–1010.

Piaget, J., & Inhelder, B. (1973). *Memory and intelligence.* New York: Basic Books.

Reyna, V. F. (1991). Class inclusion, the conjunction fallacy, and other cognitive illusions. *Developmental Review, 11,* 317–336. doi: 10.1016/0273-2297(91)90017-I.

Reyna, V. F. (1995). Interference effects in memory and reasoning: A fuzzy-trace theory analysis. In G. Wright & P. Ayton (Eds.), *Subjective probability* (pp. 239–272). New York: Wiley.

Reyna, V. F. (2004). How people make decisions that involve risk: A dual process approach. *Current Directions in Psychological Science, 13*, 60–66. doi: 10.1111/j.0963-7214.2004.00275.x

Reyna, V. F. (2005). Fuzzy-trace theory, judgment, and decision-making: A dual-processes approach. In C. Izawa & N. Ohta (Eds.), *Human learning and memory: Advances in theory and application: The 4th Tsukuba International Conference on Memory* (pp. 239–256). Mahwah, NJ: Lawrence Erlbaum Associates.

Reyna, V.F. (2008a). A theory of medical decision making and health: Fuzzy trace theory. *Medical Decision Making, 28*(6), 850–865. doi: 10.1177/0272989X08327066

Reyna, V. F. (2008b). *Understanding and communicating risk and benefit – What we have learned.* Invited address, American College of Rheumatology Annual Scientific Meeting, San Francisco, CA.

Reyna, V. F. (2012). A new intuitionism: Meaning, memory, and development in fuzzy-trace theory. *Judgment and Decision Making, 7*, 332–359.

Reyna, V. F. (in press). Dual processes in the development of reasoning: The memory side of the story. In C. Gauffroy & P. Barrouillet (Eds.), *The development of thinking and reasoning.* Hove, UK: Psychology Press.

Reyna, V. F., & Adam, M. B. (2003). Fuzzy-trace theory, risk communication, and product labeling in sexually transmitted diseases. *Risk Analysis, 23*(2), 325–342. doi: 10.1111/1539-6924.00332

Reyna, V. F., & Brainerd, C. J. (1991). Fuzzy-trace theory and framing effects in choice: Gist extraction, truncation, and conversion. *Journal of Behavioral Decision Making, 4*(4), 249–262.

Reyna, V. F., & Brainerd, C. J. (1995). Fuzzy-trace theory: An interim synthesis. *Learning & Individual Differences, 7*, 1–75. doi: 10.1016/1041-6080(95)90031-4

Reyna, V. F., & Brainerd, C. J. (2008). Numeracy, ratio bias, and denominator neglect in judgments of risk and probability. *Learning and Individual Differences, 18*, 89–107.

Reyna, V. F., & Brainerd, C. J. (2011). Dual processes in decision making and developmental neuroscience: A fuzzy-trace model. *Developmental Review, 31*, 180–206. doi: 10.1016/j.dr.2011.07.004

Reyna, V. F., & Ellis, S. C. (1994). Fuzzy-trace theory and framing effects in children's risky decision making. *Psychological Science, 5*, 275–279. doi: 10.1111/j.1467-9280.1994.tb00625.x

Reyna, V. F., & Farley, F. (2006). Risk and rationality in adolescent decision-making: Implications for theory, practice, and public policy. *Psychological Science in the Public Interest, 7*(1), 1–44. doi: 10.1111/j.1529-1006.2006.00026.x

Reyna, V. F., & Hamilton, A. J. (2001). The importance of memory in informed consent for surgical risk. *Medical Decision Making, 21*, 152–155. doi: 10.1177/0272989X0102100209

Reyna, V. F., & Kiernan, B. (1994). Development of gist versus verbatim memory in sentence recognition: Effects of lexical familiarity, semantic content, encoding instructions, and retention interval. *Developmental Psychology, 30*, 178–191. doi: 10.1037/0012-1649.30.2.178

Reyna, V. F., & Kiernan, B. (1995). Children's memory and metaphorical interpretation. *Metaphor and Symbolic Activity, 10*, 309–331. doi: 10.1207/s15327868ms1004_5

Reyna, V. F., & Lloyd, F. J. (2006). Physician decision making and cardiac risk: Effects of knowledge, risk perception, risk tolerance, and fuzzy processing. *Journal of Experimental Psychology, 12*(3), 179–195. doi: 10.1037/1076-898X.12.3.179

Reyna, V. F., Chick, C. F., Corbin, J. C., & Hsia, A. N. (2014). Developmental reversals in risky decision making: Intelligence agents show larger decision biases than college students. *Psychological Science, 25*(1), 76–86. doi: 10.1177/0956797613497022

Reyna, V. F., Estrada, S. M., DeMarinis, J. A., Myers, R. M., Stanisz, J. M., & Mills, B. A. (2011). Neurobiological and memory models of risky decision making in adolescents versus young adults. *Journal of Experimental Psychology: Learning, Memory, and Cognition, 37*(5), 1125–1142. doi: 10.1037/a0023943

Reyna, V. F., Lloyd, F. J., & Brainerd, C. J. (2003). Memory, development, and rationality: An integrative theory of judgment and decision-making. In S. Schneider & J. Shanteau (Eds.), *Emerging perspectives on judgment and decision research* (pp. 201–245). New York: Cambridge University Press.

Reyna, V. F., Lloyd, F., & Whalen, P. (2001). Genetic testing and medical decision making. *Archives of Internal Medicine, 161*(20), 2406–2408. doi: 10.1001/archinte.161.20.2406

Rivers, S. E., Reyna, V. F., & Mills, B. (2008). *Risk taking under the influence: A fuzzy-trace theory of emotion in adolescence.* Developmental review: DR, 28(1), 107–144. doi: 10.1016/j.dr.2007.11.002

Shafir, E., & LeBoeuf, R. A. (2002). Rationality. *Annual Review of Psychology, 53*, 491–517.

Sloman, S. A. (1996). The empirical case for two systems of reasoning. *Psychological Bulletin, 119*, 3–22.

Stanovich, K. E., & West, R. F. (2000). Individual differences in reasoning: Implications for the rationality debate? *Behavioral and Brain Sciences, 23*, 645–726.

Stanovich, K. E., & West, R. F. (2008). On the relative independence of thinking biases and cognitive ability. *Journal of Personality and Social Psychology, 94*(4), 672–695. doi: 10.1037/0022-3514.94.4.672

Stanovich, K. E., West, R. F., & Toplak, M. E. (2011). The complexity of developmental predictions from dual process models. *Developmental Review, 31*(2-3), 103–118. doi: 10.1016/j.dr.2011.07.003

Stanovich, K. E., West, R. F., & Toplak, M. E. (2012). Judgment and decision making in adolescence: Separating intelligence from rationality. In V. F. Reyna, S. Chapman, M. Dougherty, & J. Confrey (Eds.), *The adolescent brain: leaning, reasoning, and decision making* (pp. 337–378). Washington, DC: American Psychological Association.

Tversky, A., & Kahneman, D. (1981). The framing of decisions and the psychology of choice. *Science, 211*, 453–458. doi: 10.1126/science.7455683

Tversky, A., & Kahneman, D. (1983). Extensional versus intuitive reasoning: The conjunction fallacy in probability judgment. *Psychological Review, 90*, 293–315.

Wilhelms, E. A., & Reyna, V. F. (2013). Fuzzy trace theory and medical decisions by minors: Differences in reasoning between adolescents and adults. *J. Med. Philosophy, 38*(3), 268–282.

Wolfe, C. R. (1995). Information seeking on Bayesian conditional probability problems: A fuzzy-trace theory account. *Journal of Behavioral Decision Making, 8*, 85–108. doi: 10.1002/bdm.3960080203

Wolfe, C. R., & Reyna, V. F. (2010). Semantic coherence and fallacies in estimating joint probabilities. *Journal of Behavioral Decision Making, 23*(2), 203–223. doi: 10.1002/bdm.650

6

FROM TOOL TO THEORY

What recognition memory reveals about inductive reasoning

Aidan Feeney, Brett Hayes and Evan Heit

Generalising the unreliability of your Lada and your neighbour's Trabant to all cars made in Eastern Europe seems very different to recognising that the car in the distance is your neighbour's Trabant. Descriptively these are very different psychological phenomena: in the first case, you are making an inductive inference based on your prior knowledge, whereas in the second case, you are deciding whether a stimulus has been encountered before. Despite these apparent differences, there are at least two deep similarities between inductive inference and recognition memory. First, both draw on background knowledge, about a sample or about a previously encountered stimulus. Second, both require a decision about whether a property is shared by two (sets of) stimuli. In our reasoning example, that property is mechanical unreliability, which you know to be true of the cars in the sample and which you may or may not decide to project to all cars made in Eastern Europe. In the recognition-memory part of our example, the property is identity; you know the identity of the object in your mental representation of the car that sits on your neighbour's driveway, and you must decide whether that identity is shared with the approaching car.

In this chapter, we will describe several different lines of work that were inspired by the intuition that there are meaningful relations between inductive reasoning and recognition memory. First, we will consider the idea that different ways of making inductive inferences about objects in the world lead to differences in subsequent recognition memory for those objects. A consequence of this idea is that people's ability to recognise stimuli about which they have previously made inductive inferences has the potential to tell us something about how they made those inferences in the first place. In other words, recognition memory can be used as a tool for the study of how people make inductive inferences. Second, we will argue that people's ability to make inductive inferences about stimuli can be explained in the same way as their ability to recognise the same stimuli. More specifically, we will describe recent work (e.g. Heit & Hayes, 2011) showing that people's judgements of the strength of simple inductive arguments are captured by a model that also captures their ability to recognise the same stimuli. This line of research moves us beyond the idea that recognition memory can be a tool for the study of inductive reasoning, to a position where theories of recognition memory have been applied to the explanation of inductive reasoning. Amongst other things, we will argue that these lines of work are important because in a research environment that has become increasingly specialised, they emphasise the commonalities between different types of cognitive phenomena.

Inductive reasoning

When we reason inductively, we go beyond the information that we have been given. We can never be certain that the conclusion to an inductive argument is true, but our degree of belief is affected by a range of characteristics of the evidence. For example, the diversity of the evidence is important (see Osherson, Smith, Wilkie, Lopez & Shafir, 1990; Heit, Hahn & Feeney, 2005; Feeney, 2007a), as is the size of the sample (see Fong, Krantz & Nisbett, 1986; Osherson et al., 1990; Feeney, 2007a). In the context of economics, the Greeks and the Germans seem very different, so knowing that people in both countries favour a particular economic policy is more diverse and therefore stronger evidence that all Europeans favour that policy, than knowing, for example, that the Greeks and the Spanish favour that policy. The importance of sample size seems obvious. For example, although the Greeks, the Spanish, the Irish and the Italians are likely to hold certain economic attitudes in common, knowing that people in all four countries favour a particular policy is better evidence that all Europeans do, than knowing about people in only two of those countries.

The extended example above involves categories of people, and much of the research on inductive reasoning has been about category-based induction: our willingness to project a property known to be possessed by members of one or more categories to members of another category (for reviews see Hayes, Heit & Swendsen, 2010; and chapters in Feeney & Heit, 2007). These properties are often "blank"; that is, they are chosen so that people will have no relevant background knowledge about them. Theories of category-based induction with blank properties can be grouped in a variety of ways, but one important difference between them is whether they appeal to a category structure when predicting people's beliefs about categorical conclusions on the basis of the characteristics of the evidence. Some theories (e.g. Osherson et al., 1990; Kemp & Tenenbaum, 2009) make explicit appeals to people's knowledge about structures such as taxonomic hierarchies that relate categories to one another, whereas others (Sloman, 1993; Rogers & McClelland, 2004) eschew explanations based on category membership and account for the phenomena of inductive reasoning on the basis of the overlap between the features of the entities in the premises and the conclusion.

There have been attempts to apply some of the models of inductive reasoning that rely on category membership to development (see Lopez, Gelman, Gutheil & Smith, 1992), and one strong claim in the literature on children's reasoning is that very early in development children show an awareness of categories in terms of both their inductive potential and a more general expectation that entities belong to groups (see Gelman & Markman, 1986). There is ongoing debate about this claim (see Sloutsky & Fisher, 2012; Gelman & Davidson, 2013), and it is clear that there are problems of interpretation relating to the materials typically used to test it (see Hayes, McKinnon & Sweller, 2008). To overcome these problems, Sloutsky and Fisher (2004) developed a novel paradigm for studying the processes involved in inductive reasoning, which allowed them to make predictions about children's and adults' likely memory for the entities about which they had made inferences. This paradigm is important here because it rests on the assumption that people's recognition memory for the items they have reasoned about contains important information about their reasoning processes.

The induction-then-recognition paradigm

To investigate relations between the mental representations underlying recognition and inductive reasoning, Sloutsky and Fisher (2004) taught participants that a particular cat possessed a novel property, and then asked them whether a series of cats, bears and birds also possessed that property. Participants were given feedback after each trial, indicating that they should project the property to cats only. After this reasoning stage, participants were given a surprise recognition-memory test, in which they saw seven of the cats and seven of the bears they had seen earlier, alongside seven new cats and seven previously unencountered squirrels. Sloutsky and Fisher predicted that although five-year-old children and adults were likely to do equally well on the inference task, the children would outperform the adults on the surprise recognition-memory task. In particular, they expected adults to make more false-positive errors than the children.

The basis for Sloutsky and Fisher's predictions was that children and adults make inductive inferences in different ways. Consistent with their claims about the status of shared labels, they argued that children evaluate inductive inferences on the basis of the perceptual similarity between the base and target categories. Adults, on the other hand, reason on the basis of shared category membership. This difference in the reasoning processes that are applied by children and adults should, according to Sloutsky and Fisher, have consequences for how they process the entities that they reason about, and hence the nature of their subsequent mental representation of those entities.

These claims are derived from the well-established principles of fuzzy-trace theory (see Reyna, this volume) which holds that we construct verbatim- and gist-level representations of events. Verbatim representations are at the level of surface detail, whereas memory for the meaning of events is at the gist level. Brainerd, Reyna and Forrest (2002) examined the development of these two forms of memory using the Deese–Roediger–McDermott (DRM) paradigm (Deese, 1959; Roediger & McDermott, 1995), in which participants are presented with lists of associated words (e.g. bed, rest, yawn) and then asked to recall these items or to distinguish between presented and unpresented words. The crucial finding was that adults and eleven-year-olds were more likely than five-year-olds to recall or falsely recognise a semantically related word (e.g. "sleep") that was not present in the study list. Brainerd et al. (2002) concluded that adults and older children are more likely than young children to spontaneously construct gist-level representations of semantically related items (for a review of related work see Brainerd, Reyna & Ceci, 2008).

In a similar vein, Sloutsky and Fisher predicted that adults would have relatively poor recognition memory for the items they reasoned about, because they processed those items at the gist-level, whereas children, who process the reasoning materials at the verbatim level, would have relatively good recognition memory. In a series of experiments Sloutsky and Fisher confirmed their predictions (Sloutsky & Fisher, 2004; Fisher & Sloutsky, 2005); adults and children did equally well on the reasoning task, but children's recognition memory for the items they had reasoned about was better than adults'. Sloutsky and Fisher also showed that in a memory-control condition where adults and children were just asked to memorise the study materials, adults' recognition-memory performance was slightly better than children's. Thus, it appears that adults are capable of verbatim processing of the stimuli, but they process the gist rather than the verbatim detail when reasoning. Sloutsky & Fisher (2004, Experiment 2) showed that children who had received categorisation pre-training showed poorer recognition memory in the reasoning condition than in the memory-control condition, and Fisher and Sloutsky (2005) described results suggesting that children begin to spontaneously process reasoning stimuli at the level of gist only after the age of seven.

Although Sloutsky and Fisher's work has stimulated interest in relations between reasoning and recognition memory, the particular conclusions that they have drawn from their results have been disputed (see Feeney & Wilburn, 2008; Hayes et al., 2008; Wilburn & Feeney, 2008). The main problem with the original experiments is that inspection time was not controlled for. Wilburn & Feeney (2008) showed that five-year-old children look at the reasoning items for longer than adults (Experiment 1), and that when inspection time is limited to 250 ms (Experiment 2), children do as well as adults on the reasoning task, and equally poorly on the memory task. Hayes et al. (2008) described similar findings. It is possible that children look at the reasoning materials for longer because they are not as pragmatically sensitive as adults and so misunderstand what is required of them in the task (see Feeney & Wilburn, 2008), or perhaps their ability to disengage attention is not well developed (see Hayes et al., 2008; Hanania & Smith, 2010). Whatever the reason, there appear to be no necessary conclusions about the development of inductive reasoning to be drawn on the basis of Sloutsky and Fisher's findings.

Regardless of the controversy described above, the induction-then-recognition paradigm has great potential to elucidate the link between the mental representations underlying recognition memory and inductive reasoning. The problem of interpreting Sloutsky and Fisher's results arises because many abilities, not only those related to reasoning, develop between the ages of five years and adulthood, and perhaps the paradigm is better suited to testing claims about reasoning processes available to participants at one particular stage of development. Fisher and Sloutsky (2005) describe an experiment that is consistent with this idea. They asked adults to reason about novel artificial categories of animals. Because participants had not previously learned the categories in this experiment, they were forced to reason on the basis of the perceptual similarity between the base and target items. In other words, the experiment forced them to build verbatim representations of the materials. As a consequence, participants' recognition memory for the items was considerably better than it had been in all of the induction-then-recognition experiments with adults that we have reviewed so far. These results suggest that, within an age group, a surprise recognition-memory test could help to distinguish between inferences about category members that are made in a category-based way and those that are made on the basis of featural overlap.

Are all inductive inferences achieved by a single process?

In the previous section, we arrived at a possible use for the induction-then-recognition paradigm – distinguishing, in an adult sample, between inductive inferences that draw on different processes. However, although work on the relationship between induction and deduction suggests that both types of inference are accomplished by more than one process (see Heit & Rotello, 2010), models of category-based inductive reasoning about blank properties assume that all of the relevant experimental phenomena can be captured in the same way. Hence, there is no a priori theoretical reason to look in any particular place for category-based inductive inferences that might be made in different ways. For example, sensitivity to sample size and diversity, which we outlined at the start of the chapter, is captured in some models (e.g. Osherson et al., 1990) by assuming that a diverse set of evidential categories "cover" a more general conclusion category better than a less diverse evidence set. Similarly, larger premise sets will cover a conclusion category better than smaller premise sets. Other models work at the level of overlap between the features of the categories in the premises and in the conclusion (see Sloman, 1993; Rogers & McClelland, 2004). Once again, the features of diverse and larger sets of categories in the sample will overlap the features of the conclusion category to a greater degree than will the features of non-diverse and smaller sets of evidential categories.

Accounts of category-based induction provide the only descriptive explanations of reasoners' sensitivity to evidence diversity to be found in the psychological literature (although for a discussion of the relation between the literatures on evidence diversity in reasoning and exemplar variability in category learning, see Hahn, Bailey & Elvin, 2005). However, there are several alternative accounts of people's sensitivity to sample size when reasoning, some of which are cast as sensitivity to the law of large numbers. Kahneman and Tversky (1972) claimed that people are insensitive to the law of large numbers. However, there is considerable evidence that people do factor sample size into their judgements and decisions (see Nisbett, Krantz, Jepson & Kunda, 1983). Fong et al. (1986) argued that people possess an intuitive rule corresponding to the law of large numbers. Consistent with this view, Stanovich and West (1998) have proposed a dual-process account of thinking: on this account, sensitivity to sample size depends on the operation of a cognitively expensive process that applies normatively justified principles or rules for reasoning. When extrapolated to category-based induction, these accounts suggest that sensitivity to sample size when reasoning about categorical evidence might also be achieved by the operation of an abstract rule. Reasoning in this way is likely to lead to the construction of gist, rather than verbatim representations of the entities in the problem. These gist representations will most likely be at the category level. On the other hand, because all accounts of sensitivity to diversity suggest that it depends on processing similarity relations, on diversity trials reasoners are more likely to represent the features of the items they reason about. Such representations will contain more verbatim detail of the reasoning items than will the gist-level representations constructed for sample-size trials.

Clearly, there are contrasting predictions about people's ability to subsequently recognise materials testing for sensitivity to diversity, and materials testing for sensitivity to sample size. Sensitivity to diversity requires consideration of the similarity between the items in the sample and members of the conclusion category, and because a similarity calculation requires a comparison between the features of the relevant items, the resulting representation will be at the verbatim level, and thus is likely to lead to good performance on a subsequent recognition-memory test. As rule-based accounts of sensitivity to sample size require no similarity calculation, such accounts predict gist-level representations of the reasoning items, at the category level, which are likely to lead to relatively poor recognition-memory performance.

To test the hypothesis that people would have better recognition memory for diversity materials, we used the induction-then-recognition paradigm (Travers & Feeney, 2013). Participants pretended that they were scientists trying to ascertain the truth of generic claims about members of particular categories (e.g. dogs, roses, etc.). Next they were shown two samples side by side, each containing pictures of individual category members, and were asked which sample they would like to examine in order to test the generic claim. Participants attempted seven trials where each sample consisted of two pictures varying in diversity, and seven trials where sample size was manipulated so that one of the samples contained a picture of an additional category member. In the recognition-memory test, participants made recognition judgements about 28 old pictures (two from each trial), 28 new lure pictures (two for each trial) and a further 7 new pictures from categories that had not previously been used in the experiment.

In the reasoning part of the experiment, the results showed that although participants were significantly more likely to select diverse and large samples than would be expected by chance, they were significantly more likely to choose a large sample on the sample-size trials (82%) than they were to choose a diverse sample on the diversity trials (74%). The recognition-memory results showed that, for both sets of reasoning problems, participants' ability to distinguish new from old items was significantly greater than chance. However, participants had significantly better recognition memory for diversity items than for sample-size items. As a control measure we asked a separate group of participants to study the reasoning materials for memory. Recognition-memory performance in these participants showed that both sets of materials were equally memorable. Thus, the differences in the recognition-memory performance of participants who had reasoned about the items that they were subsequently asked to remember cannot be attributed to the different materials used in each condition. We also measured inspection times in this experiment and found that inspection times for each type of trial were similar. Furthermore, the difference in recognition-memory performance continued to be significant when inspection times for both items were included as covariates in the analysis. Accordingly, the recognition-memory results cannot be attributed to time spent looking at the different items.

The results of this experiment suggest that people's recognition memory for the items they have reasoned about can tell us something about their reasoning processes. Controlling for inspection times, the results show that people have better recognition memory for diversity items than for sample-size items. On the basis of Sloutsky and Fisher's (2004) original argument, this suggests that diversity problems are processed verbatim, whereas monotonicity problems are processed for gist. This distinction between the processes involved in sensitivity to diversity versus sensitivity to sample size is important, because it suggests that only some phenomena which are captured by theories of inductive reasoning via a consideration of associative or similarity relations between categories may actually be produced by such processes. Other phenomena, such as sensitivity to sample size, may be produced by a rule-based process. Our findings cohere with claims that all reasoning involves both associative and more deliberative, analytic processes (see Evans, 2007). However, earlier work has focused on the degree to which inductive reasoning tends to rely more on associative processing than does deductive reasoning (see Feeney, 2007b; Heit & Rotello, 2010). The results described here suggest that there may be specific phenomena in people's inductive reasoning that are produced primarily by analytic processes.

The results that we have described suggest that reasoning processes have effects on memory that can be usefully exploited in order to test hypotheses about the nature of those processes and the mental representations over which they operate. Future work might examine whether sensitivity to sample size is the only phenomenon of category-based induction that is accomplished in a rule-based way, or whether other phenomena found in inductive reasoning with blank properties also depend on the operation of rule-based processes. In addition, the findings described here lead to predictions about when sensitivity to certain characteristics of evidence emerge during development. To the extent that sensitivity to sample size relies on analytic processes, whereas sensitivity to diversity relies on associative or similarity-based processes, then we might expect the latter sensitivity to develop first. More generally, the results suggest that an inference-then-recognition paradigm may be a useful tool for reasoning researchers who are interested in psychological process (see De Neys & Glumicic, 2008).

The work we have just described illustrates a methodological relation between memory and reasoning. As should have been clear from our discussion, this methodological relation is dependent on theoretical claims that have been made about different processes and mental representations in memory (Brainerd et al., 2002). However, as we shall see in the subsequent sections of this chapter, there are strong links between theories of inductive reasoning and theories of recognition memory. Not only can we use recognition memory to test claims about inductive-reasoning processes, we can capture empirical phenomena of recognition memory and inductive reasoning using the same theoretical apparatus.

A common basis for reasoning and memory

Up to this point we have mainly focused on how performance on memory tasks can give us insights into how people do inductive reasoning. But there is evidence for an even deeper relationship between memory and reasoning. A number of researchers have suggested that the cognitive processes that underlie memory play a key role in explaining various types of reasoning. Dougherty and colleagues (Dougherty, Thomas & Lange, 2010; Lange et al., this volume) have shown how a global memory model can be adapted to explain probability judgement and decision making. In the field of artificial intelligence, Sun and Hélie (2012) have developed a cognitive architecture (CLARION) based on fundamental principles of memory that can account for a number of key reasoning phenomena.

Recently Heit, Hayes and colleagues have undertaken a systematic examination of the relationship between recognition memory and inductive reasoning (for a review see Heit, Rotello & Hayes, 2012). The cornerstone of this work is the development of a paradigm making reasoning and memory tasks as comparable as possible. In Heit and Hayes (2011), for example, people studied pictures of large dogs under either a recognition condition ("remember these animals") or under an induction condition where they were taught that the large dogs shared a novel property ("these animals have beta cells"). Subjects then made recognition judgements ("did you see this animal before?") or induction judgements ("does this animal have beta cells?") about a common test set containing old items and novel items that varied in similarity to the study instances (i.e. novel large, medium and small dogs).

Examination of positive responses to test items revealed an important difference between recognition and induction. Those given induction instructions were generally more likely to make a positive response to novel dogs than those in the recognition group. This is hardly surprising given that recognition instructions emphasise responding on the basis of identity with studied items, whereas induction instructions explicitly invite the subject to project the property to novel items.

What is more surprising and interesting is the close correspondence between many other aspects of recognition and induction performance. Heit and Hayes (2011) calculated the item-wise probability of making a positive response to each test item in recognition and induction conditions. Across six experiments, the mean item-wise correlation between test responding in induction and recognition was 0.86. In other words, performance in inductive reasoning could be predicted with a high degree of accuracy from performance on the recognition-memory task.

Another important finding is that task and subject manipulations that affect recognition often have similar effects on induction (see Table 6.1 for a summary). One such factor examined by Heit and Hayes (2011) was the frequency of exposure to study items. Each study item was presented either once or three times in the recognition and induction conditions. The effects of such a manipulation of study item frequency on recognition are well documented (e.g. Criss, 2009; Ratcliff, Clark, & Shiffrin, 1990), with increased item exposure leading to increases in hits (i.e. responding positively to old test items) and decreases in false alarms (i.e. responding positively to novel test items). Heit and Hayes (2011) found that manipulating item frequency had the same effect on inductive responding: those in the induction condition who saw the study items three times tended to limit projection of the novel property to old items and novel items that were very similar to those studied, whereas those who saw items only once showed high rates of positive responding to novel items. Likewise, factors that are known to *increase* the likelihood of making a positive response to novel items in recognition (e.g. change in item context between study and test) had a similar effect on induction.

These empirical parallels point to an even deeper relationship between memory and reasoning – they suggest that common processes may be involved in making recognition and property induction judgements. One such process may be the way people assess the similarity of test items to study instances (Heit & Hayes, 2011; Heit et al., 2012). In both recognition and induction this is thought to proceed via a comparison of the total similarity of a novel probe to a sample of studied exemplars retrieved from memory. Note that this is not a new idea for recognition. Many memory models assume that the similarity between a test probe and a sample of old instances plays a key role in whether or not the probe will be recognised (e.g. Hintzman, 1988; Ratcliff, 1990; Jones & Heit, 1993). The notion that the same exemplar-based process underlies inductive reasoning, however, is novel.

Heit and Hayes (2011) have developed a formal model of this exemplar-based approach to reasoning and memory, called GEN-EX (GENeralisation from EXamples). In the GEN-EX model the same basic mechanics for computing the similarity of a test probe to study exemplars and deciding whether to make a positive response are assumed for recognition and induction. The only substantive difference between the way the two tasks are modelled is in the GEN-EX generalisation parameter, with generalisation from study items assumed to be

TABLE 6.1 Summary of effects of task and subject manipulations on recognition and induction with a common stimulus set. (Note that in all studies the rate of positive responding to novel items was always higher in induction than recognition.)

Source	Manipulation	Effects on recognition	Effects on induction
Heit & Hayes (2011)	Frequency of presentation of study items	Increasing presentation frequency increased discrimination between old and new items (i.e. increased positive responding to old test items relative to new items)	Increasing presentation frequency increased discrimination between old and new items (i.e. increased positive responding to old test items relative to new items)
Heit & Hayes (2011)	Study list drawn from multiple categories (dogs + birds + fish)	Adding study items from multiple categories decreased discrimination between old and new items from the target category (dogs)	Adding study items from multiple categories decreased discrimination between old and new items from the target category (dogs)
Heit & Hayes (2011)	Test list drawn from multiple categories	Adding test items from multiple categories decreased discrimination between old and new items from the target category (dogs)	Adding test items from multiple categories decreased discrimination between old and new items from the target category (dogs)
Hayes & Heit (2009)	Perceptual context of study and test items	Presenting studied items in a new context at test decreased discrimination between old and new items	Presenting studied items in a new context at test decreased discrimination between old and new items
Hayes, Fritz & Heit (2013)	Age	5-6 year-olds more likely to respond positively to new items than adults	5-6 year-olds more likely to respond positively to new items than adults
Hayes & Heit (2013)	Decision time at test	For short and long decision times, responses based on overall similarity	For short decision times, responses based on overall similarity; for long decision times, responses based on multiple forms of similarity

broader in induction than recognition. This model has been shown to give a good fit to both recognition and induction data across a range of task manipulations in adults (Hayes & Heit, 2009, 2013; Heit & Hayes, 2011) and young children (Hayes et al., 2012).

Of course property induction is often much more complex than just generalising a property of large dogs to other dogs. Heit and Rubinstein (1994), for example, found that subjects used flexible forms of similarity relations to generalise different properties across animal triads. For example, generalisation of anatomical properties (e.g. has a liver with two chambers) was guided by taxonomic similarity (e.g. generalisation from *sparrows* to *hawks* was stronger than from *tigers* to *hawks*). But when the property was behavioural (e.g. "prefers to eat at night"), similarity was based on ecological relationships and led to a different pattern of property projection (e.g. generalisation from *tigers* to *hawks* was stronger) (see Coley & Vasilyeva, 2010; Heit & Rubinstein, 1994; Shafto, Kemp, Bonawitz, Coley & Tenenbaum, 2008, for similar findings). An important question is whether an exemplar-based model like GEN-EX can explain recognition and this more complicated form of induction involving flexible forms of similarity.

The answer appears to be a qualified "yes". Hayes and Heit (2013) extended their common recognition–induction paradigm to the more complex case where study items were members of the conjunctive category "marine mammals". These were presented under recognition conditions or under induction conditions where the property to be generalised was likely to direct attention to similarity along either the aquatic dimension (e.g. "an enzyme that assists in the development of water-resistant skin") or the mammalian dimension (e.g. "an enzyme in breast milk that is passed to the young during feeding"). Recognition and induction test sets contained old and new members of the conjunctive category, together with items that were similar to the study category on only one dimension (e.g. aquatic non-mammals like sharks or land animals like chimpanzees).

Hayes and Heit found that the different property types led to different patterns of induction (e.g. those given the aquatic property at study were more likely to make a positive response to aquatic non-mammals). Notably, the strength of this selective induction effect varied with the amount of time that people had to respond to each test item. Selective induction was stronger when subjects were forced to wait several seconds before responding, than when responses were made under time pressure (cf. Shafto, Coley & Baldwin, 2007).

This manipulation of response deadlines also affected the relationship between induction and recognition. When responding was fast, then the original version of GEN-EX gave a good account of both recognition and induction with different property types. When responding was slower, GEN-EX had to be modified to account for selective induction. This involved adding other types of similarity comparisons between old and new items (e.g. similarity with respect to habitat).

An important implication of this work is that the relationship between inductive reasoning and memory may depend on the amount of time that people spend thinking about their judgements. The relationship between the tasks seems especially strong when recognition and induction judgements are made quickly. This suggests a potentially interesting direction for future research − examining how different aspects of stimuli are used to make recognition and induction judgements over varying decision times. An analogous line of work (e.g. De Neys, 2006; Kahneman, 2011) has helped clarify the relationship between different forms of reasoning, with heuristic, intuitive processes found to operate relatively quickly, but analytic and deductive reasoning requiring more time.

An even more general implication of the work examining memory and induction with a common paradigm is that responses on these tasks may be viewed as facets of the same underlying process. Memory and reasoning performance may depend on a common set of lower-level mechanisms, such as generalisation (e.g. Shepard, 1987) or recollection (e.g. Rotello & Heit, 1999, 2000). There are differences between reasoning and memory tasks, to be sure, but these may be largely parametric rather than qualitative (see Heit et al., 2012, for more extensive discussion).

Whether or not this turns out to be an oversimplification of the relationship between reasoning and memory remains to be seen. What we think is certain, however, is that some of the arbitrary divisions between research on memory and reasoning are unjustified. We hope that the work reviewed here shows that research on reasoning can benefit by considering close interactions with memory and vice versa.

Alternative frameworks for modelling the relationship between reasoning and memory

In many respects the GEN-EX model compares favourably with previous theoretical accounts that have attempted to explain different types of inductive reasoning. In early work on this issue, Osherson and colleagues developed qualitatively different processing frameworks to explain induction involving blank properties (the Similarity-Coverage model, Osherson et al., 1990), and induction involving familiar, knowledge-rich properties (the GAP model, Smith, Shafir & Osherson, 1993). GEN-EX, by contrast, offers a single framework to explain both kinds of induction, and recognition as well.

Like GEN-EX, Relevance Theory (Medin, Coley, Storms & Hayes, 2003; see also Heit & Feeney, 2005) assumes that different kinds of similarity relations are primed by the use of different properties. When properties are blank, default relations, such as taxonomic or overall similarity, guide property induction. Familiar (non-blank) properties are assumed to direct attention to more distinctive or informative relations between base and target items (e.g. habitat or ecological links between animals). Relevance Theory does not specify how people identify the most informative relation within a given reasoning context. Relevance Theory has also yet to be implemented in a formal model. This means that Relevance Theory cannot make specific predictions about patterns of property generalisation across a large and diverse set of test items like those used in the current studies. Finally, Relevance Theory has not been applied to recognition memory.

Kemp and Tenenbaum (2009) have proposed a Bayesian theory of induction in knowledge-rich domains (see Heit, 1998, 2000, for an earlier, related approach). Induction is seen as a process of estimating the probability that a property generalises to a novel target, given information about which categories or objects are known to have the property. Notably, the model assumes that the hypothesis spaces that serve as priors for Bayesian computations are based on intuitive domain theories.

These are instantiated as structured models of the distribution of features across categories. Different kinds of structured representations are retrieved, depending on the type of property being generalised. For example, when induction involves taxonomic properties, the default structure is a hierarchical tree. When induction involves causal properties, category relations are represented by a directed graph (a Bayes net).

This model has been successfully applied to a range of induction data involving both blank and non-blank properties. How would such Bayesian models account for our current findings concerning reasoning and memory? Recently, Lassiter and Goodman (2012) have extended a Bayesian model to address differences between inductive reasoning and deductive reasoning, as in Rotello and Heit (2009) and Heit and Rotello (2010). One key finding was that with a small amount of positive evidence, induction judgements would be positive, while deduction judgements would be negative – requiring greater certainty. Lassiter and Goodman suggested that this difference can be explained by varying the mapping between Bayesian probabilities (from the model) and response probabilities (produced by a human subject). This mapping function follows a power law, and with different parameterisations can produce the pattern for induction (requiring a small amount of positive evidence) or deduction (requiring greater certainty). To be clear, Bayesian models of reasoning of this type have not been applied to memory (although Bayesian models of memory have been developed, e.g. Criss & McClelland, 2006; Shiffrin & Steyvers, 1997, and it has been shown that Bayesian models of induction can be generalised to categorisation: Kemp, Shafto & Tenenbaum, 2012). However, it might be possible to take Lassiter and Goodman's approach to capture some of the differences between reasoning and memory, such as the much lower false-alarm rate for recognition than for induction that we have consistently found. Namely, the mapping parameterisation that Lassiter and Goodman used to produce deduction responses requiring certainty could also be used to produce recognition responses requiring certainty.

Therefore, we think there is some hope that Bayesian models of reasoning could be adapted to address memory. However, it is currently unclear how flexible similarity would be addressed by these models. The transformation from Bayesian probabilities to response probabilities suggested by Lassiter and Goodman (2012) is monotonic, and would not allow for the flexible use of different information for different judgements (e.g. induction about habitat versus reproduction). Put another way, our results include crossover effects that Lassiter and Goodman (footnote 1) acknowledge their account cannot address.

Presumably, to address our results suggesting flexible similarity, Bayesian models would use different initial hypothesis spaces for different judgements or different time courses. Although Bayesian models are sometimes criticised for this flexibility (e.g. Jones & Love, 2011; Bowers & Davis, 2012), our own view is that the ability to put together initial hypotheses with new data is a key strength of Bayesian models (cf. Heit & Erickson, 2011). Although we would not minimise the challenges that our results pose for Bayesian models, and in fact we would emphasise that it remains to be seen how they would be applied here, it does seem entirely appropriate that flexible use of initial hypothesis spaces would be part of the explanation.

Although GEN-EX is based on exemplar models, and we would welcome the development of Bayesian models to address our results, we briefly turn to another kind of computational model, neural networks, which has also been applied to inductive reasoning (Sloman, 1993; Rogers & McClelland, 2004). Essentially, these models use similarity in distributed representations to draw inferences. For example, if horses have spleens, and the representation of horses in the network overlaps with the representation of cows, then it may be inferred that cows have spleens. The evidence that certain inductive reasoning phenomena occur due to the operation of rules, which is described in the first part of this chapter, is problematic for these models. However, here we consider whether such models could be extended to capture the findings we have described, which suggest that there are common processes in induction and recognition memory.

To address our results, one fundamental change would be to use networks to encode instances rather than propositions, as they are commonly applied. Although unusual, this is possible in principle. Also, the models would have to be conceived of as applying to both memory and reasoning. Rogers and McClelland (2004) already consider their model to apply to semantic memory, but it would need to be extended to apply to recognition judgements of an episodic nature. Again, we see this as possible in principle, by relying on overlap in representations to make recognition judgements. There would need to be further assumptions to capture the key difference between recognition and induction, of narrower generalisation for recognition. Perhaps the mapping function from Lassiter and Goodman (2012) could be applied for this purpose.

The fundamental challenge for neural network models would be to capture the use of flexible similarity, for different kinds of judgements and at different time courses. Hence, the challenge for neural networks would be akin to the challenge for Bayesian models. We would not rule out neural network models, and for some initial suggestions on addressing flexible similarity, see Glick (2011). One possibility, much like the Bayesian notion of multiple hypotheses, is that a neural network model could start with a space of sub-networks, each corresponding to a different similarity weighting (e.g. paying greater attention to behaviour or anatomy). Then, flexible judgements could be formed by taking linear combinations of the outputs of the sub-networks, as in a mixture of experts network (e.g. Jacobs, 1997; Heit & Bott, 2000; Heit, Briggs & Bott, 2004). Still, although neural network models have the potential to address these results, that remains to be demonstrated.

Summing up

In the first part of this chapter we have described evidence and arguments that different processes for inductive reasoning lead to the construction of different mental representations, which have consequences for recognition memory. Hence, the study of recognition memory can be informative with respect to reasoning processes. We went on to describe how, at a deeper level, models of recognition memory appear to capture performance on inductive-reasoning tasks, particularly when time is limited. This suggests that the same basic processes may underlie both cognitive abilities. Whether recognition memory is viewed as a tool with which to study reasoning, or as a source of inspiration for theorising about reasoning, what seems important is that reasoning is not studied in isolation. Although many of the models of inductive reasoning that we have briefly reviewed in the penultimate section have been developed to account only for reasoning performance, we have outlined how they could be extended to make predictions about recognition memory. As the development of GEN-EX demonstrates, by extending a model of one ability to another, we may uncover important processes that are common to both abilities. We work in an era of rapidly increasing expertise and research specialisation where, to paraphrase Charles Horace Mayo, we tend to know more and more about less and less. To counteract this tendency it is important to examine relations between core psychological abilities, and we hope that the work on inductive reasoning and recognition memory described here illustrates how such an enterprise might proceed.

Authors' note

This material includes work by Evan Heit while serving at the National Science Foundation (US). Any opinion, findings and conclusions or recommendations expressed in this material are those of the authors and do not necessarily reflect the views of the National Science Foundation.

References

Bowers, J. S., & Davis, C. J. (2012). Bayesian just-so stories in psychology and neuroscience. *Psychological Bulletin, 138*, 389–414.

Brainerd, C. J., Reyna. V. F., & Ceci, S. J. (2008). Developmental reversals in false memory: A review of data and theory. *Psychological Bulletin, 134*, 343–382.

Brainerd, C. J., Reyna, V. F., & Forrest, T. J. (2002). Are young children susceptible to the false-memory illusion? *Child Development, 73*, 1363–1377.

Coley, J. D., & Vasilyeva, N. Y. (2010). Generating inductive inferences: Premise relations and property effects. *Psychology of Learning and Motivation*, 53, 183–226.

Criss, A. H. (2009). The distribution of subjective memory strength: List strength and response bias. *Cognitive Psychology, 59*, 297–319.

Criss, A. H., & McClelland, J. L. (2006). Differentiating the differentiation models: A comparison of the retrieving effectively from memory model (REM) and the subjective likelihood model (SLiM). *Journal of Memory and Language, 55*, 447–460.

Deese, J. (1959). On the prediction of occurrence of certain verbal intrusions in free recall. *Journal of Experimental Psychology, 58*, 17–22.

De Neys, W. (2006). Automatic–heuristic and executive–analytic processing during reasoning: Chronometric and dual-task considerations. *The Quarterly Journal of Experimental Psychology, 59*, 1070–1100.

De Neys, W., & Glumicic, T. (2008). Conflict monitoring in dual process theories of reasoning. *Cognition 106*, 1248–1299.

Dougherty, M. R., Gettys, C. F., & Ogden, E. E. (1999). MINERVA-DM: A memory processes model for judgments of likelihood. *Psychological Review, 106*, 180–209.

Dougherty, M. R., Thomas, R. P., & Lange, N. (2010). Toward an integrative theory of hypothesis generation, probability judgment, and hypothesis testing. *The Psychology of Learning and Motivation, 52*, 300–342.

Evans, J. St. B. T. (2007). *Hypothetical Thinking*. Hove: Psychology Press.

Feeney, A. (2007a). How many processes underlie category-based induction? Effects of conclusion specificity and cognitive ability. *Memory & Cognition, 35*, 1830–1839.

Feeney, A. (2007b). Individual differences, dual processes, and induction. In A. Feeney & E. Heit (Eds.), *Inductive Reasoning* (pp. 302–327). Cambridge: Cambridge University Press.

Feeney, A., & Heit, E. (Eds.) (2007). *Inductive Reasoning: Experimental, Developmental and Computational Approaches*. Cambridge: Cambridge University Press.

Feeney, A., & Wilburn, C. J. (2008). Deciding between theories of how reasoning develops is hard. *Cognition, 108*, 507–511.

Fisher, A. V., & Sloutsky, V. M. (2005). When induction meets memory: Evidence for gradual transition from similarity-based to category-based induction. *Child Development, 76*, 583–597.

Fong, G. T., Krantz, D. H., & Nisbett, R. E. (1986). The effects of statistical training on thinking about everyday problems. *Cognitive Psychology, 18*, 253–292.

Gelman, S. A., & Davidson, N. S. (2013). Conceptual influences on category-based induction. *Cognitive Psychology, 66*, 327–353.

Gelman, S. A., & Markman, E. M. (1986). Categories and induction in young children. *Cognition, 23*, 183–209.

Glick, J. J. (2011). *Uncovering the organization of semantic structure with similarity and inductions*. Unpublished doctoral dissertation, Stanford University.

Hahn, U., Bailey, T. M., & Elvin, L. B. C. (2005). Effects of category coherence on category learning, memory, and generalization. *Memory & Cognition, 33*, 289–302.

Hanania, R., & Smith L. B. (2010). Selective attention and attention switching: Towards a unified developmental approach. *Developmental Science, 13*, 622–635.

Hayes, B. K., & Heit, E. (2009). *Exploring the relationship between inductive reasoning and recognition memory*. Boston, MA: Paper presented at the 50th Annual Meeting of the Psychonomic Society.

Hayes, B., & Heit, E. (2013). How similar are recognition memory and inductive reasoning? *Memory & Cognition. 41*, 781–795.

Hayes, B. K., Fritz, K., & Heit, E. (2013). The relationship between memory and inductive reasoning: Does it develop? *Developmental Psychology. 49*, 848–860.

Hayes, B., Heit, E., & Swendsen, H. (2010). Inductive reasoning. *Wiley Interdisciplinary Reviews: Cognitive Science, 1*, 278–292.

Hayes, B. K., McKinnon, R., & Sweller, N. (2008). The development of category-based induction: Reexamining conclusions from the induction then recognition (ITR) paradigm. *Developmental Psychology, 44*, 1430–1441.

Heit, E. (1998). A Bayesian analysis of some forms of inductive reasoning. In M. Oaksford & N. Chater (Eds.), *Rational models of cognition* (pp. 248–274). Oxford: Oxford University Press.

Heit, E. (2000). Properties of inductive reasoning. *Psychonomic Bulletin & Review, 7*, 569–592.

Heit, E., & Bott, L. (2000). Knowledge selection in category learning. *Psychology of Learning and Motivation, 39*, 163–199.

Heit, E., & Erickson, S. (2011). In praise of secular Bayesianism. *Behavioral and Brain Sciences, 34*, 202.

Heit, E. & Feeney, A. (2005). Relations between premise similarity and inductive strength. *Psychonomic Bulletin & Review, 12*, 340-344.

Heit, E., & Hayes, B. K. (2011). Predicting reasoning from memory. *Journal of Experimental Psychology: General, 140*(1), 76–101.

Heit, E., & Rotello, C. M. (2010). Relations between inductive reasoning and deductive reasoning. *Journal of Experimental Psychology: Learning, Memory, and Cognition, 36*, 805–812.

Heit, E., & Rubinstein, J. (1994). Similarity and property effects in inductive reasoning. *Journal of Experimental Psychology: Learning, Memory, and Cognition, 20*, 411–422.

Heit, E., Briggs, J., & Bott, L. (2004). Modelling the effects of prior knowledge on learning incongruent features of category members. *Journal of Experimental Psychology: Learning, Memory, and Cognition, 30*, 1065–1081.

Heit, E., Hahn, U., & Feeney, A. (2005). Defending diversity. *Categorization Inside and Outside of the Laboratory: Essays in Honor of Douglas L. Medin* (pp. 87–99). Washington: APA.

Heit, E., Rotello, C. M., & Hayes, B. K. (2012). Relations between memory and reasoning. *Psychology of Learning and Motivation, 57*, 57–101.

Hintzman, D. L. (1988). Judgments of frequency and recognition memory in a multiple trace memory model. *Psychological Review, 95*, 528–551.

Jacobs, R. A. (1997). Nature, nurture, and the development of functional specializations: A computational approach. *Psychonomic Bulletin & Review, 4*, 299–309.

Jones, C., & Heit, E. (1993). An evaluation of the total similarity principle: Effects of similarity on frequency judgments. *Journal of Experimental Psychology: Learning, Memory, and Cognition, 19*, 799–812.

Jones, M., & Love, B. C. (2011). Bayesian Fundamentalism or Enlightenment? On the explanatory status and theoretical contributions of Bayesian models of cognition. *Behavioral and Brain Sciences, 34*, 169–188.

Kahneman, D. (2011). *Thinking, Fast and Slow*. New York: Farrar, Straus, and Giroux.

Kahneman, D., & Tversky, A. (1972). Subjective probability: A judgment of representativeness. *Cognitive Psychology, 3*, 430–454.

Kemp, C., & Tenenbaum, J. B. (2009). Structured statistical models of inductive reasoning. *Psychological Review, 116*, 20–58.

Kemp, C., Shafto, P., & Tenenbaum, J. B. (2012). An integrated account of generalization across objects and features. *Cognitive Psychology, 64*, 35–73.

Lassiter, D., & Goodman, N. D. (2012). How many kinds of reasoning? Inference, probability, and natural language semantics. *Proceedings of the Thirty-Fourth Annual Conference of the Cognitive Science Society*.

Lopez, A., Gelman, S.A., Gutheil, G., & Smith, E. E. (1992). The development of category-based induction. *Child Development, 63*, 1070–1090.

Medin, D. L., Coley, J. D., Storms, G., & Hayes, B. K. (2003). A relevance theory of induction. *Psychonomic Bulletin & Review, 10*, 517–532.

Nisbett, R. E., Krantz, D. H., Jepson, C., & Kunda, Z. (1983). The use of statistical heuristics in everyday inductive reasoning. *Psychological Review, 90*, 339–363.

Osherson, D. N., Smith, E. E., Wilkie, O., Lopez, A., & Shafir, E. (1990). Category-based induction. *Psychological Review, 97*, 185–200.

Ratcliff, R. (1990). Connectionist models of recognition memory: Constraints imposed by learning and forgetting functions. *Psychological Review, 97*, 285–308.

Ratcliff, R., Clark, S. E., & Shiffrin, R. M. (1990). List-strength effect: I. Data and discussion. *Journal of Experimental Psychology: Learning, Memory, and Cognition, 16*, 163–178.

Roediger III, H. L., & McDermott, K. B. (1995). Creating false memories: Remembering words not presented in lists. *Journal of Experimental Psychology: Learning, Memory, and Cognition, 21*, 803–814.

Rogers, T. T., & McClelland, J. L. (2004). *Semantic Cognition: A Parallel Distributed Processing Approach*. Cambridge, MA: MIT Press.

Rotello, C. M., & Heit, E. (1999). Two-process models of recognition memory: Evidence for Recall-to-Reject? *Journal of Memory and Language, 40*, 432–453.

Rotello, C., & Heit, E. (2000). Associative recognition: A case of recall-to-reject processing. *Memory & Cognition, 28*, 907–922.

Rotello, C., & Heit, E. (2009). Modelling the effects of argument length and validity on inductive and deductive reasoning. *Journal of Experimental Psychology: Learning, Memory, and Cognition, 35*, 1317–1330.

Shafto, P., Coley, J., & Baldwin, D. (2007). Effects of time pressure on context-sensitive property induction. *Psychonomic Bulletin & Review, 14*, 890–894.

Shafto, P., Kemp, C., Bonawitz, E. B., Coley, J. D., & Tenenbaum, J. B. (2008). Inductive reasoning about causally transmitted properties. *Cognition, 109*, 175–192.

Shepard, R. N. (1987). Toward a universal law of generalization for psychological science. *Science, 237*(4820), 1317–1323.

Shiffrin, R. M., & Steyvers, M. (1997). A model for recognition memory: REM retrieving effectively from memory. *Psychonomic Bulletin and Review, 4*, 145–166.

Sloman, S. A. (1993). Feature-based induction. *Cognitive Psychology, 25*, 231–280.

Sloutsky, V. M., & Fisher, A. V. (2004). When development and learning decrease memory: Evidence against category-based induction in children. *Psychological Science, 15*, 553–558.

Sloutsky, V. M., & Fisher, A. V. (2012). Effects of categorical labels on similarity judgments: A critical evaluation of a critical analysis. Comment on Noles and Gelman. *Developmental Psychology, 48*, 897–900.

Smith, E. E., Shafir, E., & Osherson, D. (1993). Similarity, plausibility, and judgments of probability. *Cognition, 49*, 67–96.

Stanovich, K. E., & West, R. F. (1998). Individual differences in rational thought. *Journal of Experimental Psychology: General, 127*, 161–188.

Sun, R., & Hélie, S. (2012). Psychologically realistic cognitive agents: Taking human cognition seriously. *Journal of Experimental & Theoretical Artificial Intelligence, 25*, 65–92.

Travers, E., & Feeney, A. (2013). Diverse evidence for dissociable processes in inductive reasoning. *Proceedings of the Thirty-Fifth Annual Conference of the Cognitive Science Society*.

Wilburn, C., & Feeney, A. (2008). Do development and learning really decrease memory? On similarity and category-based induction in adults and children. *Cognition, 106*, 1451–1464.

7

KNOWLEDGE STRUCTURES INVOLVED IN EPISODIC FUTURE THINKING

Arnaud D'Argembeau

The ability to construct mental representations of possible futures is of fundamental importance for various aspects of human decision and behavior. Indeed, many of our actions are not tied to our immediate circumstances, but are instead guided by the events we anticipate, their envisioned consequences, and our goals and plans in attaining or avoiding the imagined state of affairs. Prospective thinking allows us to mentally "try out" multiple versions of the future before engaging in actual behavior, which provides us with increased behavioral flexibility and adaptability (Schacter, 2012; Suddendorf & Corballis, 2007).

Prospection involves imagining events and perspectives that transcend the here and now, and in this regard it is closely related to other forms of hypothetical thinking such as counterfactual reasoning – thoughts about what might have been (e.g., Byrne, 2002). Recent findings suggest, however, that hypothetical thinking is not necessarily governed by the same principles when the content of imagined possibilities pertains to the past or the future (De Brigard, Szpunar, & Schacter, 2013; Ferrante, Girotto, Straga, & Walsh, 2013; Van Hoeck et al., 2013). In this chapter, I focus on one particular kind of future-oriented cognition that has attracted much attention in recent years – namely episodic future thinking – and consider the knowledge structures or representational systems that support this function.

Types of future-oriented cognition and the concept of episodic future thought

We experience many future-oriented thoughts in our daily life and these thoughts can take various forms, more or less abstract or specific (D'Argembeau, Renaud, & Van der Linden, 2011). Sometimes we think about ourselves in the future in quite abstract ways; for example, we envisage, in general terms, our future social roles (e.g., being a parent), professional occupation (e.g., becoming a lawyer), and lifestyle (e.g., travel widely) (Markus & Nurius, 1986). We also think about various kinds of events that we have planned or that we think will happen; events that might happen at specific time points in the future (e.g., a dinner with friends next Saturday), categories of events that will repeatedly happen in the future (e.g., family parties), and future events that are extended in time (e.g., going on vacation in Italy next summer) (Anderson & Dewhurst, 2009). One particular form of future-oriented cognition – here referred to as *episodic future thought* – has attracted much attention in the past few years and refers to the capacity to mentally represent or simulate unique (one-time) events that might happen in one's personal future (Atance & O'Neill, 2001; Schacter, Addis, & Buckner, 2008; Suddendorf & Corballis, 2007; Szpunar, 2010). Episodic future thinking allows us to subjectively "pre-experience" events before they happen; we can imagine what it would be like to be in a particular future situation, for example, by picturing the setting, characters, and action in our mind's eye (D'Argembeau & Van der Linden, 2004).

Research on episodic future thinking has revealed the existence of a close linkage between the ability to remember past events and ability to imagine future events. The intuition of this link is not new and can be found, for example, in Roman mythology; according to a legend, Janus had received the gift to see both the past and the future, which is symbolized by his two heads facing opposite directions, one oriented towards the past and the other towards the future (Berens, 2010). Recent evidence from different fields of psychology provides support for this intuition by showing that episodic memory plays a critical role in allowing the mental simulation of future events (for review, see D'Argembeau, 2012; Schacter et al., 2012; Szpunar, 2010). Perhaps the most convincing evidence comes from the study of patients with episodic memory deficits. Tulving (1985) made the interesting observation that a severe amnesic patient (known as K.C.; Rosenbaum et al., 2005) was not only unable to remember any specific episodes from his life, but was also incapable of imagining anything that would likely happen in his personal future; K.C. describes his state of mind as "blank" when he tries to think about both the past and the future. Subsequent investigations of other amnesic patients confirmed that deficits in remembering past events often co-occur with deficits in imagining future events (e.g., Hassabis, Kumaran, Vann, & Maguire, 2007; Klein, Loftus, & Kihlstrom, 2002; Race, Keane, & Verfaellie, 2011; for review, see Addis & Schacter, 2012) and a similar link between episodic memory and episodic future thought abilities has been observed in other populations as well, including young children (Atance & Jackson, 2009; Suddendorf, 2010), older adults (Addis, Wong, & Schacter, 2008), patients with Alzheimer's disease (Addis, Sacchetti, Ally, Budson, & Schacter, 2009), and patients with various psychopathological conditions (Brown et al., 2013; D'Argembeau, Raffard, & Van der Linden, 2008; Lind & Bowler, 2010; Williams et al., 1996).

The relationship between episodic remembering and future thinking is also evidenced in the finding that a number of factors have similar effects on the representation of past and future events. For example, some studies have shown that temporal distance influences the representation of past and future events in similar ways; for both temporal directions, temporally close events are associated with more sensory details, clearer contextual information, and a stronger feeling of experiencing the imagined situations compared to temporally distant events (Berntsen & Bohn, 2010; D'Argembeau & Van der Linden, 2004). Other studies have revealed that the characteristics of future event representations depend on the quality of the memorial information used to construct the future images; for example, people construct representations of future events that include more sensory details, a clearer context, and a greater feeling of pre-experiencing when the events are imagined in familiar settings (e.g., a friend's apartment) compared to unfamiliar settings (e.g., the jungle) (Szpunar & McDermott, 2008). Recent studies, in fact, suggest that the effect of temporal distance on the vividness of episodic future thought is largely mediated by the familiarity of the constitutive elements (e.g., the location, persons, and objects) of the imagined event (Arnold, McDermott, & Szpunar, 2011; D'Argembeau & Van der Linden, 2012). Together, these findings demonstrate that the quality of future event representations depends on the quality of the memorial information used for imagining the events.

Further support to the idea that the remembrance of past events and the imagination of future events are closely related comes from functional neuroimaging studies. In one of the first functional magnetic resonance imaging (fMRI) studies on episodic future thought, Addis, Wong, and Schacter (2007) asked a group of young adults to remember specific episodes from their past and to imagine specific events that might happen in their future. On each trial, participants were first instructed to bring a past or future event to mind (construction phase) and then to retrieve as much detail as possible about this event (elaboration phase). The fMRI results showed that, compared to semantic retrieval and visual imagery control tasks, the past and future tasks recruited many of the same brain regions, both for the construction phase and the elaboration phase. A common pattern of brain activations when remembering past events and imagining future events has been repeatedly observed in other functional neuroimaging studies (e.g., Botzung, Denkova, & Manning, 2008; Okuda et al., 2003; Spreng & Grady, 2010; Szpunar, Watson, & McDermott, 2007), thus confirming that episodic remembering and episodic future thinking rely on largely similar neural substrates.

In summary, there is growing evidence that one particular kind of future-oriented cognition — the ability to mentally represent or simulate unique events that might happen in one's personal future — is closely related to the ability to remember specific episodes from one's life. Notwithstanding this relationship, it should be noted that there are also clear differences between remembering past events and imagining future events; for example, memories refer to events that have been previously experienced (or, at least, that the rememberer believes to have experienced), whereas future thoughts represent events that have yet to take place and that are, by definition, imbued with uncertainty. These differences are in part reflected in the phenomenology of past and future event representations. Indeed, although past and future event representations are similarly influenced by a number of factors, overall, representations of past events typically contain more sensory and contextual details than representations of future events (Berntsen & Bohn, 2010; D'Argembeau & Van der Linden, 2004, 2006). On the other hand, representations of future events tend to be more positive and idyllic (Berntsen & Bohn, 2010; Berntsen & Jacobsen, 2008; D'Argembeau & Van der Linden, 2006), perhaps because they are less constrained by reality considerations than are memories of past events (Van Boven, Kane, & McGraw, 2009).

Contributions of episodic memory and semantic knowledge to episodic future thought

The evidence showing that the ability to imagine future events is closely related to the ability to remember past events has led to a number of theoretical proposals as to the role of episodic memory in the ability to simulate possible futures. Tulving (1985, 2002) put forth the idea that episodic memory allows people to mentally travel through subjective time, and that such travel can take place in both temporal directions, not only in the past (allowing one to re-experience previous experiences), but also in the future (allowing one to pre-experience forthcoming situations). Suddendorf and Corballis (2007) argued that elements that are stored in episodic memory provide a "vocabulary" from which to construct planned future events. Schacter and Addis (2007) proposed the constructive episodic simulation hypothesis, according to which the constructive nature of episodic memory allows the flexible recombination of elements of previous experiences to simulate future scenarios. Hassabis and Maguire (2007) argued that the imagination of future events, and more generally the imagination of any fictitious experience, be it located in time or not, requires the construction of a complex and coherent scene or event, which involves the retrieval and integration of multiple elements in a coherent spatial context. All these proposals share the idea that episodic memory provides the constitutive elements or building blocks (e.g., details about previously encountered objects, persons, and locations) from which we construct representations of future episodes.

Notwithstanding the role of episodic memory in episodic future thinking, it is likely that the mental simulation of future events draws on other sources of information as well. Szpunar (2010) suggested that most episodic future thoughts are likely composed of a mixture of various episodic and semantic details, and that the extent to which episodic and semantic representations are drawn upon in simulating a future event depends on their respective accessibility. When the individual has extensive experience with a particular event feature, an abstracted representation of this feature will likely be more accessible for use in episodic future thinking. For example, the location in which an imagined future event is represented to take place may not necessarily be extracted from the memory of a specific past experience that occurred in that place, but may instead rely on an abstracted (generalized) representation of the location that has been formed over multiple past episodes. Episodic representations may only be used in episodic future thought when repeated experience with specific aspects of the imagined event is lacking. When people do not have previous experience at all with a particular event feature, they may make use of sources of information other than personal experiences, such as the experiences of friends or information gleaned from the media (Anderson, 2012).

A recent study by Anderson (2012) supports this idea that episodic future thinking relies on a combination of information drawn from episodic events and schematized representations of repeated events. After having imagined a series of future scenarios, participants were asked to look back at the details constituting the imagined events and to consider whether each of these details reminded them of anything of their personal past. If it did, they recorded brief details of up to two memories and were asked whether they had consciously used each memory when generating the future event. A further question ascertained whether or not each memory represented a personal episodic recollection. Specifically, participants categorized the type of memory (specific, categoric, extended) by choosing one of three options: "This memory is of a single event that occurred on one particular day in the past"; "This memory is a summary or merging of many similar or related events"; or "This memory is of an event or lifetime period that lasted longer than one day." The results showed that 90% of details reported when imagining future events were associated with at least one memory, and that 52% of details were associated with the conscious use of at least one memory. These findings suggest that people consciously access information stored in memory quite frequently when imagining future events. Looking more specifically at the types of information used for imagining future events, Anderson found that categoric memories were used at least as frequently as (and sometimes even more frequently than) specific memories.

Further evidence for the role of abstracted representations in episodic future thought has come from the study of patients with semantic dementia, a syndrome characterized by progressive temporal lobe atrophy and multimodal loss of semantic memory. Irish, Addis, Hodges, and Piguet (2012a) found that, while they had relatively intact episodic memory for recent past events, patients with semantic dementia showed significant impairments in episodic future thinking. Furthermore, voxel-based morphometry analyses demonstrated that atrophy in the left inferior temporal gyrus and bilateral temporal poles, regions strongly implicated in semantic memory, correlated significantly with deficits in episodic future thinking in these patients. In a follow-up study, the same authors conducted a fine-grained analysis of the types of details provided during past retrieval and future simulation (Irish, Addis, Hodges, & Piguet, 2012b). They found that patients with semantic dementia reported fewer details – across different subcategories (event, time, place, perceptual, and emotion details) – when imagining future events, while they scored at control levels for past event details. Another study showed that patients with semantic dementia had impaired future self-representations despite relatively intact past self-representations; patients appeared unable to project themselves forward in time and were only able to imagine a few semanticized and episodic personal events relating to their future self-representations (Duval et al., 2012). Together, these findings show that the disintegration of the conceptual knowledge base in semantic dementia has serious detrimental consequences for the imagination of future events. Irish et al. (2012a) suggested that semantic knowledge is critical for the construction of novel future events because it provides the conceptual framework or scaffolding into which episodic details can be integrated.

The contribution of semantic knowledge to episodic future thought is also supported by functional neuroimaging studies. There is substantial evidence that the imagination of future events recruits a specific set of frontal, parietal, and temporal regions (e.g., Addis, Pan, Vu, Laiser, & Schacter, 2009; Addis et al., 2007; Botzung et al., 2008; Okuda et al., 2003; Spreng & Grady, 2010; Szpunar et al., 2007; Weiler, Suchan, & Daum, 2010; for review, see Schacter et al., 2012). Interestingly, a quantitative meta-analysis of 120 neuroimaging studies shows that some of these brain areas (including inferior parietal, lateral temporal, medial prefrontal, and posterior cingulate cortices, especially in the left hemisphere) are consistently involved in semantic processing tasks (Binder, Desai, Graves, & Conant, 2009). This set of brain regions may support the storage, retrieval, and manipulation of conceptual knowledge about the particular attributes that are used for imagining future events (Binder & Desai, 2011).

In summary, there is growing evidence that, in addition to episodic memory, abstract or semantic representations significantly contribute to the imagination of future events. The precise contribution of semantic knowledge to episodic future thinking, however, has to be further elucidated. I see at least three kinds of conceptual knowledge that could potentially contribute to the imagination of future events: abstract representations of entities and features (e.g., locations, objects, persons, actions, emotions, and so on) that are used for representing the event (as discussed by Szpunar, 2010, and Binder & Desai, 2011; see above), schematic knowledge about how these entities interrelate and combine with each other to form events (Radvansky & Zacks, 2011), and general representations of one's personal future that locate and contextualize imagined events within one's life story (D'Argembeau & Mathy, 2011). In the next section, I focus on the contribution of the latter type of conceptual knowledge.

Episodic future thought in context: the role of autobiographical knowledge structures

As briefly noted in the first section of this chapter, there is evidence that people frequently form abstract representations of their personal future – representations that do not refer to specific events (Anderson & Dewhurst, 2009; D'Argembeau et al., 2011). An intriguing question is whether this sort of conceptual knowledge about one's personal future somehow contributes to the construction of episodic future thought, and if so, what is the nature of this contribution. In this section, I review a series of studies in which we drew on a model of the structure of autobiographical memory to investigate these issues.

Extensive research over the past twenty-five years has led to the view that autobiographical memory relies on a knowledge base that comprises three broad classes of information: conceptual knowledge about features (e.g., significant others, common locations, typical activities, personal goals, and so on) that characterized broad lifetime periods, such as "when I was in primary school" for example; summary representations of repeated events (e.g., "Sundays at Grandma's house") or events extended in time (e.g., "our vacation in Italy last summer"), together referred to as general events; and episodic memories, which are themselves constituted by episodic details that represent components of a specific past experience (e.g., a visual image of my friend snorkeling in the Mediterranean) (Conway, 2005, 2009; Conway & Pleydell-Pearce, 2000). These knowledge domains are organized in partonomic hierarchies (Barsalou, 1988), in which specific events are part of general events, which in turn are part of lifetime periods. A specific autobiographical memory is conceived of as a stable pattern of activation over these knowledge structures and, therefore, it typically contains knowledge at different levels of specificity: episodic details are contextualized within a general event that in turn is associated with one or more lifetime periods that locate the more specific knowledge within an individual's entire life story (Conway, 2005). Further, research has shown that when actively searching for specific memories, people typically access general autobiographical knowledge first (i.e., a lifetime period and/or an associated general event), and then use this knowledge to identify a specific event (Haque & Conway, 2001; but see Uzer, Lee, & Brown, 2012, for recent evidence that directly retrieved memories may be more frequent than previously thought).

Drawing on this conception of autobiographical memory, we hypothesized that the selection of episodic details for constructing episodic future thoughts is not random, but rather is guided by more general knowledge structures (D'Argembeau & Mathy, 2011). Specifically, people may hold conceptual knowledge about their personal future, including abstract knowledge about goals and possible selves (e.g., "I would like to become an architect"), anticipated lifetime periods (e.g., "when I'll be married") and general events (e.g., "my trip to India next summer"), which might guide the construction of specific future events and provide a context or frame for integrating and interpreting imagined scenarios with respect to the individual's life story. If this is the case, when generating episodic future thoughts, people should frequently activate general knowledge about their personal future before a specific event is constructed. We tested this hypothesis using a think-aloud procedure (Fox, Ericsson, & Best, 2011) in which we asked participants to verbalize the content of their thought flow (i.e., to report whatever comes to mind) while they attempted to imagine a series of specific future events in response to cue words (D'Argembeau & Mathy, 2011, Study 1). We found that in 84% of trials, participants activated abstract autobiographical representations (i.e., personal semantic information and/or general events) before producing a specific future event, thus providing initial support to the hypothesis that general autobiographical knowledge plays an important role in the construction of episodic future thought (see Table 7.1, for an example of think-aloud protocol).

TABLE 7.1: Example of a think-aloud protocol produced by a participant in D'Argembeau and Mathy (2011, Study 1).

Task: The participant had to imagine a specific future event in response to the cue-word "trip" and was instructed to say aloud everything that came to mind during the imagination process.

Protocol: "Well, I'm thinking about next summer, about the last week of July, this will be a time period when I will have to write my Master's thesis but I'd like to go on vacation for a week to relax a bit and I plan to rent a cottage in Provence with my mother, my sister, and my father-in-law's family … I will have to work a bit, so I can see myself one day with my laptop working on the Discussion section of my thesis, while the children are taking a nap. I will be outside, in the garden, working on a wooden table. The weather will be good and my thesis will be almost done, so that's positive."

In this example, the participant starts accessing general knowledge about an extended event (a vacation that would take place next summer in Provence) and then imagines a specific situation that might happen during this extended event.

Further evidence for the contribution of higher-order autobiographical knowledge structures in episodic future thought has recently come from the finding that many future events are not represented in isolation, but are instead part of broader themes and causal sequences. To investigate the organizational structure of episodic future thought, we used an adaptation of an event-cueing paradigm originally devised by Brown and Schopflocher (1998). Participants first imagined a series of future events, and each of these events (which were called the cueing events) was used to cue the imagination of another related future event (called the cued event). Then, participants looked back at each pair of events to answer questions about various ways in which the cueing and cued events could be related to each other (i.e., the two events could involve the same persons, the same location, and/or the same activity; one event could cause the other; one event could be included in the other; both events could be part of a single broader event). The results of two studies showed that the cueing and cued events were frequently embedded in an *event cluster*, meaning that they were causally and/or thematically related to each other (D'Argembeau & Demblon, 2012; for similar findings regarding event memories, see Brown, 2005; Brown & Schopflocher, 1998). This finding suggests that episodic future thought involves higher-order knowledge structures that link and organize imagined events in broader themes and causal sequences.

In other studies, we sought to further investigate the nature of this general knowledge that intervenes in episodic future thought and, more specifically, to test the hypothesis that knowledge about personal goals might play an important role in envisioning possible future events. Indeed, an important adaptive function of episodic future thought may be to allow the representation of specific events that incarnate personal goals and the construction of scenarios that implement efficient ways to achieve these goals (D'Argembeau & Mathy, 2011; Schacter, 2012; Taylor, Pham, Rivkin, & Armor, 1998). Therefore, when attempting to envision events that might happen in their future, people might often access abstract knowledge about their personal goals first, and then progressively specify goal features (e.g., consider the most likely place and time, the persons that would be present, the actions that might be possible, and so on) to construct a specific event. For example, a person might first consider the fact that she plans to go to India next summer (a personal goal) and then envision a specific experience that might happen in relation to that goal (e.g., she might imagine a specific place she would like to visit during her trip).

If this hypothesis is correct, then increasing the accessibility of goal-related knowledge should facilitate the construction of episodic future thoughts. To investigate whether this is the case, we asked participants to provide information about their personal goals and other personal features (i.e., personally known individuals and familiar locations), and this information was used to create cues for a future-event construction task that took place one week later (D'Argembeau & Mathy, 2011, Study 3). On each trial, participants were asked to imagine a specific future event in relation to one of the goals, persons, and locations they previously reported, and they were also instructed to verbalize the content of their thought flow during the construction process. In line with our previous findings, the results showed that, on most trials, participants accessed general personal knowledge before producing a specific event. Interestingly, however, we found that participants directly produced a specific event more frequently when they were cued with their personal goals (35% of trials) compared to other classes of personal information (27% and 18% of trials for person and location cues, respectively). Furthermore, even when participants recruited generative processes to construct specific future events (i.e., in the absence of direct access to a particular episode), they generated specific events more easily when cued with personal goals compared to familiar persons and locations. These findings suggest that activating knowledge about personal goals may be a common first step in episodic future thinking, which is used to guide the construction of relevant events.

Other findings suggest that goal-related knowledge also plays an important role in linking imagined future events to each other and organizing them in overarching themes and causal sequences. Using the event-cueing paradigm described above, we found that the frequency of event clusters in episodic future thought increased with the personal importance attributed to the cueing events (D'Argembeau & Demblon, 2012). If one assumes that important events are mostly events that are relevant to personal goals, this suggests that goal-related knowledge helps structure imagined events in broader event sequences. More direct evidence for the organizational role of personal goals comes from an unpublished study in which I manipulated the kind of cues provided to initiate the imagination of future events; I found that future events that were produced in response to goal cues were more often part of an event cluster than future events that were elicited by cues referring to other kinds of personal information (i.e., known individuals and familiar locations).

Recent neuroimaging studies have started to investigate the neural correlates of goal processing in relation to episodic future thought. D'Argembeau et al. (2010) used fMRI to examine brain activity when participants imagined future episodes that were related to their personal goals (e.g., moving into a new apartment in two months, getting married next summer) versus future events that were plausible and could be easily imagined, but were not related to personal goals (e.g., buying a clock at the flea market in two months, taking a pottery lesson next summer). The results showed that the act of imagining events related to personal goals was associated with increased activity in the ventral medial prefrontal cortex (MPFC) and posterior cingulate cortex (PCC) relative to imagining nonpersonal events. The ventral MPFC is involved in self-referential and affective processing (e.g., D'Argembeau et al., 2012; Northoff & Bermpohl, 2004; Roy, Shohamy, & Wager, 2012; Schmitz & Johnson, 2007) and may contribute to appraise and code the relevance of future simulations with respect to personal goals, while the PCC may contribute to contextualize and integrate imagined events with more general autobiographical knowledge structures (Northoff et al., 2006). Another study by Spreng, Stevens, Chamberlain, Gilmore, and Schacter (2010) suggests that autobiographical planning (i.e., considering the steps and possible obstacles in meeting specific goals in one's personal future) relies on the coupling of brain regions such as the MPFC and PCC with the frontoparietal control network, a network that may support executive processes involved in integrating the envisioned steps and obstacles into a cohesive plan that would allow goal achievement (see also Gerlach, Spreng, Gilmore, & Schacter, 2011).

In summary, a number of recent findings suggest that, in addition to relying on specific representations of event features, episodic future thinking commonly recruits higher-order autobiographical knowledge structures. These knowledge structures, and in particular representations of personal goals, may guide the construction of episodic future thoughts and may organize imagined events in broader themes and causal sequences.

A dual-knowledge structure account of episodic future thinking

The evidence considered in the previous section suggests that episodic future thinking involves multiple knowledge structures or representational systems. In this section, I draw on a prominent conception of autobiographical memory (Conway, 2005; Conway & Pleydell-Pearce, 2000) to propose that episodic future thinking is supported by at least two main kinds of representational systems – a pool of event details and an autobiographical knowledge base (see Figure 7.1).

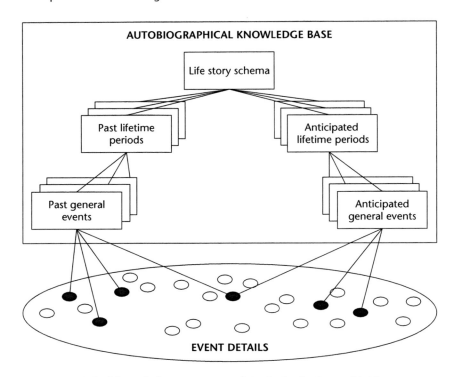

FIGURE 7.1 A dual-knowledge structure model of episodic future thinking.

In line with others (e.g., Schacter & Addis, 2007; Suddendorf & Corballis, 2007), I endorse the view that episodic memories and episodic future thoughts are, at least in part, built from a common pool of event details. These details are event components (e.g., persons, objects, locations, and so on) that may be conceived of as simulations in the brain's modality-specific systems for perception, action, emotion, and introspection (Barsalou, 2008; Rubin, 2006). As discussed in a previous section, such event details may consist of elements that have been extracted from a single past event (e.g., a visual image that represents the appearance of my friend Steve when I saw him this morning) or elements that are more abstract (in the sense that they summarize multiple past experiences) and yet simulate experience (e.g., a visual image that represents what my friend Steve typically looks like); of course, these two possibilities are not mutually exclusive, and it is likely that both episodic memories and episodic future thoughts are frequently composed of a mixture of both kinds of elements. Note also that the details used to mentally represent possible future events might not only consist of elements that have been extracted from first-hand personal experiences, but also of information gleaned more indirectly, for example through the media (e.g., television, magazines, and so on).

Besides this pool of event details, episodic future thinking may rely on general knowledge about facts and events that people anticipate will happen in their personal future. Here I propose to extend the scope of the autobiographical knowledge base described by Conway (2005) to include knowledge about the personal future. People may construct a life story schema that provides an overall representation of their entire life, covering both the past and the future (McAdams, 2001). In parallel to knowledge about past lifetime periods, people may possess conceptual knowledge about various features (e.g., relationships, locations, activities, goals, and so on) that they believe will characterize future lifetime periods – such as "when I'll have children" or "when I'll own my own business", for example. This knowledge about expected lifetime periods may, in part, be transmitted culturally through life scripts (i.e., knowledge about a series of events that represents a prototypical life course in a given culture, such as graduation, marriage, and children (Berntsen & Bohn, 2010; Berntsen & Rubin, 2004), or may be more idiosyncratic. In addition, people may form general representations of events that they anticipate to happen, including summary representations of repeated events (e.g., "taking children to school") and events extended in time (e.g., "going on vacation in France next summer"). As with autobiographical knowledge of the past, these different knowledge domains about the personal future may be organized in partonomic hierarchies – with representations of future general events being part of anticipated lifetime periods, which in turn constitute the future aspect of the life story schema – and personal goals may play a particularly important role in this organizational scheme.

A fundamental premise of this framework is that information stored in the autobiographical knowledge base guides the construction of episodic future thoughts, and locates or contextualizes imagined events within the individual's life story. This leads me to conclude with a note on the possible difference between episodic future thought and the imagination of "purely fictitious" events (Hassabis et al., 2007). There is clear evidence that remembering past events, envisioning future events, and imagining atemporal scenes (i.e., events not set in the past or future) all rely on a common constructive process – the mental generation of a complex and coherent scene through the retrieval and integration of relevant event details (Hassabis & Maguire, 2007). Indeed, envisioning future events and imagining atemporal scenes recruit many of the same brain regions (Hassabis & Maguire, 2009), and they are indistinguishable in terms of phenomenological features such as the amount of event detail experienced (de Vito, Gamboz, & Brandimonte, 2012). The question that arises, then, is what gives people the subjective sense that they are projecting themselves in their personal future (rather than merely fantasizing)? An intriguing possibility is that this feeling depends, at least in part, on the extent to which an imagined event is linked to general knowledge about one's personal future: while episodic future thoughts are contextualized within higher-order autobiographical knowledge structures (e.g., are part of a set of causally and thematically related events; D'Argembeau & Demblon, 2012), representations of atemporal events may not be meaningfully linked to such knowledge structures. Recent findings suggest that the extent to which an imagined event is linked to personal goals may play an important role in this respect. Indeed, when participants imagine future events that are more connected to their personal goals, they feel that they are pre-experiencing the situations to a greater extent, and believe that the imagined events will actually materialize in the future (D'Argembeau & Van der Linden, 2012). The essence of episodic future thinking – the subjective sense of pre-experiencing one's personal future – might thus lie not only in the construction of a detailed representation of a complex event, but also in the value attributed to this event with respect to one's personal goals.

Summary

Episodic future thinking – the ability to imagine or simulate unique events that might happen in one's personal future – has become the subject of intense research interest over the past few years. Growing evidence from different fields of psychology points to the critical role of episodic memory in the ability to imagine future events, yet it is unlikely that episodic future thought relies solely on episodic representations. In this chapter, I have proposed a framework that conceives of episodic future thought as relying on two broad kinds of knowledge structures. A pool of event details provides the constitutive elements or building blocks (e.g., representations of persons, objects, locations, and so on) from which to construct future events and scenarios. This pool may be used for mentally representing any specific episode or scene, be it located in time or not. A constructed event may acquire its past or future status only when linked to more general knowledge structures that place episodic details in different temporal contexts. General knowledge about the personal future (e.g., conceptual knowledge about personal goals and anticipated events) may be an integral part of an individual's autobiographical knowledge base that complements knowledge of the personal past and provides a context or frame for constructing and organizing episodic future thoughts.

Acknowledgments

Arnaud D'Argembeau is Research Associate of the Fund for Scientific Research (F.R.S.-FNRS), Belgium.

References

Addis, D. R., Pan, L., Vu, M. A., Laiser, N., & Schacter, D. L. (2009). Constructive episodic simulation of the future and the past: Distinct subsystems of a core brain network mediate imagining and remembering. *Neuropsychologia, 47*(11), 2222–2238. doi: 10.1016/j.neuropsychologia.2008.10.026

Addis, D. R., Sacchetti, D. C., Ally, B. A., Budson, A. E., & Schacter, D. L. (2009). Episodic simulation of future events is impaired in mild Alzheimer's disease. *Neuropsychologia, 47*, 2660–2671. doi: 10.1016/j.neuropsychologia.2009.05.018

Addis, D. R., & Schacter, D. L. (2012). The hippocampus and imagining the future: Where do we stand? *Front Hum Neurosci, 5*, 173. doi: 10.3389/fnhum.2011.00173

Addis, D. R., Wong, A. T., & Schacter, D. L. (2007). Remembering the past and imagining the future: Common and distinct neural substrates during event construction and elaboration. *Neuropsychologia, 45,* 1363–1377.

Addis, D. R., Wong, A. T., & Schacter, D. L. (2008). Age-related changes in the episodic simulation of future events. *Psychological Science, 19,* 33–41.

Anderson, R. J. (2012). Imagining novel futures: The roles of event plausibility and familiarity. *Memory, 20*(5), 443–451. doi: 10.1080/09658211.2012.677450

Anderson, R. J., & Dewhurst, S. A. (2009). Remembering the past and imagining the future: Differences in event specificity of spontaneously generated thought. *Memory, 17*(4), 367–373. doi: 10.1080/09658210902751669

Arnold, K. M., McDermott, K. B., & Szpunar, K. K. (2011). Imagining the near and far future: The role of location familiarity. *Memory & Cognition, 39*(6), 954–967. doi: 10.3758/s13421-011-0076-1

Atance, C. M., & Jackson, L. K. (2009). The development and coherence of future-oriented behaviors during the preschool years. *Journal of Experimental Child Psychology, 102*(4), 379–391. doi: 10.1016/j.jecp.2009.01.001

Atance, C. M., & O'Neill, D. K. (2001). Episodic future thinking. *Trends in Cognitive Science, 5*(12), 533–539.

Barsalou, L. W. (1988). The content and organization of autobiographical memories. In U. Neisser & E. Winograd (Eds.), *Remembering reconsidered: Ecological and traditional approaches to the study of memory* (pp. 193–243). New York: Cambridge University Press.

Barsalou, L. W. (2008). Grounded cognition. *Annual Review of Psychology, 59,* 617–645. doi: 10.1146/annurev.psych.59.103006.093639

Berens, E. M. (2010). *The myths and legends of Ancient Greece and Rome: A handbook of mythology.* Bremen, Germany: Europaeischer Hochschulverlag (original work published 1894).

Berntsen, D., & Bohn, A. (2010). Remembering and forecasting: The relation between autobiographical memory and episodic future thinking. *Memory & Cognition, 38*(3), 265–278. doi: 10.3758/MC.38.3.265

Berntsen, D., & Jacobsen, A. S. (2008). Involuntary (spontaneous) mental time travel into the past and future. *Consciousness and Cognition, 17,* 1093–1104.

Berntsen, D., & Rubin, D. C. (2004). Cultural life scripts structure recall from autobiographical memory. *Memory & Cognition, 32*(3), 427–442.

Binder, J. R., & Desai, R. H. (2011). The neurobiology of semantic memory. *Trends in Cognitive Science, 15*(11), 527–536. doi: 10.1016/j.tics.2011.10.001

Binder, J. R., Desai, R. H., Graves, W. W., & Conant, L. L. (2009). Where is the semantic system? A critical review and meta-analysis of 120 functional neuroimaging studies. *Cerebral Cortex, 19*(12), 2767–2796. doi: 10.1093/cercor/bhp055

Botzung, A., Denkova, E., & Manning, L. (2008). Experiencing past and future personal events: Functional neuroimaging evidence on the neural bases of mental time travel. *Brain and Cognition, 66*(2), 202–212.

Brown, A. D., Root, J. C., Romano, T. A., Chang, L. J., Bryant, R. A., & Hirst, W. (2013). Overgeneralized autobiographical memory and future thinking in combat veterans with posttraumatic stress disorder. *Journal of Behavior Therapy and Experimental Psychiatry, 44*(1), 129–134. doi: 10.1016/j.jbtep.2011.11.004

Brown, N. R. (2005). On the prevalence of event clusters in autobiographical memory. *Social Cognition, 23,* 35–69.

Brown, N. R., & Schopflocher, D. (1998). Event clusters: An organization of personal events in autobiographical memory. *Psychological Science, 9*(6), 470–475.

Byrne, R. M. (2002). Mental models and counterfactual thoughts about what might have been. *Trends in Cognitive Science, 6*(10), 426–431.

Conway, M. A. (2005). Memory and the self. *Journal of Memory and Language, 53*, 594–628.

Conway, M. A. (2009). Episodic memories. *Neuropsychologia, 47*(11), 2305–2313. doi: 10.1016/j.neuropsychologia.2009.02.003

Conway, M. A., & Pleydell-Pearce, C. W. (2000). The construction of autobiographical memories in the self-memory system. *Psychological Review, 107*(2), 261–288.

D'Argembeau, A. (2012). Autobiographical memory and future thinking. In D. Berntsen & D. C. Rubin (Eds.), *Understanding Autobiographical Memory: Theories and Approaches* (pp. 311–330) New York: Cambridge University Press.

D'Argembeau, A., & Demblon, J. (2012). On the representational systems underlying prospection: Evidence from the event-cueing paradigm. *Cognition, 125*(2), 160–167. doi: 10.1016/j.cognition.2012.07.008

D'Argembeau, A., Jedidi, H., Balteau, E., Bahri, M., Phillips, C., & Salmon, E. (2012). Valuing one's self: Medial prefrontal involvement in epistemic and emotive investments in self-views. *Cerebral Cortex, 22*(3), 659–667. doi: 10.1093/cercor/bhr144

D'Argembeau, A., & Mathy, A. (2011). Tracking the construction of episodic future thoughts. *Journal of Experimental Psychology: General, 140*, 258–271.

D'Argembeau, A., Raffard, S., & Van der Linden, M. (2008). Remembering the past and imagining the future in schizophrenia. *Journal of Abnormal Psychology, 117*(1), 247–251.

D'Argembeau, A., Renaud, O., & Van der Linden, M. (2011). Frequency, characteristics, and functions of future-oriented thoughts in daily life. *Applied Cognitive Psychology, 25*, 96–103.

D'Argembeau, A., Stawarczyk, D., Majerus, S., Collette, F., Van der Linden, M., Feyers, D., Maquet, P., & Salmon, E. (2010). The neural basis of personal goal processing when envisioning future events. *Journal of Cognitive Neuroscience, 22*(8), 1701–1713. doi: 10.1162/jocn.2009.21314

D'Argembeau, A., & Van der Linden, M. (2004). Phenomenal characteristics associated with projecting oneself back into the past and forward into the future: Influence of valence and temporal distance. *Consciousness and Cognition, 13*(4), 844–858.

D'Argembeau, A., & Van der Linden, M. (2006). Individual differences in the phenomenology of mental time travel: The effect of vivid visual imagery and emotion regulation strategies. *Consciousness and Cognition, 15*(2), 342–350.

D'Argembeau, A., & Van der Linden, M. (2012). Predicting the phenomenology of episodic future thoughts. *Consciousness and Cognition, 21*(3), 1198–1206. doi: 10.1016/j.concog.2012.05.004

De Brigard, F., Szpunar, K. K., & Schacter, D. L. (2013). Coming to grips with the past: Effect of repeated simulation on the perceived plausibility of episodic counterfactual thoughts. *Psychological Science.* doi: 10.1177/0956797612468163

de Vito, S., Gamboz, N., & Brandimonte, M. A. (2012). What differentiates episodic future thinking from complex scene imagery? *Consciousness and Cognition, 21*, 813–823.

Duval, C., Desgranges, B., de La Sayette, V., Belliard, S., Eustache, F., & Piolino, P. (2012). What happens to personal identity when semantic knowledge degrades? A study of the self and autobiographical memory in semantic dementia. *Neuropsychologia, 50*(2), 254–265. doi: 10.1016/j.neuropsychologia.2011.11.019

Ferrante, D., Girotto, V., Straga, M., & Walsh, C. (2013). Improving the past and the future: A temporal asymmetry in hypothetical thinking. *Journal of Experimental Psychology: General, 142*(1), 23–27. doi: 10.1037/a0027947

Fox, M. C., Ericsson, K. A., & Best, R. (2011). Do procedures for verbal reporting of thinking have to be reactive? A meta-analysis and recommendations for best reporting methods. *Psychological Bulletin, 137*(2), 316–344. doi: 10.1037/a0021663

Gerlach, K. D., Spreng, R. N., Gilmore, A. W., & Schacter, D. L. (2011). Solving future problems: Default network and executive activity associated with goal-directed mental simulations. *Neuroimage, 55*(4), 1816–1824. doi: 10.1016/j.neuroimage.2011.01.030

Haque, S., & Conway, M. A. (2001). Sampling the process of autobiographical memory construction. *European Journal of Cognitive Psychology, 13*(4), 529–547.

Hassabis, D., Kumaran, D., Vann, S. D., & Maguire, E. A. (2007). Patients with hippocampal amnesia cannot imagine new experiences. *Proceedings of the National Academy of Sciences of the United States of America, 104*(5), 1726–1731.

Hassabis, D., & Maguire, E. A. (2007). Deconstructing episodic memory with construction. *Trends in Cognitive Science, 11*(7), 299–306.

Hassabis, D., & Maguire, E. A. (2009). The construction system of the brain. *Philosophical Transactions of the Royal Society of London: B Biological Sciences, 364*(1521), 1263–1271. doi: 10.1098/rstb.2008.0296

Irish, M., Addis, D. R., Hodges, J. R., & Piguet, O. (2012a). Considering the role of semantic memory in episodic future thinking: Evidence from semantic dementia. *Brain, 135*(7), 2178–2191. doi: 10.1093/brain/aws119

Irish, M., Addis, D. R., Hodges, J. R., & Piguet, O. (2012b). Exploring the content and quality of episodic future simulations in semantic dementia. *Neuropsychologia, 50*(14), 3488–3495. doi: 10.1016/j.neuropsychologia.2012.09.012

Klein, S. B., Loftus, J., & Kihlstrom, J. F. (2002). Memory and temporal experience: The effects of episodic memory loss on an amnesic patient's ability to remember the past and imagine the future. *Social Cognition, 20*, 353–379.

Lind, S. E., & Bowler, D. M. (2010). Episodic memory and episodic future thinking in adults with autism. *Journal of Abnormal Psychology, 119*(4), 896–905. doi: 10.1037/a0020631

Markus, H., & Nurius, P. (1986). Possible selves. *American Psychologist, 41*, 954–969.

McAdams, D. P. (2001). The psychology of life stories. *Review of General Psychology, 5*, 100–122.

Northoff, G., & Bermpohl, F. (2004). Cortical midline structures and the self. *Trends in Cognitive Science, 8*, 102–107.

Northoff, G., Heinzel, A., de Greck, M., Bermpohl, F., Dobrowolny, H., & Panksepp, J. (2006). Self-referential processing in our brain: A meta-analysis of imaging studies on the self. *Neuroimage, 31*, 440–457.

Okuda, J., Fujii, T., Ohtake, H., Tsukiura, T., Tanji, K., Suzuki, K., Kawashima, R., Fukuda, H., Itoh, M., & Yamadori, A. (2003). Thinking of the future and past: The roles of the frontal pole and the medial temporal lobes. *Neuroimage, 19*(4), 1369–1380.

Race, E., Keane, M. M., & Verfaellie, M. (2011). Medial temporal lobe damage causes deficits in episodic memory and episodic future thinking not attributable to deficits in narrative construction. *Journal of Neuroscience, 31*(28), 10262–10269. doi: 10.1523/JNEUROSCI.1145-11.2011

Radvansky, G., & Zacks, J. M. (2011). Event perception. *Wiley Interdisciplinary Reviews: Cognitive Science, 2*(6), 608–620. doi: 10.1002/wcs.133

Rosenbaum, R. S., Kohler, S., Schacter, D. L., Moscovitch, M., Westmacott, R., Black, S. E., Gao, F., & Tulving, E. (2005). The case of K.C.: Contributions of a memory-impaired person to memory theory. *Neuropsychologia, 43*(7), 989–1021. doi: 10.1016/j.neuropsychologia.2004.10.007

Roy, M., Shohamy, D., & Wager, T. D. (2012). Ventromedial prefrontal-subcortical systems and the generation of affective meaning. *Trends in Cognitive Science, 16*(3), 147–156. doi: 10.1016/j.tics.2012.01.005

Rubin, D. C. (2006). The basic-systems model of episodic memory. *Perspectives on Psychological Science, 1*, 277–311.

Schacter, D. L. (2012). Adaptive constructive processes and the future of memory. *American Psychologist, 67*(8), 603–613. doi: 10.1037/a0029869

Schacter, D. L., & Addis, D. R. (2007). The cognitive neuroscience of constructive memory: remembering the past and imagining the future. *Philosophical Transactions of the Royal Society of London: B Biological Sciences, 362*(1481), 773–786.

Schacter, D. L., Addis, D. R., & Buckner, R. L. (2008). Episodic simulation of future events: Concepts, data, and applications. *Annals of the New York Academy of Sciences, 1124*, 39–60.

Schacter, D. L., Addis, D. R., Hassabis, D., Martin, V. C., Spreng, R. N., & Szpunar, K. K. (2012). The future of memory: Remembering, imagining, and the brain. *Neuron, 76*(4), 677–694. doi: 10.1016/j.neuron.2012.11.001

Schmitz, T. W., & Johnson, S. C. (2007). Relevance to self: A brief review and framework of neural systems underlying appraisal. *Neuroscience and Biobehavioral Reviews, 31*(4), 585–596.

Spreng, R. N., & Grady, C. L. (2010). Patterns of brain activity supporting autobiographical memory, prospection, and theory of mind, and their relationship to the default mode network. *Journal of Cognitive Neuroscience, 22*(6), 1112–1123. doi: 10.1162/jocn.2009.21282

Spreng, R. N., Stevens, W. D., Chamberlain, J. P., Gilmore, A. W., & Schacter, D. L. (2010). Default network activity, coupled with the frontoparietal control network, supports goal-directed cognition. *Neuroimage, 53*(1), 303–317. doi: 10.1016/j.neuroimage.2010.06.016

Suddendorf, T. (2010). Linking yesterday and tomorrow: Preschoolers' ability to report temporally displaced events. *British Journal of Developmental Psychology, 28*(2), 491–498. doi: 10.1348/026151009x479169

Suddendorf, T., & Corballis, M. C. (2007). The evolution of foresight: What is mental time travel and is it unique to humans? *Behavioral and Brain Sciences, 30*, 299–351.

Szpunar, K. K. (2010). Episodic future thought: An emerging concept. *Perspectives on Psychological Science, 5*, 142–162.

Szpunar, K. K., & McDermott, K. B. (2008). Episodic future thought and its relation to remembering: Evidence from ratings of subjective experience. *Consciousness and Cognition, 17*, 330–334.

Szpunar, K. K., Watson, J. M., & McDermott, K. B. (2007). Neural substrates of envisioning the future. *Proceedings of the National Academy of Sciences of the United States of America, 104*(2), 642–647.

Taylor, S. E., Pham, L. B., Rivkin, I. D., & Armor, D. A. (1998). Harnessing the imagination. Mental simulation, self-regulation, and coping. *American Psychologist, 53*(4), 429–439.

Tulving, E. (1985). Memory and consciousness. *Canadian Psychologist, 26*, 1–12.

Tulving, E. (2002). Episodic memory: From mind to brain. *Annual Review of Psychology, 53*, 1–25.

Uzer, T., Lee, P. J., & Brown, N. R. (2012). On the prevalence of directly retrieved autobiographical memories. *Journal of Experimental Psychology: Learning, Memory, and Cognition, 38*(5), 1296–1308. doi: 10.1037/a0028142

Van Boven, L., Kane, J. M., & McGraw, A. P. (2009). Temporally asymmetric constraints on mental simulation: Retrospection is more constrained than prospection. In K. D. Markman, W. M. P. Klein, & J. A. Suhr (Eds.), *Handbook of Imagination and Mental Simulation* (pp. 131–147). New York: Psychology Press.

Van Hoeck, N., Ma, N., Ampe, L., Baetens, K., Vandekerckhove, M., & Van Overwalle, F. (2013). Counterfactual thinking: An fMRI study on changing the past for a better future. *Social Cognitive and Affective Neuroscience, 8*(5), 556–564. doi: 10.1093/scan/nss031

Weiler, J. A., Suchan, B., & Daum, I. (2010). Foreseeing the future: Occurrence probability of imagined future events modulates hippocampal activation. *Hippocampus, 20*(6), 685–690. doi: 10.1002/hipo.20695

Williams, J. M. G., Ellis, N. C., Tyers, C., Healy, H., Rose, G., & MacLeod, A. K. (1996). The specificity of autobiographical memory and imageability of the future. *Memory & Cognition, 24*(1), 116–125.

8

INTUITION

Introducing affect into cognition

Sascha Topolinski

One of the most enigmatic human capabilities is the faculty of intuition; that is, holding knowledge without knowing the basis for this knowledge (Epstein, 2008; Vaughan, 1979). Starting with the well-known phenomenon of *artificial grammar learning* (Reber, 1967), in which individuals are able to detect patterns without being able to report the rule that generated the pattern, cognitive and social psychology have demonstrated several impressive intuitive performances in which individuals express knowledge that is beyond their analytic, conscious abilities; and they cannot verbally report the basis of this knowledge (for reviews, see Kahneman, 2003; Kihlstrom, 1999; Pothos, 2007).

Intuitions play a major role in memory and reasoning, namely when no clear information is yet available (Frank, O'Reilly, & Curran, 2006). For instance, when we seek a memory content but cannot currently retrieve it, we still have reliable intuitions about whether this information is part of our memory and will later be retrieved or not (the *feeling of knowing*, Yaniv & Meyer, 1987). During learning, when no actual feedback on later recall performance is available yet, we assess the progress of our learning attempts intuitively, using a variety of cues (Koriat, 1997). Also, our confidence in having found a correct answer to a problem is often only an intuition that comes before verifying the veracity of the answer (e.g., Kelley & Lindsay, 1993; Koriat, 2012; Topolinski & Reber, 2010a).

Theorizing the underlying causal mechanisms of intuition in general has been a major aim in psychology (e.g., Kihlstrom, 1999; Pothos, 2007). Most explanatory approaches to intuition assume purely perceptual and cognitive mechanisms to be at work (e.g., Kahneman, 2003; Kihlstrom, 1999; Pothos, 2007), for instance "implicit thought" (Kihlstrom, 1999) or "impressions" (Kahneman, 2003) and neglect affective processes (but see Baumann & Kuhl, 2002; Epstein, 2008). For instance, among the various theories of artificial grammar learning, no account assumes affective or emotional mechanisms (Pothos, 2007). This comes as a surprise, since intuition itself is often characterized as a feeling that essentially involves an affective component (e.g., Epstein, 2008; Topolinski & Hertel, 2007).

The same is true for intuitions during memory and reasoning. While influential theoretical accounts identified a variety of causal determinants of meta-memory and meta-reasoning judgments, affective states as procedural mediators of how meta-mnemonic judgments are construed or how reasoning steps are guided have not been considered yet (e.g., for learning confidence, Koriat, 1997; for the feeling of knowing, Koriat, 1993; for subjective confidence itself, Koriat, 2012; but see, for instance, Bechara, Damasio, Tranel, & Damasio, 1997, for affective responses in intuition during strategic decisions; Topolinski & Reber, 2010a, for insight). The present chapter features a procedural account of the general case of intuition that assumes an essential involvement of affective processes within the causal architecture of intuitive judgments (Topolinski, 2011). This account was first developed and tested for the case of coherence intuitions (Bowers, Regehr, Balthazard, & Parker, 1990). This phenomenon shall first be described before the current intuition model is introduced and then supporting evidence is reviewed. Finally, implications for other intuitions in reasoning and memory are drawn.

Sensing the web without seeing the spider – intuitive judgments of coherence

Coherence, or consistency, is an essential goal of our mental representation of the inner and outer world; one model of the brain's functions is as a device that detects and establishes coherence. In some cases coherence is easily detected, for instance when we choose white instead of red wine to go with the fish for dinner. In other cases, coherence is much harder to detect explicitly, because there are many items and complex relations between them that constitute a possible coherence. In a meanwhile classical paper, Bowers and colleagues (Bowers et al., 1990) have provided several tasks to examine such subtle coherence detections and tested whether individuals would still be able to sense coherence intuitively. In one example, they used RAT items (Remote Associate Test; Mednick, 1962); that is, triads of words that are each connected to a common remote associate. For instance, the three words, SHINE, BEAM, and STRUCK, are each remotely semantically related to the word MOON, or the words OVER, PLANT, and HORSE are each related to the word POWER (Bowden & Jung-Beeman, 2003). Since this connection is only remote, individuals have to think a while and consider several possible solution candidates before they retrieve the actual solution (e.g., Harkins, 2006). Bowers et al. (1990) presented such coherent word triads together with completely random, that is, incoherent word triads (e.g., DREAM BALL BOOK) to participants for only a few seconds and asked participants whether the given triad was coherent or not. Since the time provided for rendering this judgment was too brief to consciously ponder and retrieve the solution word, participants had to rely on their intuition to rate the coherence. It turned out that participants were actually able to discriminate above chance between coherent and incoherent triads (see also, for replications, Baumann & Kuhl, 2002; Bolte, Goschke, & Kuhl, 2003).

In the context of problem solving, this impressive faculty can also be conceptualized as a *judgment of solvability* (JOS; Thompson, 2009). In their basic use as creativity measure (Mednick, 1962), RAT items are not to be judged on coherence, but are to be solved; that is, the common remote associate should be found by the participants. The initial intuitive feeling that there is a solution or not constitutes a judgment of solvability (for other cases, see Ackermann & Thompson, this volume; also see the feeling-of-rightness of an initial solution intuition: Thompson, Prowse Turner, & Pennycook, 2011), which might guide the reasoning process in the basic RAT: If this initial intuition is strong, individuals will invest more time and effort in finding the solution compared to when the intuition is weak, since the search promises to be successful eventually (cf., De Neys, Rossi, & Houdé, 2013).

The question is how individuals are able to achieve this performance, the driving mechanisms of which remained unclear for two decades (Kihlstrom, 1999). Recently, Fritz Strack and I (Topolinski & Strack, 2008, 2009a, 2009b, 2009d) have developed a model mapping the underlying mechanisms of this intuition, the fluency–affect intuition model (FAIM, Topolinski, 2011). In this account, the dynamics of cognitive operations as well as brief affective responses are assumed to be the operating principles in coherence intuitions. The present chapter will first outline the FAIM and will then review several lines of experimental research that have systematically tested its predictions. But before that, the core concept of processing fluency should be introduced.

Fluency – the smooth operator of the mind

Processing fluency is the speed or efficiency with which a mental operation is executed (e.g., Reber, Schwarz, & Winkielman, 2004). Independent from the content that is processed, the information processing can be relatively fluent and fast or disfluent and slow. FoR iNsTaNcE, tHiS sEnTeNcE iS HaRdEr To ReAd ThAn ThE rEsT oF tHe TeXt. Processing fluency applies to any kind of mental operation, from perception (e.g., Reber, Wurtz, & Zimmermann, 2004) and semantic processing (e.g., Whittlesea, 1993) to motor execution (Leder, Bär & Topolinski, 2013; Topolinski, 2010, 2012; Topolinski, Lindner, & Freudenberg, 2014; Topolinski & Strack, 2009c, 2010). Fluency can be experimentally manipulated, for example by increasing the visual contrast of a stimulus (Reber & Schwarz, 1999) or by repeating a stimulus (e.g., Bornstein & D'Agostino, 1994). In numerous experiments manipulating fluency it has been shown that fluency variations influence judgments concerning the more or less fluently processed stimulus on many kinds of dimensions. For instance, high fluency triggers a feeling of familiarity (e.g., Whittlesea, 1993), fame (Jacoby, Kelley, Brown, & Jasechko, 1989; Topolinski & Strack, 2010), funniness (Topolinski, 2014), and even truth (e.g., Topolinski & Reber, 2010a, 2010b). Also, fluency has been shown to be a causal determinant of many meta-memory and meta-reasoning judgments, for instance the *feeling of knowing* (Koriat, 1993; Koriat & Levy-Sadot, 2001), the feeling that an answer is correct (Kelley & Lindsay, 1993; Topolinski & Reber, 2010a, 2010b), or judgments of the progress of one's own learning (Koriat, 1997).

The common denominator of all these judgmental influences is not a cognitive, but rather an affective one. High fluency simply feels good because it triggers a brief positive affect (e.g., Harmon-Jones & Allen, 2001; Winkielman and Cacioppo, 2001) that can be used for any kind of judgment, and as the basis of a preference judgment. Accordingly, it has been shown repeatedly that more fluent stimuli are liked more than less fluent stimuli (e.g., Gordon & Holyoak, 1983; Moreland & Topolinski, 2010).

This concept of processing fluency, and particularly its affective consequences, is the core notion of our intuition model, which will be described in the following.

The fluency-affect intuition model (FAIM)

Aiming to elucidate the underlying operational mechanisms of intuitive judgments of semantic coherence, we assumed that semantic coherence increases processing fluency and thus triggers positive affect (Topolinski & Strack, 2009a, 2009b, 2009d). Concerning the first link, fluency, we assumed that when reading a coherent word triad, the three word constituents each semantically prime the remote solution word (Beeman et al., 1994; Topolinski & Strack, 2008), which in turn facilitates the processing of coherent compared to incoherent word triads (see Whittlesea, 1993, for the first demonstration that semantic coherence can increase fluency). Note that the current notion of fluency is confined to encoding fluency, i.e., perceptual and semantic fluency of the triads, but not to the fluency in retrieving any answer (cf., Thompson et al., 2013).

Furthermore, as was reviewed above, this fluency gain due to coherence automatically triggers a brief positive affective state (cf., Reber, Schwarz et al., 2004), which is then used as a gut feeling when one is asked to judge the coherence of a given word triad. Note that this fluency-affect link runs automatically (Topolinski & Strack, 2008) and completely independently from searching for or retrieving the solution word. Thus, in this account intuition relies on by-products of semantic encoding and memory processes which are partly affective in nature. In the following, several lines of research are reviewed that systematically tested each step of this fluency-affect link.

Assessing cognitive dynamics and their affective consequences in intuition

A first line of experiments tested these predictions in a deductive fashion; that is, assessing the variations of processing fluency caused by (in)coherence and the resulting affective responses that were predicted by the FAIM. Importantly, FAIM predicts that these cognitive and affective variations occur automatically when processing word material (e.g., Reber, Schwarz et al., 2004); that is, they arise independently from the goal to judge coherence or to find a solution word for a given triad (cf., Topolinski & Strack, 2008). Thus, the following experiments were largely done outside of any task-set, with participants incidentally reading over word triads without any goal to judge coherence or use their intuition. Moreover, to demonstrate that the fluency-affect chain runs as a default automatic mechanism, participants were not even informed about the underlying semantic structure of the word triads. In the following, first experiments assessing the cognitive dynamics (fluency) are described, then studies on affective consequences, and later studies will be presented that manipulated both fluency and affect.

Cognitive dynamics caused by (in)coherence

The assertion that coherent triads would be processed more fluently than incoherent triads was assessed using different methods. In a first experiment we employed the logic of a lexical decision-task to assess processing speed for coherent and incoherent word triads in the following way (Topolinski & Strack, 2009a, Experiment 1). Participants received intact coherent (e.g., RABBIT CLOUD CREAM) and incoherent (e.g., DREAM BALL BOOK) as well as both coherent and incoherent triads for which a randomly chosen word was replaced by a pronounceable letter string (e.g., DREAM TRULG BOOK). The latter nonword containing triads were only fillers to justify the lexical decision-task for the participant, and have no conceptual importance. Participants were presented with all these triads in a random order and were asked to judge as quickly and as accurately as possible whether the given triad was intact, i.e., contained only real words, or was violated, i.e., contained a nonword. This task naturally requires that participants semantically process all three words of the given triad. Crucially, if coherence facilitates semantic processing, then coherent triads should be judged faster than incoherent triads in this task. And this was actually what we found, with a speed gain of 57 ms. In various analyses on possible psycholinguistic differences in the item pool, coherent and incoherent triads did not differ in task-relevant linguistic features, such as word length, word classes, or frequency in everyday language (Topolinski & Strack, 2009a, Experiment 1).

In a further experiment, we assessed mere reading speed as a further measure of processing ease. Participants received coherent and incoherent word triads in a random fashion and were asked to simply read the triads as fast as possible and to push a key when they had accomplished reading the triad. Once again, coherent triads were read faster than incoherent triads, yielding a significant processing gain of 58 ms (Topolinski & Strack, 2009d, Experiment 1).

In sum, these two experiments suggest that mere semantic coherence actually facilitates semantic processing, although participants had no idea that there existed a hidden coherence for some of the triads, as follow-up debriefings revealed.

Affective consequences of coherence

Numerous previous approaches have shown that high processing efficiency, i.e., fluency, is hedonically marked (e.g., Harmon-Jones & Allen, 2001; Reber & Schwarz, 1999; Winkielman & Cacioppo, 2001). Consequently, FAIM predicts that the coherence-induced high fluency would elicit a brief positive affective state.

As an indirect assessment of arising affective responses to coherence, we used a physiological measure that has been shown before to be sensitive to fluency-triggered affect, namely facial electromyography (fEMG, Winkielman & Cacioppo, 2001). As earlier research in social psychology has shown, the activity of two muscles in the face are indicative of affective responses, namely the smiling muscle Zygomaticus Major for positive, and the frowning muscle Corrugator Supercilii for negative affect (Cacioppo, Petty, Losch, & Kim, 1986). Thus, we assessed the activity of these muscles while participants – who were again ignorant about the hidden coherence of some of the triads– merely read coherent and incoherent word triads (Topolinski, Likowski, Weyers, & Strack, 2009). As a cover story, we told participants that this reading task was simply a calibration phase to get used to the laboratory session. We found that during incidental reading of coherent compared to incoherent triads, the smiling muscle showed higher averaged activity, which suggests an increase in positive affect, and the frowning muscle showed lower averaged activity, which suggests a decrease in negative affect (Topolinski et al., 2009). These subtle facial responses appeared and decayed within a few seconds after reading a given triad, indicating the subtle and transient nature of fluency-induced affective responses (cf., phasic affect, Topolinski & Deutsch, 2012, 2013).

We also used self-reports of preference. The crucial question here was whether the subtle affective responses elicited by coherence-induced fluency could be strong enough to become consciously experienced (Topolinski & Strack, 2009d) and could thus be explicitly reported (e.g., Reber & Schwarz, 1999). Participants preferred coherent over incoherent triads (Topolinski & Strack, 2009a, Experiment 3; Topolinski & Strack, 2009d, Experiment 1). Again, in careful stimulus analyses we made sure that the stimulus pool of coherent and of incoherent triads, respectively, did not differ in terms of valence of the containing words themselves.

In conclusion, hidden semantic coherence in word triads altered cognitive processing by increasing processing ease, which further triggered positive affect. In further experiments using an inductive method, we examined whether fluency and affect also causally determined intuitions.

Experimental manipulations of fluency and affect in intuition

In additional lines of research we actively manipulated processing fluency and infused affect experimentally to test whether such manipulations would influence intuition. If so, fluency and affect could be regarded as the causal determinants of intuitive judgments.

For this purpose, we replicated the basic paradigm of intuitive judgments of semantic coherence (e.g., Baumann & Kuhl, 2002), in which word triads are presented to participants for only 1,500 ms, and participants are asked to judge coherence within an additional time window of only 500 ms after offset of the triad. This forced task prompts participants to judge intuitively, since the time given does not allow them to strategically ponder and combine the triad's constituents and to find a solution word analytically (Bolte & Goschke, 2005). To nevertheless control for an incidental retrieval of the solution word (which would thus disqualify the given judgment as being intuitive), participants are asked for the solution word after each trial. Typically, in this paradigm participants find the actual solution word in only a few trials, which are discarded from later analyses. Within this established intuition task, we manipulated fluency and affect, as is reviewed in the following.

Experimental manipulations of processing fluency

As mentioned before, the current notion of fluency refers to the encoding fluency of the word triads, not to the retrieval or answer fluency (cf., Thompson et al., 2013) for the solution word. Thus, the following manipulations of fluency involved perceptual and semantic fluency. As a first method to alter fluency, we experimentally changed the contrast with which a word triad was presented against a white background (Reber & Schwarz, 1999; Unkelbach, 2007) using different colorings of the triads and changing the intensity of the coloring, with some items appearing in a pale shade (low contrast against the white background, thus low fluency) and some in a darker shade (high contrast, high fluency). This manipulation was done orthogonally to actual coherence. As a result, we found two main effects, i.e., of coherence and fluency, on the likelihood for a given triad to be judged as being coherent (Topolinski & Strack, 2009b, Experiment 1). Specifically, the likelihood to be judged as being coherent was higher for coherent compared to incoherent triads, which is the basic intuition effect. However, in addition, for both coherent and incoherent triads the likelihood to be judged as being coherent was higher when the given triad was presented in a high than in a low contrast. Thus, experimentally induced fluency did have an impact on intuition.

As another way of altering processing ease we used repeated exposure (Bornstein & D'Agostino, 1994), which trains encoding and yields increased fluency for repeated compared to novel stimuli (e.g., Topolinski, 2012; Topolinski & Strack, 2009c, 2010). Thus, in a preceding task we pre-exposed a random set of coherent and incoherent word triads before the actual intuition task. Again, we found a main effect of both coherence and exposure on intuitive judgments. While participants again judged coherent triads more often as being coherent than incoherent triads, they also judged pre-exposed triads more often as being coherent than novel triads, an effect that held both for coherent and incoherent triads (Topolinski & Strack, 2009b, Experiment 2).

Yet another and very unobtrusive way to increase fluency is subliminal contour priming (Winkielman & Cacioppo, 2001), in which the gist of a stimulus is presented very briefly immediately before the stimulus itself appears. Thus, we presented word triads, and for some of them flashed (17 ms) a visually degraded version of the third word of the triad immediately before onset of the given triad. For the other triads, we flashed an irrelevant nonword. Again, both coherent and incoherent triads were more likely judged as being coherent when they were primed with their own word than with a nonword (Topolinski & Strack, 2009b, Experiment 3).

In sum, three very different fluency manipulations reliably influenced intuition. In further experiments, we exploited several means to alter current affect.

Experimental inductions of affect

If fluency-triggered positive affect is the causal gut feeling in intuitions, infusing brief affective states (or *phasic affect*, Topolinski & Deutsch, 2012, 2013) during an intuition task should influence intuitions. Specifically, brief positive compared to negative affect should increase the likelihood that participants perceive coherence and thus judge a given triad as being coherent, independent from its veridical coherence.

First, we implemented phasic facial feedback (Larsen, Kasimatis, & Frey, 1992; Strack, Martin, & Stepper, 1988) during an intuitive task. For this purpose, participants held a pen in their mouth (Strack et al., 1988), and golf tees were affixed to the inner edges of their brows (Larsen et al., 1992). Upon a specific prompting signal (which the participants had learned before), they should either lift their lips off the pen or move the golf tees in a way that the end of the golf tees would touch each other. By simple biomechanical means, the lifting of the lips off the pen can only be achieved by contracting the Zygomaticus Major, the smiling muscle (which induces positive affect, Strack et al., 1988), and the moving of the tees can only be achieved by furrowing the brows and contracting the Corrugator Supercilii, the frowning muscle (which induces negative affect, Larsen et al., 1992). This facial feedback exercise was implemented in a way that participants held the particular contraction during encoding of the to-be-judged triad. Randomly, for some triads, participants contracted the smiling muscle (positive affect) and for other triads participants contracted the furrowing muscle (negative affect), again, as the fluency manipulations had been, orthogonally to actual coherence of the given triad. As a result, additionally to the main effect of coherence, the likelihood of judging a triad as being coherent was reliably higher for triads encoded under smiling-muscle contraction than for triads encoded under furrowing-muscle contraction (Topolinski & Strack, 2009b, Experiment 4).

As another affect infusion, we used *subliminal facial primes* (Murphy & Zajonc, 1993). Specifically, immediately before a given triad would appear, a photo of either a happy or a sad face was flashed for 17 ms, succeeded by a backward mask of a neutral face presented for 350 ms to distract from perceiving the affective face.

This affective priming was so unobtrusive that participants did not report awareness of the affective primes in later funneled debriefings. Yet, participants were more likely to judge a triad as being coherent if a happy face had preceded the triad than if a sad face had preceded it (Topolinski & Strack, 2009b, Experiment 5).

In a final manipulation of affect, we used the word triads themselves as containers for brief affect. Specifically, we constructed our own set of word triads that were constituted of either positive, or negative, words, respectively. For instance, the word triad FRESH HOLY LIQUID contains relatively positive words, while the word triad SALT DROWN RAIN contains relatively negative words, although both triads have the same rather neutral solution word WATER. From such positive and negative coherent triads we derived positive and negative incoherent triads by simply intermixing the triad constituents within each valence category. This yielded positive coherent, negative coherent, positive incoherent, and negative incoherent word triads that were then used as stimuli in an intuition task. As a result, in addition to the basic effect of coherence, participants were more likely to judge a triad as being coherent when the triad contained positive than when the triad contained negative words, regardless of its actual coherence (Topolinski & Strack, 2009b, Experiment 8).

In sum, these findings show that incidentally infused brief affect, either stemming from proprioception, visual stimuli, or even word triads themselves, influenced intuition. Taken together with the above reviewed evidence that coherence itself triggers positive affect as measured deductively, this inductive evidence strongly suggests that affect plays a causal role in intuitive judgments of semantic coherence. Finally, because FAIM assumes that both fluency and affect play a role in intuition, we manipulated both of these factors within the same paradigm.

Joint manipulations of fluency and affect

FAIM assumes that the coherence of a word triad alters the processing ease of that triad and thereby triggers an automatic affective reaction, which is the eventual gut feeling used in intuition. If fluency and affect causally influence intuitions, then manipulating them orthogonally should yield independent main effects of each variable. This was tested in an experiment that used color contrast as fluency and the valenced word triads mentioned above as affect manipulation. All three factors – actual coherence, fluency, and affect – were manipulated orthogonally to each other and in a within-subjects design. This procedure did indeed yield three independent main effects of coherence, fluency, and affect, with high compared to low fluency and positive compared to negative affect increasing the likelihood of a triad to be judged as being coherent (Topolinski & Strack, 2009b, Experiment 9). Most interestingly, for the conditions in which fluency and affect ran against actual coherence, intuitive judgments were even reversed. Triads that were coherent, but low-fluent and negative, were actually judged *less* likely to be coherent than *in*coherent but highly fluent positive triads. Thus, a feeling of coherence was artificially created in the absence of veridical coherence.

The question remains whether the fluency-affect link is only valid for intuitions of semantic coherence or also for other intuitive paradigms. This was addressed in additional experiments reviewed in the following section.

Fluency and affect also determine intuitions of Gestalt and grammaticality

In further research, we generalized the fluency-affect link proposed in FAIM to other classical examples of intuitions in cognitive psychology, namely to *artificial grammar learning* (Pothos, 2007; Reber, 1967) and to visual *Gestalt intuitions* (Bowers et al., 1990). Although already semantic coherence seems a rather affect-free phenomenon – and thus affective influences in such a task are surprising – artificial grammaticality and visual Gestalt seem even more distant to affective processes, since they employ abstract and meaningless (grammaticality) or neutral (Gestalt) stimuli. Nevertheless, processing ease and particularly affective responses might also mediate these intuitive performances, as shown in the following.

Artificial grammar learning

Surely the most well-known demonstration of intuition is the paradigm of artificial grammar learning (Reber, 1967). In this paradigm, participants study examples of neutral letter strings that conform to a hidden rule (or grammar) that is so complex that recognizing the rule consciously, and thus using this explicit knowledge in later judgments, is beyond human capability (Pothos, 2007; Reber, 1967). Then, in a later test phase, participants receive novel letter strings, some of which conform to the rule of the studied strings, and some of which do not. When forced to guess whether a given string conforms to the earlier rule (the grammar) or not, participants can reliably discriminate above chance grammatical from agrammatical strings (for a review, see Pothos, 2007) without being able to justify their guess (Reber, 1967).

For this task, fluency has already been shown to be a causal determinant (as already theoretically proposed by Servan-Schreiber & Anderson, 1990) of grammaticality judgments, since Buchner (1994) showed that grammatical strings are more efficiently processed than agrammatical strings, and Kinder, Shanks, Cock, and Tunney (2003) showed that increasing visual fluency of strings leads to higher probabilities of judging a string to be coherent. Furthermore, at least deductively, there is even evidence that grammaticality is also associated with affective responses, since it has been shown that grammatical strings are liked more than agrammatical strings (Gordon & Holyoak, 1983).

Thus, we manipulated fluency and affect simultaneously in an artificial grammar task (Topolinski & Strack, 2009b, Experiment 11). Specifically, in the test phase, we manipulated the visual fluency of strings by figure-ground contrast and current affect by subliminal facial primes. Once again, while the likelihood of judging a given string as being grammatical was reliably higher for actually grammatical than for agrammatical strings (the basic effect), it was also higher for highly fluent compared to disfluent strings, and positively primed compared to negatively primed strings. All main effects were reliable, but not any of the interaction effects (Topolinski & Strack, 2009b, Experiment 11).

Gestalt intuitions

Yet another intuition paradigm is *visual Gestalts* (Bowers et al., 1990). In this task, participants receive black-and-white drawings of everyday objects, with the drawing visually degraded and distorted to such a degree that the object cannot be verbally identified anymore, yet its visual Gestalt remains intact. From these Gestalt-like images, purely random but perceptually similar images are constructed by randomly intermixing parts of the image. When participants are presented such Gestalt-like, yet unidentifiable, images along with completely random visual noise images and are asked to guess whether the current image depicts a real object, they can reliably discriminate Gestalt from random images above chance, without being able to name the object, which again, is an intuitive judgment.

We employed repeated exposure (see above) as the fluency manipulation, and subliminal facial primes as the affect manipulation; as above, these variables were orthogonal to actual Gestaltness. Once again, we detected three independent main effects of Gestalt, fluency, and affect in the same direction as in the above-reviewed experiments (Topolinski & Strack, 2009b, Experiment 10). In sum, a causal fluency-affect link also appears to exist in other intuitions in addition to intuitions of semantic coherence, namely in intuitions of grammaticality and visual Gestalt.

Conclusion of the FAIM and connections to dual-process theories of reasoning

In conclusion, the presently reviewed research demonstrates how the cognitive dynamics of processing efficiency and the resulting affective consequences form the causal architecture of intuitive judgments. The affective input into these judgments is particularly interesting in light of the claim that intuitions –epistemologically and psychologically – fall between feelings and rational judgments (e.g., Kahneman, 2003; Thompson et al., 2011).

A question closely related to this intermediate state between feeling and thinking is where intuitive judgments are generally located in the topology of current dual-process theories (e.g., Smith & DeCoster, 2000). These accounts hold that reasoning (Evans, 2007), but also any other psychological faculty (Stanovich & West, 2000; Strack & Deutsch, 2004), is determined by two independent systems, an associative primary system that is fast, effortless (e.g., System 1, Stanovich & West, 2000; Type 1, Evans, 2007) and impulsive (Strack & Deutsch, 2004), and a propositional secondary system that is slow, effortful (e.g., System 2, Stanovich & West, 2000; Type 2, Evans, 2007) and reflective (Strack & Deutsch, 2004). Generally, intuitions are mapped with System 1 by conceptualizing that any automatic output from System 1 that is not further elaborated or corrected by

System 2 is an intuition (e.g., Kahneman, 2003; Evans, 2007; see Thompson et al., 2011, for inductions how System 2 engagement can be triggered). Integrating the current fluency-affect link into dual-process accounts, one might posit that fluency, which arises from automatically occurring processing dynamics in the associative store, and affect, which is an automatically triggered hedonic consequence of fluency, are Type 1 processes, while the eventual intuitive judgment that uses affect as a judgmental cue is a product of Type 2 processes (see Topolinski & Strack, 2009a, 2009d, for a detailed account of this).

Implications of the FAIM for reasoning and memory

In the following section, I propose some future avenues for research that apply the fluency-affect link to judgments concerning meta-memory and reasoning. The overarching hypothesis is that any judgment that draws on processing fluency might also be causally mediated by (or at least might be susceptible to) affective cues. This research agenda would introduce the causal role of affect that stems from memory-retrieval and reasoning processes to a variety of cognitive phenomena.

Judgments of solvability (JOS) (Ackerman & Thompson, this volume; Thompson, 2009), or also judgments of rightness (i.e., the faith in an initial solution intuition, Thompson et al., 2011)

Given that high fluency and positive affect increase the initial hunch that a problem is solvable, the prediction to be tested is whether individuals would also invest more time and effort in a cognitive problem, such as water-jar problems or anagrams (Novick & Sherman, 2003; Payne & Duggan, 2011) when this problem is presented with high fluency and a concomitant positive affect. Interestingly, this prediction runs counter to the general *cognitive tuning* prediction (Clore et al., 2001) that positive, relative to negative, affective states normally reduce effortful processing (such as low compared to high fluency increases effortful processing, Alter, Oppenheimer, Epley, & Eyre, 2007). The crucial difference might be, however, that individuals used their current affective state as a meta-reasoning cue for the solvability of a problem. If they discounted affect as a cue, as, for instance, when they are told that all of the problems they are faced with are actually solvable, then positive should be less solvable than negative items (according to cognitive tuning, Clore et al., 2001). In contrast, if they relied on affect as a cue to guide their cognitive investment into the task, as, for instance, when they are told that only some of the problems would actually be solvable and they should decide beforehand in which of the problems to invest time, positive items should be solved more frequently than negative ones.

Feeling of knowing (FOK)

Given that FOKs (see above) rely on both the encoding fluency of the memory question and the retrieval fluency of memory content (Koriat & Levy-Sadot,

2001), it is highly likely that FOKs can also be influenced by brief affective responses. In support of this hypothesis is the finding that the probability of feeling that something is on the "tip of the tongue" was increased for emotionally arousing compared to neutral items (Schwartz, 2010). However, in that study, valence itself was not an independent factor of the experimental design. The FAIM, however, predicts that positive compared to negative emotional content would increase the likelihood of a FOK (since it signals the positive feeling of a successful memory search). In future research, both the valence of questions and the valence of the to-be-retrieved answers should be manipulated independently to assess the affective impact on FOKs.

Judgments of learning (JOL)

In JOLs, individuals judge the probability that they will recall a recently learned item on a later recall attempt. Like other meta-memory judgments, this meta-mnemonic judgment draws on heuristic cues. According to the cue-utilization view (Koriat, 1997), these comprise intrinsic (e.g., word imagery value), extrinsic (e.g., conditions of learning), and, most important for the present argumentation, mnemomic cues, such as phenomenlogical experiences during learning. Fluency, as well as affect, falls into this third category of cues. While fluency manipulations have been shown to affect JOLs, with higher fluency increasing judged probability of later successful retrieval (Rhodes & Castel, 2008; but see Koriat & Ma'ayan, 2005, for a more differentiated pattern regarding encoding and retrieval fluency manipulations), the impact of affective cues has yet to be demonstrated.

Again, FAIM predicts that relative to negatively valenced material and concomitant negative affective cues (such as flashed faces or sounds, Topolinski & Deutsch, 2013), positive cues would increase JOLs. A corollary to this question is how phasic affect during study would influence the actual performance during later recall, since JOLs and actual recall performance are not necessarily related. The (perceptual) fluency manipulation in Rhodes and Castel (2008), for instance, increased JOLs, but left later recall performance unaffected. In contrast, the cognitive-tuning hypothesis (Clore et al., 2001), which predicts less thorough encoding and elaboration under positive compared to negative affect, would predict that valence of study material (or brief stimulus-unrelated affective state during study) would have an opposite impact on later recall than it has on JOLs, with decreased performance for positive compared to negative trials.

Subjective confidence and insight

While prior work has shown retrieval fluency to be a mediating force behind the subjective confidence in having an insight or finding an answer to a reasoning problem (e.g., Kelley & Lindsay, 1993), affective precursors of subjective confidence have not yet been investigated. Recently, a theoretical account of such affective determinants has been sketched by Topolinski and Reber (2010a; see also

Topolinski & Deutsch, 2012) who developed a fluency-affect account for the subjective experience of having an insight. Again, phasic positive affect has been identified as a causal contributor to this feeling. Consequently, FAIM predicts that subjective confidence would be enhanced by positivity stemming either from the material an insight is generated from, or from the insight idea itself.

Conclusion

A procedural model of intuition is reviewed that highlights affective components as causal mechanisms in intuitive judgments. Furthermore, future research questions are developed that apply a fluency-*affect* link also for intuitions in memory and reasoning.

Author's note

I thank Rakefet Ackerman and Valerie Thompson for their stimulating and rigorous input into this chapter. This review is partially based on the author's doctoral dissertation. I thank Fritz Strack for his great input into the original research.

References

Ackerman, R., & Thompson, V. (this volume). Meta-reasoning: What can we learn from meta-memory? In A. Feeney & V. Thompson (Eds.), *Reasoning as Memory*.

Alter, A. L., Oppenheimer, D. M., Epley, N., & Eyre, R. N. (2007). Overcoming intuition: Metacognitive difficulty activates analytic reasoning. *Journal of Experimental Psychology: General, 136*, 569–576.

Baumann, N., & Kuhl, J. (2002). Intuition, affect, and personality: Unconscious coherence judgments and self-regulation of negative affect. *Journal of Personality and Social Psychology, 83*, 1213–1223.

Bechara, A., Damasio, H., Tranel, D., & Damasio, A. R. (1997). Deciding advantageously before knowing the advantageous strategy. *Science, 275*, 1293–1294.

Beeman, M., Friedman, R. B., Grafman, J., Perez, E., Diamond, S., & Beadle Lindsay, M. (1994). Summation priming and coarse semantic coding in the right hemisphere. *Journal of Cognitive Neuroscience, 6*, 26–45.

Bolte, A., & Goschke, T. (2005). On the speed of intuition: Intuitive judgments of semantic coherence under different response deadlines. *Memory & Cognition, 33*, 1248–1255.

Bolte, A., Goschke, T., & Kuhl, J. (2003). Emotion and intuition: Effects of positive and negative mood on implicit judgments of semantic coherence. *Psychological Science, 14*(5), 416–421.

Bornstein, R. F. (1989). Exposure and affect: Overview and meta-analysis of research, 1968–1987. *Psychological Bulletin, 106*, 265–289.

Bornstein, R. F., and D'Agostino, P. R. (1994). The attribution and discounting of perceptual fluency: Preliminary tests of a perceptual fluency/attributional model of the mere exposure effect. *Social Cognition 12*, 103–128.

Bowden, E. M. & Jung-Beeman, M. (2003). One hundred forty-four compound remote associate problems: Short insight-like problems with one-word solutions. *Behavioral Research, Methods, Instruments, and Computers, 35*, 634–639.

Bowden, E. M., Jung-Beeman, M., Fleck, J., & Kounios, J. (2005). New approaches to demystifying insight. *Trends in Cognitive Sciences, 9*, 322–328.

Bowers, K. S., Regehr, G., Balthazard, C., & Parker, K. (1990). Intuition in the context of discovery. *Cognitive Psychology, 22*, 72–110.

Buchner, A. (1994). Indirect effects of synthetic grammar learning in an identification task. *Journal of Experimental Psychology: Learning, Memory, and Cognition, 20*, 550–566.

Cacioppo, J. T., Petty, R. E., Losch, M. E., & Kim, H. S. (1986). Electromyographic activity over facial muscle regions can differentiate the valence and intensity of affective reactions. *Journal of Personality and Social Psychology, 50*, 260–268.

Clore, G. L., Wyer, R. S. J., Dienes, B., Gasper, K., Gohm, C., & Isbell, L. (2001). Affective feelings as feedback: Some cognitive consequences. In L. L. Martin & G. L. Clore (Eds.), *Theories of Mood and Cognition: A User's Guidebook* (pp. 27–62). Mahwah, NJ: Lawrence Erlbaum.

De Neys, W. (2012). Bias and conflict: A case for logical intuitions. *Perspectives on Psychological Science, 7*(1), 28–38.

De Neys, W., Rossi, S., & Houdé, O. (2013). Bats, balls, and substitution sensitivity: Cognitive misers are no happy fools. *Psychonomic Bulletin & Review, 20*, 269–273.

Dijksterhuis, A. (2004). Think different: The merits of unconscious thought in preference development and decision making. *Journal of Personality and Social Psychology, 87*, 586–598.

Epstein, S. (2008). Intuition from the perspective of cognitive-experiential self-theory. In H. Plessner, C. Betsch, & T. Betsch (Eds.), *Intuition in Judgment and Decision Making*. Mahwah, NJ: Lawrence Erlbaum.

Evans, J. St. B. T. (2007). *Hypothetical Thinking: Dual Processes in Reasoning and Judgment*. New York: Psychology Press.

Frank, M. J., O'Reilly, R. C., & Curran, T. (2006). When memory fails, intuition reigns. Midazolam enhances implicit inference in humans. *Psychological Science, 17*, 700–707.

Gordon, P. C., & Holyoak, K. J. (1983). Implicit learning and generalization of the "mere exposure" effect. *Journal of Personality and Social Psychology, 45*, 492–500.

Harkins, S. (2006). Mere effort as the mediator of the evaluation-performance relationship. *Journal of Personality and Social Psychology, 91*(3), 436–455.

Harmon-Jones, E., & Allen, J. B. (2001). The role of affect in the mere exposure effect: Evidence from psychophysiological and individual differences approaches. *Personality and Social Psychology Bulletin, 27*, 889–898.

Jacoby, L. L., Kelley, C. M., Brown, J., & Jasechko, J. (1989). Becoming famous overnight: Limits on the ability to avoid unconscious influences of the past. *Journal of Personality and Social Psychology, 56*, 326–338.

Kahneman, D. (2003). A perspective on judgment and choice: Mapping bounded rationality. *American Psychologists, 58*, 697–720.

Kelley, C. M., & Lindsay, D. S. (1993). Remembering mistaken for knowing: Ease of retrieval as a basis for confidence in answers to general knowledge questions. *Journal of Memory and Language, 32*(1), 1–24.

Kihlstrom, J. F. (1999). The psychological unconscious. In L. R. Pervin & O. John (Eds.), *Handbook of Personality*, 2nd edn. (pp. 424–442). New York: Guilford.

Kinder, A., Shanks, D. R., Cock, J., & Tunney, R. J. (2003). Recollection, fluency, and the explicit/implicit distinction in artificial grammar learning. *Journal of Experimental Psychology: General, 132*, 551–565.

Koriat, A. (1993). How do we know that we know? The accessibility model of the feeling of knowing. *Psychological Review, 100*(4), 609–639.

Koriat, A. (1997). Monitoring one's own knowledge during study: A cue-utilization approach to judgments of learning. *Journal of Experimental Psychology: General, 126,* 349–370.

Koriat, A. (2012). The self-consistency model of subjective confidence. *Psychological Review, 119,* 80–113.

Koriat, A., & Levy-Sadot, R. (2001). The combined contributions of the cue-familiarity and accessibility heuristics to feelings of knowing. *Journal of Experimental Psychology: Learning, Memory, and Cognition, 27*(1), 34–53.

Koriat, A., & Ma'ayan, H. (2005). The effects of encoding fluency and retrieval fluency on judgments of learning. *Journal of Memory and Language, 52,* 478–492.

Larsen, R. J., Kasimatis, M., & Frey, K. (1992). Facilitating the furrowed brow: An unobtrusive test of the facial feedback hypothesis applied to unpleasant affect. *Cognition & Emotion, 6*(5), 321–338.

Leder, H., Bär, S., & Topolinski, S. (2013). Covert painting simulations influence aesthetic appreciation of artworks. *Psychological Science, 23*(12), 1479–1481.

Mednick, S. A. (1962). The associative basis of the creative process. *Psychological Review, 69,* 220–232.

Moreland, R. L., & Topolinski, S. (2010). The mere exposure phenomenon: A lingering melody by Robert Zajonc. *Emotion Review, 2*(4), 329–339.

Murphy, S. T., & Zajonc, R. B. (1993). Affect, cognition and awareness: Affective priming with optimal and suboptimal stimulus exposures. *Journal of Personality and Social Psychology, 64,* 723–739.

Novick, L. R., & Sherman, S. J. (2003). On the nature of insight solutions: Evidence from skill differences in anagram solution. *The Quarterly Journal of Experimental Psychology, 56*(2), 351–382.

Payne, S. J., & Duggan, G. B. (2011). Giving up problem solving. *Memory & Cognition, 39*(5), 902–913.

Pothos, E. M. (2007). Theories of artificial grammar learning. *Psychological Bulletin, 133,* 227–244.

Reber, A. S. (1967). Implicit learning of artificial grammars. *Journal of Verbal Learning and Verbal Behavior, 6,* 855–863.

Reber, R., & Schwarz, N. (1999). Effects of perceptual fluency on judgments of truth. *Consciousness and Cognition, 8,* 338–342.

Reber, R., Schwarz, N., & Winkielman, P. (2004). Processing fluency and aesthetic pleasure: Is beauty in the perceiver's processing experience? *Personality and Social Psychology Review, 8,* 364–382.

Reber, R., Winkielman, P., & Schwarz, N. (1998). Effects of perceptual fluency on affective judgments. *Psychological Science, 9*(1), 45–48.

Reber, R., Wurtz, P., & Zimmermann, T. D. (2004). Exploring "fringe" consciousness: The subjective experience of perceptual fluency and its objective bases. *Consciousness and Cognition, 13,* 47–60.

Rhodes, M. G., & Castel, A. D. (2008). Memory predictions are influenced by perceptual information: Evidence for metacognitive illusions. *Journal of Experimental Psychology: General, 137*(4), 615–625.

Schwartz, B. L. (2010). The effects of emotion on tip-of-the-tongue states. *Psychonomic Bulletin & Review, 17*(1), 82–87.

Servan-Schreiber, E., & Anderson, J. R. (1990). Learning artificial grammars with competitive chunking. *Journal of Experimental Psychology: Learning, Memory, and Cognition, 16,* 592–608.

Smith, E. R., & DeCoster, J. (2000). Dual process models in social and cognitive psychology: Conceptual integration and links to underlying memory systems. *Personality and Social Psychology Review, 4,* 108–131.

Stanovich, K. E., & West, R. F. (2000). Individual differences in reasoning: Implications for the rationality debate? *Behavioral and Brain Sciences, 23*(5), 645–665.

Strack, F., & Deutsch, R. (2004). Reflective and impulsive determinants of social behavior. *Personality and Social Psychology Review, 8,* 220–247.

Strack, F., Martin, L., & Stepper, S. (1988). Inhibiting and facilitating conditions of the human smile: A nonobtrusive test of the facial feedback hypothesis. *Journal of Personality and Social Psychology, 54,* 768–777.

Thompson, V. A. (2009). Dual process theories: A metacognitive perspective. In J. Evans & K. Frankish (Eds.), *In Two Minds: Dual Processes and Beyond* (pp. 171–195). Oxford: Oxford University Press.

Thompson, V. A., Prowse Turner, J., & Pennycook, G. (2011). Intuition, reason, and metacognition. *Cognitive Psychology, 63*(3), 107–140.

Thompson, V. A., Turner, J. A. P., Pennycook, G., Ball, L. J., Brack, H., Ophir, Y., & Ackerman, R. (2013). The role of answer fluency and perceptual fluency as metacognitive cues for initiating analytic thinking. *Cognition.*

Topolinski, S. (2010). Moving the eye of the beholder: Motor components in vision determine aesthetic preference. *Psychological Science, 21*(9), 1220–1224.

Topolinski, S. (2011). A process model of intuition. *European Review of Social Psychology, 22*(1), 274–315.

Topolinski, S. (2012). The sensorimotor contributions to implicit memory, familiarity, and recollection. *Journal of Experimental Psychology: General, 14*(2), 260–281.

Topolinski, S. (2014). A processing fluency-account of funniness: Running gags and spoiling punchlines (in press). *Cognition and Emotion, 28*(5), 811–820.

Topolinski, S., & Deutsch, R. (2012). Phasic affective modulation of creativity. *Experimental Psychology, 59*(5), 302–310.

Topolinski, S., & Deutsch, R. (2013). Phasic affective modulation of semantic priming. *Journal of Experimental Psychology: Learning, Memory, and Cognition, 39,* 414–436.

Topolinski, S., & Hertel, G. (2007). The role of personality in psychotherapists' careers: Relationships between personality traits, therapeutic schools, and job satisfaction. *Psychotherapy Research, 17*(3), 378–390.

Topolinski, S., & Reber, R. (2010a). Gaining insight into the "Aha"-experience. *Current Directions in Psychological Science, 19*(6), 402–405.

Topolinski, S., & Reber, R. (2010b). Immediate truth – Temporal contiguity between a cognitive problem and its solution determines experienced veracity of the solution. *Cognition, 114,* 117–122.

Topolinski, S., & Strack, F. (2008). Where there's a will – there's no intuition: The unintentional basis of semantic coherence judgments. *Journal of Memory and Language, 58*(4), 1032–1048.

Topolinski, S., & Strack, F. (2009a). The analysis of intuition: Processing fluency and affect in judgements of semantic coherence. *Cognition and Emotion, 23*(8),1465–1503.

Topolinski, S., & Strack, F. (2009b). The architecture of intuition: Fluency and affect determine intuitive judgments of semantic and visual coherence, and of grammaticality in artificial grammar learning. *Journal of Experimental Psychology: General, 138*(1), 39–63.

Topolinski, S., & Strack, F. (2009c). Motormouth: Mere exposure depends on stimulus-specific motor simulations. *Journal of Experimental Psychology: Learning, Memory, and Cognition, 35*(2), 423–433.

Topolinski, S., & Strack, F. (2009d). Scanning the "fringe" of consciousness: What is felt and what is not felt in intuitions about semantic coherence. *Consciousness and Cognition, 18,* 608–618.

Topolinski, S., & Strack, F. (2010). False fame prevented – avoiding fluency-effects without judgmental correction. *Journal of Personality and Social Psychology, 98*(5), 721–733.

Topolinski, S., Likowski, K. U., Weyers, P., & Strack, F. (2009). The face of fluency: Semantic coherence automatically elicits a specific pattern of facial muscle reactions. *Cognition and Emotion, 23*(2), 260–271.

Topolinski, S., Lindner, S., & Freudenberg, A. (2014). Popcorn in the cinema: Oral interference sabotages advertising effects. *Journal of Consumer Psychology, 24*(2), 167–176.

Unkelbach, C. (2007). Reversing the truth effect: Learning the interpretation of processing fluency in judgments of truth. *Journal of Experimental Psychology: Learning, Memory, and Cognition, 33,* 219–230.

Vaughan, F. E. (1979). *Awakening Intuition.* Garden City, NJ: Anchor Press/Doubleday.

Volz, K. G., & von Cramon, D. Y. (2006). What neuroscience can tell about intuitive processes in the context of perceptual discovery. *Journal of Cognitive Neuroscience, 18*(12), 2077–2087.

Whittlesea, B. W. A. (1993). Illusions of familiarity. *Journal of Experimental Psychology: Learning, Memory, and Cognition, 19,* 1235–1253.

Winkielman, P., & Cacioppo, J. T. (2001). Mind at ease puts a smile on the face: Psychophysiological evidence that processing facilitation leads to positive affect. *Journal of Personality and Social Psychology, 81,* 989–1000.

Yaniv, I., & Meyer, D. E. (1987). Activation and metacognition of inaccessible stored information: Potential bases for incubation effects in problem solving. *Journal of Experimental Psychology: Learning, Memory, and Cognition, 2,* 187–205.

Zajonc, R. B. (1968). Attitudinal effects of mere exposure. *Journal of Personality and Social Psychology Monographs, 9*(2, 2), 1–27.

9

META-REASONING

What can we learn from meta-memory?

Rakefet Ackerman and Valerie A. Thompson

The past few decades have witnessed a surge of research in the area of metacognition in general, and meta-memory in particular. The foundational principles for this work were articulated in the framework developed by Nelson and Narens (1990). Although there have been substantial developments since then, the basic principles articulated there remain widely accepted (see Bjork, Dunlosky, & Kornell, 2013). These differentiate object-level from meta-level cognition: meta-level processes monitor and regulate ongoing object-level processes. To date, the bulk of the metacognitive literature is focused on the processes associated with learning, particularly, memorizing word lists. Here, object-level processes involve the transfer of information from an external source to the learner's memory system via one or more learning strategies (e.g., rehearsal, imagery, elaboration, etc.). The meta-level regulates these processes by setting goals, deciding among appropriate strategies, monitoring their progress and terminating an activity (Bjork et al., 2013).

Although these basic principles are clearly relevant for regulating the performance of many other cognitive tasks, relatively little is known about the meta-level processes involved in them. The present chapter is focused on meta-level processes involved in reasoning, including tasks such as logical reasoning, and problem solving. In some respects, there are strong analogies that can be made between meta-memory and meta-reasoning. For example, some reasoning tasks may be solved by retrieving an answer from memory. However, others cannot be solved in that way, and instead rely on deliberate, working-memory demanding processes that evolve over time (see Beilock & DeCaro, 2007). Even when a solution can be retrieved from memory, higher-order cognitive processes may be recruited to evaluate the adequacy of the answer and consider alternatives. Nevertheless, the meta-level in this context will involve processes that are similar to those that regulate learning, such as setting goals, deciding among strategies, monitoring progress and terminating an activity.

We first provide an overview of object-level processes in reasoning and then highlight well-established principles of meta-memory, with a focus on those that we think most appropriate for drawing analogies to reasoning. Our second goal is to consider ways in which the meta-level of reasoning may necessitate qualitatively different processes than those postulated to monitor and regulate memory. Finally, as the literature in meta-reasoning is in its infancy, one of our primary goals is to suggest productive avenues for further research, specifically with regards to meta-level processes unique to reasoning.

A. Object-level processes in reasoning

Our analysis of object-level processes in reasoning derives from a Dual Process perspective, which suggests that high-level cognition is accomplished by two qualitatively different types of processes (Evans & Stanovich, 2013). Type 1 processes are autonomous processes that are executed in the presence of their triggering conditions. These can produce instant judgments based on categorization, stereotypes, affect, linguistic processes, and memory retrievals (see Kahneman, 2003; Stanovich, 2004 for detailed analyses). Type 2 processes are differentiated from Type 1 processes by the fact that they require effortful thinking (Evans & Stanovich, 2013). These processes include inhibiting the prepotent Type 1 response, considering alternative responses, hypothetical thinking, searching memory for confirmatory or disconfirmatory evidence, applying rules of probability and logic, etc. We should note that there is no sharp distinction between the domains that are served by each type of process. In particular, there are processes, like memory retrieval and categorization, that can both be accomplished by instant Type 1 and by deliberate Type 2 processing.

The key assumption from a Dual Process perspective is that Type 1 processes can occur autonomously, and suggest an immediate answer to reasoning challenges, as per the two examples below. The reasoning and decision making literature is replete with dozens of such tasks, which are designed to promote an intuitive, but erroneous, initial answer (see Kahneman, 2011; Lehrer, 2009 for descriptions of real-world decisions that are similarly misleading). These initial answers can be overridden by Type 2 processes.

EXAMPLE 1:

If it takes 5 machines 5 minutes to make 5 widgets, how long will it take 100 machines to make 100 widgets? _____ minutes.

(Frederick, 2005)

(100 is the immediate answer, while 5 is the correct one)

EXAMPLE 2:

Please generate a word, which when combined with each of the three following words would result in a common compound word or phrase: PLATE, BROKEN, SHOT.

(Wiley, 1998)

('home' comes immediately to mind, but fits only the first two words; 'glass' is correct)

In other cases, when no instant solution comes to mind, the problem can only be solved by recourse to explicit, working-memory demanding (Type 2) processes, as per the examples below. For solving such challenging tasks, deliberate processing is required to represent the problem information, and/or for applying strategies such as means end analysis, hypothetical thinking, rules of logic and probability, and others (see Wang & Chiew, 2010).

EXAMPLE 3:

Some of the artists are not beekeepers.
None of the carpenters are beekeepers.
Therefore, does it follows that none of the carpenters are artists?

('no' is correct)

EXAMPLE 4:

Generate a word, which when combined with each of the three following words would result in a common compound word or phrase: PEA, SHELL, CHEST.

(Bowden & Jung-Beeman, 2003)

('nut' is the correct answer provided after 30 sec. by only 23% of the sample)

The role of meta-reasoning processes in this framework is to determine the circumstances under which the initial Type 1 process suffices and when the more effortful Type 2 processes should be engaged (De Neys, 2012; Thompson, 2009). Meta-reasoning processes are also engaged during Type 2 processes for estimating the probability of success, judging progress towards a solution, and for allocating working-memory resources, selecting among potential solving strategies, and deciding when the process should be terminated (Ackerman, in press; Payne & Duggan, 2011). We now introduce the meta-memory processes that may form a useful basis for theorizing about meta-reasoning processes.

B. Meta-memory judgments

Metacognitive monitoring of memory begins when the "to-be-remembered" item is encountered and continues during encoding and retrieval of the item (Nelson & Narens, 1990). Monitoring processes assess the outcome of the object-level process, estimate the probability of successful recall, and regulate the amount and type of effort allocated to achieve one's goals. Table 1 summarizes the monitoring processes that we believe most likely to provide useful analogies to meta-reasoning. The table also includes the meta-reasoning judgment we see as being closest in nature to each meta-memory judgment. We begin by providing a brief introduction to each meta-memory judgment and the activities it is hypothesized to control.

TABLE 9.1 Parallels between meta-memory and meta-reasoning judgments.

Name	Meta-memory judgment Object	Reference time	Meta-reasoning judgment
Ease of Learning (EOL)	A particular study item or a complex study unit	Future	Judgment of Solvability (JOS)
Judgment of Learning (JOL)	A particular study item (e.g., a word)	Future	Judgments of ongoing reasoning processes
Judgment of Comprehension, comprehension rating or metacomprehension judgment	A complex study unit (e.g., a text)	Present	Judgments of ongoing reasoning processes
Prediction of Performance	A complex study unit	Future	Judgments of ongoing reasoning processes
Feeling of Knowing (FOK)	A particular test question	Future	Judgments of ongoing reasoning processes
Feeling of Familiarity (FOF)	A particular memory retrieval	Present	Feeling of Rightness (FOR)
Confidence	A particular test answer	Present	Final Confidence Judgment (FCJ)

All the monitoring judgments that we describe are thought to be based on heuristic cues (Koriat, 1997; see Dunlosky & Tauber, 2014 for a review). On this view, people do not have direct access to their underlying cognitive processes, and instead, base their judgments on the cues that are available to them. One such cue is fluency (the ease or speed with which a cognitive task is completed), which is thought to underlie most meta-memory judgments. For example, easy or efficient processing of an item gives rise to the attribution that the item has been previously experienced, even when it has not (Jacoby, Kelley, & Dywan, 1989; Whittlesea, Jacoby, & Girard, 1990). The potentially misleading nature of the heuristic cues highlights the fact that meta-level judgments are independent from object-level processes, i.e., the cognitive processes themselves. Consequently, the predictive accuracy of these judgments depends greatly on the diagnosticity of the cues that underlie them.

Ease of Learning (EOL) judgment

EOLs are judgments of how easy or difficult something will be to learn, and are usually made after a brief exposure to the to-be-remembered item and before deliberate learning is undertaken. EOLs are thought to control the choice of processing strategy (Nelson & Narens, 1990) as well as the amount of effort invested in the task. For example, participants will allocate more study time to those items that they deem to be difficult (e.g., Son & Metcalfe, 2000). Interestingly, however, this effect reverses under time pressure, both for word pairs and complex texts (Son & Metcalfe, 2000; Thiede & Dunlosky, 1999). Thus, when the time is limited, people skip the items they judge to be time consuming and strategically invest effort in easier ones.

Studies have shown EOLs, like other monitoring judgments, have low to medium predictive value for test performance (e.g., Karpicke, 2009). Koriat (1997) suggested that EOLs are based on participants' a priori beliefs about how easy or challenging items of this type are to learn (see also Dunlosky & Tauber, 2014). Thus, the predictive value of EOLs will vary as a function of how well calibrated these a priori beliefs are with actual difficulty.

In the next section, we consider Judgments of Solvability (JOS; Thompson, 2009) as a possible analogue to EOLs in reasoning.

Judgment of Learning (JOL)

JOLs concern the likelihood of remembering a particular item at a later recall attempt and are hypothesized to control the allocation of study time during learning. One model of how this is achieved is the discrepancy reduction model (Nelson & Narens, 1990), which suggests that people set a target that reflects their current motivation to succeed. They monitor their progress, studying each item until their knowledge is judged satisfactory (see Figure 1 in Ackerman & Goldsmith, 2011 for illustration). The control function of JOLs was revealed by the finding that, when JOLs were experimentally manipulated to deviate from actual degree of learning, it was the JOLs, rather than degree of learning, that predicted later study time (Metcalfe & Finn, 2008). Below, we suggest analogous mechanisms by which reasoners may regulate the effort they invest in problem solving.

JOLs, like other metacognitive judgments, are thought to be based on heuristic cues (Koriat, 1997). Koriat, Ma'ayan, and Nussinson (2006) suggested that people use a memorizing effort heuristic, in which longer learning times (i.e., lower fluency) indicate a lower probability that it will later be recalled. In most cases, this heuristic is reliable, as items that take longer to learn are, indeed, harder to recall. Other cues are less reliable, for example, when JOLs are based on surface properties of the to-be-learned items. Rhodes and Castel (2008) had college students memorize words, half of which were printed in large font. JOLs were significantly higher for words printed in large font than those printed in smaller font, while recall did not differ as a function of font size. Conversely, there are variables that have large effects on performance to which JOLs are less sensitive: Rehearsal improves recall, and long delays between learning and test cause substantial forgetting, yet JOLs are not very sensitive to either (Koriat, 1997). Thus, the accuracy of JOLs, like other metacognitive judgments, depends on the validity of the utilized cues. The analogy to meta-reasoning suggests that the accuracy of judgments that accompany reasoning also depends on the reliability of the underlying heuristic cues.

Judgment of comprehension, comprehension rating, metacomprehension judgment, and predictions of performance

Arguably, memorizing words provides few parallels to reasoning, given the discrepancy in the amount of time and effort required. However, metacognitive processes have also been studied in the context of learning from texts, which involves more complex object-level and meta-level processes. The object-level involves multi-level processing of word meaning and the integrative understanding of high-order ideas (Kintsch, 1998). The meta-level is correspondingly multi-dimensional and involves monitoring of memory for details and of higher-order comprehension (Ackerman & Goldsmith, 2011; Thiede, Wiley, & Griffin, 2011), and which can focus either on the current level of comprehension (Ackerman & Leiser, 2014; Zaromb, Karpicke, & Roediger, 2010) or on predicting future test performance (e.g., Ackerman & Goldsmith, 2011; Maki, 1998). As was the case for JOLs, these judgments predict the allocation of study time (Thiede, Anderson, & Therriault, 2003).

The discrepancy reduction model described above (Nelson & Narens, 1990) has been adapted to these more complex tasks. Ackerman and Goldsmith (2011) had undergraduate students study texts that took about 9–10 minutes to learn. In one condition, participants stopped every 3 minutes, provided a prediction of performance based on their knowledge, and decided explicitly whether to continue or to take the test. The pattern of intermediate ratings followed a power law, consistent with the classic learning curve (Ebbinghaus, 1885/1964): Judgments started low, increased quickly and then levelled off, presumably at participants' stopping criterion. Below, we outline parallels between this regulation of effort and that occurring during reasoning (see section regarding ongoing judgments).

Unlike JOLs, judgments of comprehension have been found to have little predictive validity for performance (see Dunlosky & Lipko, 2007). One reason might be that it is difficult to judge the state of one's learning when there is uncertainty about the information that will be solicited at test. Another is that monitoring of comprehension has been found to rely on misleading surface-level cues. For example, the presence of illustrations can increase the *perceived* comprehensibility of the text (Chandler & Sweller, 1991; Serra & Dunlosky, 2010) and mislead the regulatory processes like those that underlie allocation of study time (Ackerman & Leiser, 2014).

Feeling of Knowing (FOK)

While the preceding judgments are used to monitor learning, FOK is associated with testing. The FOK is typically a judgment about the probability of recognizing the answer to a question (e.g., "In which city is the Uffizi Gallery located?", Costermans, Lories, & Ansay, 1992) on a subsequent multiple-choice test. In cases where the answer to the question is currently unrecallable, FOKs have been shown to control the amount of effort participants invest in the item. For example, Reder and Ritter (1992) presented participants with a long list of arithmetic problems (e.g., 23 * 34). Some of the problems were presented several times, so that participants could retrieve their solution quickly instead of engaging in effortful calculations. Immediately after presentation, the participants had to quickly decide whether they could retrieve the solution from memory or would have to calculate it. Participants who had previously encountered problems with similar components (e.g., 23 + 34), tended to mistakenly indicate that they could retrieve the answer from memory. Thus, familiar components misled the participants to expect quick retrieval even for novel problems. Below, we propose that Judgement of Solvability and Feeling of Rightness exert a similar monitoring and regulatory function in reasoning.

Two heuristic cues are known to underlie FOKs. The first cue is the familiarity of the question terms. The above-described study by Reder and Ritter (1992) is a case in point (see also Costermans et al., 1992). The second cue is accessibility, which reflects the number of associations that come to mind during a retrieval attempt, regardless of whether this information contributes to retrieving the correct answer (Koriat, 1993). For example, Koriat and Levy-Sadot (2001) composed general knowledge questions that differed in the familiarity of the terms (e.g., the ballets *Swan Lake* vs. *The Legend of Joseph*) and in accessibility, which was operationalized as the amount of names people can provide for a category (e.g., people tend to know more composers than choreographers). These cues contributed additively to FOKs, such that FOKs were higher for the more familiar objects, but this effect was more pronounced for the highly accessible items.

Feeling of Familiarity (FOF)

Jacoby and his colleagues (Jacoby et al., 1989) referred to the FOF as the *sine qua non* of remembering, without which a retrieval experience would not be labelled as a memory and have a sense of "pastness". At its heart is the attributional nature of the experience, which was postulated to arise from experiences associated with retrieval, such as the ease or fluency with which the recalled item comes to mind (Jacoby et al., 1989; Whittlesea et al., 1990). For example, Fazendeiro, Winkielman, Luo, and Lorah (2005) had participants make "old" or "new" judgments of studied words (e.g., table), unstudied words that were semantically associated with studied words (e.g., chair), and unstudied and unrelated words. They found that the associated words were judged as "old" more often than the unstudied and unrelated words. The authors suggested that increased processing fluency of the associated words relative to the unstudied and unrelated words underlie this finding. Below, we draw parallels between the FOF and the Feeling of Rightness judgment regarding reasoning tasks.

Confidence

Confidence is a retrospective judgment that refers to the assessed probability that a question has been answered correctly. Confidence is often conceived of as a static, post-answer judgment (Nelson & Narens, 1990). However, Koriat and Goldsmith (1996) suggested that monitoring confidence is part of a cyclical process that occurs prior to as well as after giving an answer. Specifically, if an answer does not meet a threshold of confidence, it can be withheld in favour of either a "don't know" response, or be given additional processing that may reformulate the answer. For example, if one is asked about the year of an event and one thinks that it was in 1995, but is not sure about it, a possible answer would be "I don't know" or that it was "sometime in the '90s" (Ackerman & Goldsmith, 2008). Below, we consider a similar process to be involved in assessing the quality of intermediate and final outcomes in reasoning.

As with other metacognitive judgments described above, confidence varies with the fluency of production. Fluency of providing an answer can be a reliable cue when the questions are not misleading (Ackerman & Koriat, 2011). However, because judgments based on fluency are inferential, this cue may be also misleading (Kelley & Lindsay, 1993). Below, we propose that similar mechanisms underlie confidence in reasoning.

C. Meta-reasoning

In this section, we offer a framework for the metacognitive monitoring and regulation of reasoning, which is extrapolated from our discussion of meta-memory. At the object-level, learning and question answering share with reasoning tasks processes such as understanding meaning of words and syntax, identifying key information, retrieving relevant knowledge, and activating mental operations to achieve task goals (Kintsch, 1998; Wang & Chiew, 2010). At the meta-level, we consider several judgments hypothesized to take place during reasoning, and, as was the case with meta-memory judgments, we consider the associated regulatory processes as well as the heuristic basis for each judgment. Where available, we provide concrete evidence; but, because this research is still in the early stages, much of our discussion is speculative and is intended as a framework for future research.

Judgment of Solvability (JOS)

When asked to memorize words, there is usually little doubt that any given single item can be learned. In contrast, in many reasoning tasks, it is possible that the task may not be solvable at all, or that the participant lacks the requisite knowledge or capacity to solve it. In keeping with the principle of cognitive miserliness, people should be reluctant to invest time and effort in a task that has a low probability of success (e.g., De Neys, Rossi, & Houdé, 2013; see Stanovich, 2009 for a review). Thus, the very first decision that should take place is whether to attempt a solution at all. It may well be the case that the amount of effort thought to be required will be greater than the perceived benefits of solving the problem (Kruglanski et al., 2012). Thus, as was the case with ease of learning judgments (EOL), problems that are accompanied by low JOS are expected to lead to "giving up" when motivation is low or when under time pressure, and to result in a high investment when motivation is high.

What might be the basis of JOSs? That is, how might one judge, without having solved the problem, how difficult it will be to solve? As was the case with EOLs, we would expect that JOSs will be based on beliefs about the task at hand, about one's experience with solving such tasks, and on whatever surface-level cues are available from the problem that might signal difficulty. For example, metacognitive beliefs about reasoning ability can be measured using questionnaires such as the Rational Experiential Inventory (REI, Pacini & Epstein, 1999), which measures self-reported tendency to rely on analytic approaches to solving problems or to rely on past experiences and intuitions. Prowse Turner and Thompson (2009) demonstrated that rationality scores from the REI were positively correlated with confidence in solving complex logic problems; by extension, these types of metacognitive beliefs might also inform JOSs.

To the extent that JOSs are based on cues available from the problem, like EOL and FOKs, they should reflect some consensus among reasoners (Price & Murray, 2012). That is, one might expect consensus among participants regarding which items would be more difficult to solve. One such cue might be the difficulty of forming a representation or model of the problem (Johnson-Laird & Byrne, 1991). Consider the following two sets of premises:

| 1. All of the artists are bakers |
| All of the bakers are carpenters |

| 2. All of the bakers are artists |
| All of the bakers are chemists |

The first set of premises allows an easy integration of the problem information, whereas the second requires considerable re-working to align the common terms. On a reasoning task, reasoners are more confident with answers made from the first premises than the second (Stupple, Ball, & Ellis, 2013); it also seems reasonable to expect that similar differences would be observed in their JOSs.

Another cue that might be utilized is an apprehension of coherence among the problem elements. Topolinski (this volume) provides an overview of JOSs in the Remote Associate Test (Example 4, p. 166). Specifically, he reviewed several studies demonstrating that people can distinguish between triads of words that are coherent (i.e., solvable) from those that are not. Importantly, these JOSs are produced in less time than it would take to produce the solution. Topolinski (this volume) argues that coherent items are processed more fluently than non-coherent ones, and this gives rise to a positive, affective response allowing participants to make very fast JOSs. As is the case for inferential meta-memory judgments, however, such heuristic cues can be misleading (Alter & Oppenheimer, 2009). In particular, making some triads disfluent (by manipulating the contrast of the print) and inducing negative affect (by including negatively valenced words) lowered the probability that items were judged coherent.

In the absence of such cues, however, it seems unlikely that people will be able to judge the solvability of a problem. Using unsolvable water-jar problems, Payne and Duggan (2011) found that participants can only determine that a problem is insoluble after a lengthy attempt to solve it, if at all. Nevertheless, the ability to calibrate JOSs may increase with experience, at least with simpler tasks. Using anagrams (scrambled words), Novick and Sherman (2003) elicited solvability judgments under short deadlines (<1sec.). Accuracy increased with the amount of time allowed for the judgment. It also increased with experience, which probably allowed the extraction of reliable cues not apparent to novices.

Feeling of Rightness (FOR)

Thompson and colleagues (Thompson, 2009; Thompson, Prowse Turner, & Pennycook, 2011; Thompson et al., 2013) have proposed FOR as a monitoring mechanism for those cases in which Type 1 processes have produced a quick intuitive answer to a reasoning problem (Examples 1 and 2 above, pp. 165–166). FOR is proposed to determine the extent to which the initial answer is subsequently analyzed by more deliberate, Type 2 processes. To test this hypothesis, Thompson and colleagues (Thompson et al., 2011, 2013) developed a two-response paradigm in which participants are asked to provide an initial, intuitive answer to a problem and then rate their FOR about that answer. They are then given free time to rethink their response. They found, in a variety of reasoning tasks, that low FORs are associated with more time spent rethinking the initial answer and a higher probability of changing the initial answer than high FORs. Thus, FOR judgments appear to play a monitoring role regarding Type 1 outputs and a regulatory role in initiating analytic thinking.

The monitoring and regulation processes associated with FOR judgments combine the roles of several of the meta-memory processes described above. Because Type 1 processes are fast and autonomous, these answers pop into mind in a fashion similar to quick memory retrieval (Topolinski & Reber, 2010). Thus, feeling of familiarity (FOF) provides one good analogue for thinking about FOR. That is, both the FOR and FOF are attributions one makes about the "rightness" of an answer that has just come to mind. In the case of the FOR, this subjective experience of "rightness" also plays a regulatory function over the subsequent investment of effort in the task, similar to that played by the Feeling of Knowing (FOK) and Judgment of Learning (JOL). The analogy to JOL suggests that the discrepancy reduction model described above may be relevant. On this hypothesis, reasoners would set a target for the level of confidence they want to have in their final answers, monitor their reasoning processes, and stop when they judge their level of confidence to suffice (see Ackerman, in press; Evans, 2006).

What mediates the strength of FORs? Like the meta-memory judgments we have discussed, the FOR is assumed to involve an attribution based on the experience of producing the initial answer. Thompson and colleagues (Thompson et al., 2011, 2013) examined fluency of producing the first answer that comes to mind as one of the cues underlying FOR. Across a wide range of tasks, they observed that a) answer fluency, operationalized as the speed with which an initial answer is produced, predicts FOR judgments, such that fluent responding is associated with strong FORs, and that b) factors that increase answer fluency, such as the ready availability of a heuristic strategy, increase FOR, while those that reduce fluency, like a problem that elicits competing answers, decrease FOR. Thus, the fluency of answering a reasoning problem may form a basis of an attribution of rightness.

Although FORs appear similar in many respects to the meta-memory judgments described above, there is an important way in which they differ. There, we described how meta-memory judgments are sensitive to perceptual fluency, such as making text easier to read by presenting it in large print (e.g., Jacoby et al., 1989; Kleider & Goldinger, 2004; Kornell, Rhodes, Castel, & Tauber, 2011; Rhodes & Castel, 2008). The initial reports appeared to indicate perceptual fluency also played a role in reasoning, such that making problems difficult to read increased participants' solution rates, presumably by creating a sense of metacognitive unease (e.g., Alter, Oppenheimer, Epley, & Eyre, 2007). The generalizability of these findings, however, turns out to be limited, as perceptual fluency was not found to affect either FORs or retrospective confidence judgments for a variety of reasoning tasks (Thompson et al., 2013). We speculate that perceptual fluency may be too subtle a cue to manifest itself in FOR judgments, particularly in the presence of a very salient alternative, such as answer fluency.

What other cues may underlie FOR? As mentioned in our discussion of FOKs, Reder and Ritter (1992) found that the familiarity of the terms included in the question was related to FOKs. Similarly, Shynkaruk and Thompson (2006) found that reasoners expressed lower levels of confidence in conclusions about unfamiliar concepts than familiar ones, suggesting that familiarity may play a similar role in FOR judgments. FOKs are also known to vary with the accessibility of associations that come to mind during a retrieval attempt (Koriat, 1993). A similar process can be posited for reasoning, in that FORs and confidence judgments may increase with the amount of available information that is consistent with a conclusion; in the case of FOR, this might happen by automatic priming, whereas for final confidence judgments, it may be as a result of a deliberate memory search.

Ongoing judgments: warmth ratings, intermediate confidence ratings, and dynamic Prediction of Knowing (dPOK)

In contrast to the situations described above, for many reasoning tasks, an answer does not easily come to mind (Examples 3 and 4 above). Instead, deliberate processing is required to generate even an initial solution. Not much is known about metacognitive processes that might be involved; the few relevant findings are discussed below.

Metcalfe and Wiebe (1987) solicited intermediate metacognitive judgments while solving insight problems (e.g., water lilies problem, Frederick, 2005) and non-insight problems (e.g., Tower of Hanoi). Participants were asked to indicate every 15 seconds how "warm" they were getting on a cold–hot Likert scale (1–7). Warmth ratings increased over the solution interval; however, the increase was incremental for the non-insight problems and sudden for the insight problems.

Ackerman (in press) provided a more detailed look at the regulatory function of intermediate confidence ratings while solving maths and word problems, similar to Examples 1 and 4 above. The confidence ratings were elicited by a 0–100% scale ranging from "I still have no idea" to "I've got it". As Metcalfe and Wiebe (1987) observed, confidence increased over the problem-solving interval. In addition, Ackerman observed that the very first confidence judgments, made about 5–10 seconds after the presentation of the problem, had strong predictive power: High levels of initial confidence were associated with less additional time spent solving the problem, similar to the relationship observed between FOR and analytic thinking (see Thompson et al., 2011, 2013).

Finally, Vernon and Usher (2003) collected ongoing dynamic Predictions of Knowing (dPOK) every 4 seconds until 12 seconds had elapsed. In one study, they primed the words for some of their Remote Associate Task items (Example 4 above), generating a familiar (or fluent) set of problems, while the others were unfamiliar. The familiar items showed higher initial dPOK than unfamiliar items, but both increased over time. The observed pattern resembled a power function, similar to the intermediate predictions of performance collected by Ackerman and Goldsmith (2011) during text learning.

As with text comprehension, monitoring of problem solving may be misled by the provision of irrelevant cues. For example, Ackerman, Leiser, and Shpigelman (2013) presented college students with difficult-to-solve problems. Immediately after attempting each problem, participants read an explanation for how to solve the problem, and were then asked to solve a near-transfer problem (Sasson & Dori, 2012) to test their understanding of the explanation. For some of the explanations, the text was accompanied by a non-informative illustration of an object mentioned in the explanation, while the other included just the text. Judgments of comprehension were higher for the illustrated explanations, while performance on the transfer problems was lower. Thus, the vulnerability of metacognitive monitoring to surface-level cues extends to reasoning and problem-solving domains.

Final Judgments of Confidence (FJC)

Thompson and colleagues coined this phrase to differentiate this judgment from the intermediate confidence judgments just described (Thompson et al., 2011). FJC refers to confidence in the final answer, after the reasoning or problem-solving is complete. As with answering knowledge questions, confidence is conceived as a post-answer judgment. However, as was the case with meta-memory judgments, intermediate levels of confidence could regulate the decision to provide an answer or withhold it. For example, performance on the Remote Associations Task (Example 4) can be improved by providing reasoners a "don't know" option (Ackerman, in press), similar to the effect observed for answering general knowledge questions (Koriat & Goldsmith, 1996). However, on problems that produce an initial misleading answer (Example 1), participants rarely used the "don't know" option, despite a very low success rate (about 35%). A potential reason may be that for these problems, Type 1 processes produce an answer candidate that comes to mind accompanied by high FOR, so that reasoners are not aware of having made an error (Ackerman & Zalmanov, 2012).

Not much is known about the processes that give rise to FJCs in reasoning tasks. From the existing research, it is apparent that reasoners are often overconfident in their answers and that their answers are poorly calibrated with accuracy (Ackerman & Zalmanov, 2012; Prowse Turner & Thompson, 2009; Shynkaruk & Thompson, 2006). One reason for the poor relationship between confidence and accuracy could be that participants rely on non-diagnostic cues to confidence. For example, as was the case for answering knowledge questions (Kelley & Lindsay, 1993), it appears that there is a negative relationship between solution time and FJC: Ackerman and Zalmanov (2012) found that participants were more confident in solutions that were produced quickly than solutions that were produced slowly. Notably, this negative time–confidence correlation was persistent even for misleading problems, like Example 1 above, for which fluency is not related to success and is thus a non-diagnostic cue to confidence.

The negative correlation between metacognitive judgments and fluency is often explained by positing reliance on a fluency heuristic that works in a bottom-up fashion (e.g., Ackerman & Zalmanov, 2012; Koriat et al., 2006). In contrast, Ackerman (in press) recently suggested that, in contrast to rapidly accomplished tasks, such as memorizing word pairs, fluency may not be the only source for the persistent negative time–confidence correlation in lengthier tasks, such as problem solving. According to her Diminishing Criterion Model, the negative correlation stems from a top-down regulatory process: Lengthy engagement in solving a problem is accompanied by increasing willingness to compromise on the stopping criterion. That is, the stopping criterion diminishes over time, and this leads to negative time–confidence correlations. Note that this idea does not rule out fluency effects. It is possible that both a bottom-up fluency and top-down shifting of the stopping criterion jointly contribute to a negative time–confidence correlation.

These findings raise the question of whether the negative time–confidence correlations observed when answering knowledge questions (e.g., Ackerman & Koriat, 2011; Kelley & Lindsay, 1993) might also reflect top-down regulatory processes, above and beyond bottom-up effects of fluency. Thus, just as it is possible to draw useful analogues from meta-memory to meta-reasoning, findings about meta-reasoning may provide useful hypotheses about potentially similar processes in meta-memory.

Conclusions

Although reasoning processes evolve over a much longer time period than required for memorization or retrieval, the principles of meta-memory have nonetheless provided a useful starting place to theorize about meta-reasoning. For example, it seems clear that meta-level judgments in both domains are based, at least in part, on heuristic cues, such as fluency. Thus, the accuracy of meta-reasoning judgments, like their meta-memory counterparts, is determined by the validity of the cues on which they are based, so that judgments of reasoning performance, like judgments of memory, may be very inaccurate (Ackerman & Zalmanov, 2012; De Neys et al., 2013; Prowse Turner & Thompson, 2009; Shynkaruk & Thompson, 2006). On the other hand, the fact that reasoning unfolds over a longer period of time means that the contribution of those cues to meta-judgments may be different. For example, Vernon and Usher (2003) found that although initial dPOK judgments were higher for familiar than unfamiliar items, this difference disappeared over time, and Ackerman (in press) found that bottom-up fluency might be less dominant in problem-solving situations than is posited to be the case for memory.

Indeed, one of the main challenges for meta-reasoning research, going forward, will be to examine how people monitor their progress during lengthy reasoning tasks, and how they decide to allocate effort to that task. A promising starting point is the discrepancy reduction model initially proposed by Nelson and Narens (1990), which suggests that reasoners continue to invest time and effort in a task until a threshold of confidence has been reached. Once again, the fact that reasoning unfolds over a long period of time means that the process may operate quite differently in reasoning than in memory. That is, in reasoning, Ackerman (in press) has shown that one way reasoners can achieve the target threshold is simply to lower it!

It is clear from our review that meta-reasoning judgments play an important role in regulating object-level processes, as is the case for meta-memory judgments. Both Thompson et al., (2011, 2013) and Ackerman, (in press) have shown that judgments such as FOR and intermediate confidence judgments are related to the amount of subsequent effort that reasoners invest in a task. A promising direction for future work will be to examine this relationship in more detail to see how such meta-reasoning judgments are related to strategy choice. For example, in cases where there is a strong, initial level of confidence or FOR, reasoners may engender a relatively superficial form of analysis, such as rationalization of the initial answer, whereas lower levels of initial confidence may result in strategies aimed at finding an alternative solving approach (Thompson, 2009).

Finally, we hope that the issues raised, the methodologies we reviewed, and the directions we pointed to will stimulate future meta-reasoning and meta-memory research. There are, moreover, tasks in related fields, such as judgment and decision making, that are seldom studied through a metacognitive lens. In some cases, the analogy may be easy, as Dual Process models have been widely applied to decision-making tasks, making the link with the framework we have developed here (Kahneman, 2011). However, decision making can also involve quite different tasks, such as medical diagnosis (e.g., Norman & Eva, 2010), professional self-regulation (e.g., Dunning, Heath, & Suls, 2004), the challenges investigators face in forensic contexts (e.g., Lindsay, Nilsen, & Read, 2000), and organizational decisions (e.g., See, Morrison, Rothman, & Soll, 2011). In these tasks, errors in monitoring may have critical consequences. In theory, this should influence metacognitive processes by inducing people to set high confidence thresholds and critical self-assessment of the ongoing process. Does it really happen? And if so, under what conditions? Moreover, we know very little about metacognitive monitoring and regulation of open-ended decisions, like choosing among several products (e.g., Alba & Hutchinson, 2000) and other financial decisions (e.g., Biais, Hilton, Mazurier, & Pouget, 2005). As we argued above, with regard to text learning, vagueness in the target state may produce a low correspondence between metacognitive judgments and decision outcomes, as assessed by external criteria. Metacognitive processes in creative tasks, such as writing (e.g., Harris, Graham, MacArthur, Reid, & Mason, 2011) and design (e.g., Adams, Turns, & Atman, 2003), are likewise poorly understood. We hope that the analogy we made between meta-reasoning and meta-memory will inspire research into these and other tasks to facilitate our understanding of the regulatory processes that are central to all cognitive tasks.

Authors' note

We would like to thank Ian Newman, Florence Scheepers, and Nicole Therriault for their comments on an earlier draft of this manuscript.

References

Ackerman, R. (in press). The Diminishing Criterion Model for metacognitive regulation of time investment. *Journal of Experimental Psychology: General.*

Ackerman, R., & Goldsmith, M. (2008). Control over grain size in memory reporting – With and without satisficing knowledge. *Journal of Experimental Psychology: Learning, Memory, and Cognition, 34*(5), 1224–1245.

Ackerman, R., & Goldsmith, M. (2011). Metacognitive regulation of text learning: On screen versus on paper. *Journal of Experimental Psychology: Applied, 17*(1), 18–32.

Ackerman, R., & Koriat, A. (2011). Response latency as a predictor of the accuracy of children's reports. *Journal of Experimental Psychology: Applied, 17*(4), 406–417.

Ackerman, R., & Leiser, D. (2014). The effect of concrete supplements on metacognitive regulation during learning and open-book test taking. *British Journal of Educational Psychology*, 84(2), 329–348.

Ackerman, R., Leiser, D., & Shpigelman, M. (2013). Is comprehension of problem solutions resistant to misleading heuristic cues? *Acta Psychologica, 143*(1), 105–112.

Ackerman, R., & Zalmanov, H. (2012). The persistence of the fluency–confidence association in problem solving. *Psychonomic Bulletin & Review, 19*(6), 1189–1192.

Adams, R. S., Turns, J., & Atman, C. J. (2003). Educating effective engineering designers: The role of reflective practice. *Design Studies, 24*(3), 275–294.

Alba, J. W., & Hutchinson, W. J. (2000). Knowledge calibration: What consumers know and what they think they know. *Journal of Consumer Research, 27*(2), 123–156.

Alter, A. L., & Oppenheimer, D. M. (2009). Uniting the tribes of fluency to form a metacognitive nation. *Personality and Social Psychology Review, 13*(3), 219–235.

Alter, A. L., Oppenheimer, D. M., Epley, N., & Eyre, R. N. (2007). Overcoming intuition: Metacognitive difficulty activates analytic reasoning. *Journal of Experimental Psychology: General, 136*(4), 569–576.

Beilock, S. L., & DeCaro, M. S. (2007). From poor performance to success under stress: Working memory, strategy selection, and mathematical problem solving under pressure. *Journal of Experimental Psychology: Learning, Memory, and Cognition, 33*(6), 983–998.

Biais, B., Hilton, D., Mazurier, K., & Pouget, S. (2005). Judgemental overconfidence, self-monitoring, and trading performance in an experimental financial market. *The Review of Economic Studies, 72*(2), 287–312.

Bjork, R. A., Dunlosky, J., & Kornell, N. (2013). Self-regulated learning: Beliefs, techniques, and illusions. *Annual Review of Psychology, 64*, 417–444.

Bowden, E. M., & Jung-Beeman, M. (2003). Normative data for 144 compound remote associate problems. *Behavior Research Methods, 35*(4), 634–639.

Chandler, P., & Sweller, J. (1991). Cognitive load theory and the format of instruction. *Cognition and Instruction, 8*(4), 293–332.

Costermans, J., Lories, G., & Ansay, C. (1992). Confidence level and feeling of knowing in question answering: The weight of inferential processes. *Journal of Experimental Psychology: Learning, Memory, and Cognition, 18*(1), 142–150.

De Neys, W. (2012). Bias and conflict: A case for logical intuitions. *Perspectives on Psychological Science, 7*(1), 28–38.

De Neys, W., Rossi, S., & Houdé, O. (2013). Bats, balls, and substitution sensitivity: Cognitive misers are no happy fools. *Psychonomic Bulletin & Review, 20*, 269–273.

Dunlosky, J., & Lipko, A. R. (2007). Metacomprehension: A brief history and how to improve its accuracy. *Current Directions in Psychological Science, 16*(4), 228–232.

Dunlosky, J., & Tauber, S. K. (2014). Understanding people's metacognitive judgments: An isomechanism framework and its implications for applied and theoretical research. In

T. Perfect & D. S. Lindsay (Eds.), *Handbook of Applied Memory* (pp. 444–464). Thousand Oaks, CA: Sage.

Dunning, D., Heath, C., & Suls, J. M. (2004). Flawed self-assessment. *Psychological Science in the Public Interest, 5*(3), 69–106.

Ebbinghaus, H. (1885/1964). *Memory: A Contribution to Experimental Psychology* (H. A. Ruger & C. E. Bussenius, Trans.). New York: Dover.

Evans, J. S. B. T. (2006). The heuristic-analytic theory of reasoning: Extension and evaluation. *Psychonomic Bulletin & Review, 13*(3), 378–395.

Evans, J. S. B. T., & Stanovich, K. E. (2013). Dual-process theories of higher cognition advancing the debate. *Perspectives on Psychological Science, 8*(3), 223–241.

Fazendeiro, T., Winkielman, P., Luo, C., & Lorah, C. (2005). False recognition across meaning, language, and stimulus format: Conceptual relatedness and the feeling of familiarity. *Memory & Cognition, 33*(2), 249–260.

Frederick, S. (2005). Cognitive reflection and decision making. *Journal of Economic Perspectives, 19*(4), 25–42.

Harris, K. R., Graham, S., MacArthur, C., Reid, R., & Mason, L. H. (2011). Self-regulated learning processes and children's writing. In B. Zimmerman & D. H. Schunk (Eds.), *Handbook of Self-Regulation of Learning and Performance* (pp. 187–202). New York: Routledge.

Jacoby, L. L., Kelley, C. M., & Dywan, J. (1989). Memory attributions. In H. L. Roediger III & F. I. M. Craik (Eds.), *Varieties of Memory and Consciousness: Essays in Honor of Endel Tulving* (pp. 391–422). Hillsdale, NJ: Lawrence Erlbaum Associates.

Johnson-Laird, P. N., & Byrne, R. M. (1991). *Deduction.* Hove, U.K.: Lawrence Erlbaum Associates.

Kahneman, D. (2003). A perspective on judgment and choice: Mapping bounded rationality. *American Psychologist, 58*(9), 697–720.

Kahneman, D. (2011). *Thinking, Fast and Slow.* New York: Farrar, Straus, and Giroux.

Karpicke, J. D. (2009). Metacognitive control and strategy selection: Deciding to practice retrieval during learning. *Journal of Experimental Psychology: General, 138*(4), 469–486.

Kelley, C. M., & Lindsay, D. S. (1993). Remembering mistaken for knowing: Ease of retrieval as a basis for confidence in answers to general knowledge questions. *Journal of Memory and Language, 32*, 1–24.

Kintsch, W. (1998). *Comprehension: A Paradigm for Cognition.* New York: Cambridge.

Kleider, H. M., & Goldinger, S. D. (2004). Illusions of face memory: Clarity breeds familiarity. *Journal of Memory and Language, 50*(2), 196–211.

Koriat, A. (1993). How do we know that we know? The accessibility model of the feeling of knowing. *Psychological Review, 100*(4), 609–639.

Koriat, A. (1997). Monitoring one's own knowledge during study: A cue-utilization approach to judgments of learning. *Journal of Experimental Psychology: General, 126*, 349–370.

Koriat, A., & Goldsmith, M. (1996). Monitoring and control processes in the strategic regulation of memory accuracy. *Psychological Review, 103*(3), 490–517.

Koriat, A., & Levy-Sadot, R. (2001). The combined contributions of the cue-familiarity and accessibility heuristics to feelings of knowing. *Journal of Experimental Psychology: Learning, Memory, and Cognition, 27*(1), 34–53.

Koriat, A., Ma'ayan, H., & Nussinson, R. (2006). The intricate relationships between monitoring and control in metacognition: Lessons for the cause-and-effect relation between subjective experience and behavior. *Journal of Experimental Psychology: General, 135*(1), 36–68.

Kornell, N., Rhodes, M. G., Castel, A. D., & Tauber, S. K. (2011). The ease-of-processing heuristic and the stability bias. *Psychological Science, 22*(6), 787–794.

Kruglanski, A. W., Bélanger, J. J., Chen, X., Köpetz, C., Pierro, A., & Mannetti, L. (2012). The energetics of motivated cognition: A force-field analysis. *Psychological Review, 119*(1), 1–20. doi: 10.1037/a0025488

Lehrer, J. (2009). *How We Decide.* New York: Houghton Mifflin.

Lindsay, S. D., Nilsen, E., & Read, D. J. (2000). Witnessing-condition heterogeneity and witnesses' versus investigators' confidence in the accuracy of witnesses' identification decisions. *Law and Human Behavior, 24*(6), 685–697.

Maki, R. H. (1998). Test predictions over text material. In D. J. Hacker (Ed.), *Metacognition in Educational Theory and Practice* (pp. 117–144). Mahwah, NJ: Lawrence Erlbaum Associates.

Metcalfe, J., & Finn, B. (2008). Evidence that judgments of learning are causally related to study choice. *Psychonomic Bulletin & Review, 15*(1), 174–179.

Metcalfe, J., & Wiebe, D. (1987). Metacognition in insight and noninsight problem solving. *Memory & Cognition, 15*, 238–246.

Nelson, T. O., & Narens, L. (1990). Metamemory: A theoretical framework and new findings. In G. Bower (Ed.), *The Psychology of Learning and Motivation: Advances in Research and Theory* (Vol. 26, pp. 125–173). San Diego, CA: Academic Press.

Norman, G. R., & Eva, K. W. (2010). Diagnostic error and clinical reasoning. *Medical Education, 44*(1), 94–100.

Novick, L. R., & Sherman, S. J. (2003). On the nature of insight solutions: Evidence from skill differences in anagram solution. *The Quarterly Journal of Experimental Psychology, 56*(2), 351–382.

Pacini, R., & Epstein, S. (1999). The relation of rational and experiential information processing styles to personality, basic beliefs, and the ratio-bias phenomenon. *Journal of Personality and Social Psychology, 76*(6), 972–987.

Payne, S. J., & Duggan, G. B. (2011). Giving up problem solving. *Memory & Cognition, 39*(5), 902–913.

Price, J., & Murray, R. G. (2012). The region of proximal learning heuristic and adult age differences in self-regulated learning. *Psychology and Aging, 27*(4), 1120–1129.

Prowse Turner, J. A., & Thompson, V. A. (2009). The role of training, alternative models, and logical necessity in determining confidence in syllogistic reasoning. *Thinking & Reasoning, 15*(1), 69–100.

Reder, L. M., & Ritter, F. E. (1992). What determines initial feeling of knowing? Familiarity with question terms, not with the answer. *Journal of Experimental Psychology: Learning, Memory, and Cognition, 18*(3), 435–451.

Rhodes, M. G., & Castel, A. D. (2008). Memory predictions are influenced by perceptual information: Evidence for metacognitive illusions. *Journal of Experimental Psychology: General, 137*(4), 615–625.

Sasson, I., & Dori, Y. J. (2012). Transfer skills and their case-based assessment. *The Second International Handbook of Science Education* (pp. 219–250). Netherlands: Springer.

See, K. E., Morrison, E. W., Rothman, N. B., & Soll, J. B. (2011). The detrimental effects of power on confidence, advice taking, and accuracy. *Organizational Behavior and Human Decision Processes, 116*(2), 272–285.

Serra, M. J., & Dunlosky, J. (2010). Metacomprehension judgements reflect the belief that diagrams improve learning from text. *Memory, 18*(7), 698–711.

Shynkaruk, J. M., & Thompson, V. A. (2006). Confidence and accuracy in deductive reasoning. *Memory & Cognition, 34*(3), 619–632.

Son, L. K., & Metcalfe, J. (2000). Metacognitive and control strategies in study-time allocation. *Journal of Experimental Psychology. Learning, Memory, and Cognition, 26*(1), 204–221.

Stanovich, K. E. (2004). *The Robot's Rebellion: Finding Meaning in the Age of Darwin.* Chicago: The University of Chicago Press.

Stanovich, K. E. (2009). Distinguishing the reflective, algorithmic, and autonomous minds: Is it time for a tri-process theory? In J. Evans & K. Frankish (Eds.), *In Two Minds: Dual Processes and Beyond* (pp. 55–88). Oxford: Oxford University Press.

Stupple, E. J. N., Ball, L. J., & Ellis, D. (2013). Matching bias in syllogistic reasoning: Evidence for a dual-process account from response times and confidence ratings. *Thinking & Reasoning, 19*(1), 54–77.

Thiede, K. W., Anderson, M. C. M., & Therriault, D. (2003). Accuracy of metacognitive monitoring affects learning of texts. *Journal of Educational Psychology, 95*(1), 66–73.

Thiede, K. W., & Dunlosky, J. (1999). Toward a general model of self-regulated study: An analysis of selection of items for study and self-paced study time. *Journal of Experimental Psychology: Learning, Memory, and Cognition, 25*, 1024–1037.

Thiede, K. W., Wiley, J., & Griffin, T. D. (2011). Test expectancy affects metacomprehension accuracy. *British Journal of Educational Psychology, 81*, 264–273.

Thompson, V. A. (2009). Dual-process theories: A metacognitive perspective. In J. Evans & K. Frankish (Eds.), *In Two Minds: Dual Processes and Beyond* (pp. 171–195). Oxford: Oxford University Press.

Thompson, V. A., Prowse Turner, J., & Pennycook, G. (2011). Intuition, reason, and metacognition. *Cognitive Psychology, 63*(3), 107–140.

Thompson, V. A., Prowse Turner, J. A., Pennycook, G., Ball, L. J., Brack, H., Ophir, Y., & Ackerman, R. (2013). The role of answer fluency and perceptual fluency as metacognitive cues for initiating analytic thinking. *Cognition, 128*, 237–251.

Topolinski, S. (this volume). Intuition: Introducing affect into cognition. In A. Feeney & V. Thompson (Eds.), *Reasoning as Memory.*

Topolinski, S., & Reber, R. (2010). Gaining insight into the "aha" experience. *Current Directions in Psychological Science, 19*(6), 402–405.

Vernon, D., & Usher, M. (2003). Dynamics of metacognitive judgments: Pre- and postretrieval mechanisms. *Journal of Experimental Psychology: Learning, Memory, and Cognition, 29*(3), 339–346.

Wang, Y., & Chiew, V. (2010). On the cognitive process of human problem solving. *Cognitive Systems Research, 11*(1), 81–92.

Whittlesea, B. W. A., Jacoby, L. L., & Girard, K. (1990). Illusions of immediate memory: Evidence of an attributional basis for feelings of familiarity and perceptual quality. *Journal of Memory and Language, 29*(6), 716–732.

Wiley, J. (1998). Expertise as mental set: The effects of domain knowledge in creative problem solving. *Memory & Cognition, 26*(4), 716–730.

Zaromb, F. M., Karpicke, J. D., & Roediger, H. L. (2010). Comprehension as a basis for metacognitive judgments: Effects of effort after meaning on recall and metacognition. *Journal of Experimental Psychology: Learning, Memory, and Cognition, 36*(2), 552–557.

INDEX

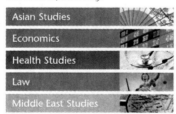